The Programmer's Guide to SCSI

Brian Sawert

ADDISON–WESLEY
An imprint of Addison Wesley Longman, Inc.

Reading, Massachusetts • Harlow, England • Menlo Park, California
Berkeley, California • Don Mills, Ontario • Sydney
Bonn • Amsterdam • Tokyo • Mexico City

Many of the designations used by manufacturers and sellers to distinguish their products are claimed as trademarks. Where those designations appear in this book, and Addison-Wesley was aware of a trademark claim, the designations have been printed in initial capital letters or all capital letters.

The author and publisher have taken care in preparation of this book, but make no expressed or implied warranty of any kind and assume no responsibility for errors or omissions. No liability is assumed for incidental or consequential damages in connection with or arising out of the use of the information or programs contained herein.

The publisher offers discounts on this book when ordered in quantity for special sales. For more information please contact:

Corporate, Government, and Special Sales Department
Addison Wesley Longman
One Jacob Way
Reading, Massachusetts 01867

Library of Congress Cataloging-in-Publication Data

Sawert, Brian
    The programmer's guide to SCSI / Brian Sawert.
        p.   cm.
    Includes bibliographical references and index.
    ISBN 0-201-18538-5
    1. Microcomputers—Programming.   2. Computer interfaces.   3. SCSI
(Computer bus)   I. Title.
QA76.6.S29   1998
004.6'4—dc21   97-44773
                                              CIP

ISBN: 0-201-18538-5
Text printed on acid-free paper
1 2 3 4 5 6 7 8 9—MA—0201009998
First printing, February 1998

This book is lovingly dedicated to my wife Mary.
Thank you for your endless encouragement and support.

Contents

Preface

In the years since the *Small Computer Systems Interface* (SCSI) first appeared, it has gained wide acceptance as the interface standard for high-performance computer peripherals. Once confined to mainframes and high-end workstations, SCSI devices are now supported by most desktop operating systems running on personal computers.

There is a reason for this near universal support. The SCSI standard was designed as a high-performance interface to a wide range of devices types. Disk drives, optical and tape drives, scanners, and printers all come equipped with SCSI interfaces. As faster machines become more common, the demand for faster peripherals follows. SCSI technology offers a way to meet this demand.

Though manufacturers and end users have embraced the Small Computer Systems Interface, information about programming SCSI devices is still scarce. This book attempts to fill that gap by describing SCSI from a programmer's point of view.

Intended Audience

This book is intended as a tutorial and a reference for programmers writing software to support SCSI peripherals. Whether you are writing low-level code for a SCSI device driver or high-level code for an application, you will find information you can use.

Maybe you have waded through the details of the ANSI specification documents. Maybe you have tried to decipher another programmer's source code. There is no doubt that learning the fundamentals of SCSI programming through trial and error can be a source of endless frustration. Our goal is to plant a few guideposts to steer you in the right direction, so as to flatten the learning curve for this complex but fascinating technology.

The presentation is slanted toward software development. Information about signal characteristics, timing protocols, and hardware details only appear when they directly relate to a programming task. We assume that if you are reading this book, you're more comfortable with a keyboard than a soldering iron. We also assume some experience with C, C++, and assembly language.

How This Book Is Organized

This book begins with an overview of SCSI. We describe the design philosophy behind the standard, and how it has evolved to incorporate new features and capabilities. We also describe variations of the SCSI standard that offer faster transfers, wider data paths, or other features.

Anyone working with SCSI must understand some fundamental concepts. How do SCSI devices communicate? How are commands executed and data transferred? What roles do the initiator and the target play? We address these questions by describing the SCSI transaction model. This provides a foundation for a more detailed discussion of the elements of a SCSI transaction.

Next we present a layered approach to SCSI programming, starting with high-level programming interfaces. We explore the *Advanced SCSI Programming Interface* (ASPI) under DOS and Windows, and ASPI32 extensions under Windows 95 and NT.

Windows NT offers its own built-in SCSI support. We explore how it works by examining the Windows NT device model and how the ASPI layer uses it.

Then we tackle more advanced material as we look at low-level programming using common SCSI I/O processors and scripting languages such as Symbios Logic's SCRIPTS. We demonstrate both initiator and target operations.

SCSI enjoys wide support on UNIX systems. Unfortunately, the specifics of SCSI support differ greatly between UNIX implementations. The UNIX chapter highlights SCSI support under different systems, then focuses on SCSI under Linux. This platform is widely available, and open enough to encourage experimentation.

Last of all, we develop a SCSI class library and use it to develop a sample application under Windows. This should encourage you to use and extend the library for your own projects.

The final chapter offers advice in troubleshooting and debugging. Appendix B lists SCSI resources in print and electronic form.

What You Will Need

The sample code in this book was designed for portability. We developed most of the code using Microsoft Visual C++. The SCRIPTS sample code uses Borland's C++ compiler and Turbo Assembler. Either should port with little effort. The sample application uses Microsoft's Foundation Classes library, also available with other compilers. The Linux code uses the compiler that comes with the operating system.

We recommend using an Iomega Zip drive as a test device for the sample code. Some of the samples demonstrate disk drive operations. When testing these, it's nice to have something besides your system disk to work with.

Zip drives come in SCSI or parallel port versions. The parallel port device uses an ASPI compatible driver.

The low-level code uses the Symbios Logic SCRIPTS compiler and host adapters equipped with 53C8XX family processors. The compiler is available from the Symbios Logic FTP site. The code should be compatible with other adapters in the same family. If your host adapter uses a chip from another manufacturer, you will not be able to use this code. If you wish to contact Symbios Logic, refer to the manufacturer listing in Appendix B.

The ASPI code will work with almost any host adapter that comes with an ASPI compatible driver. For more advanced work, you may wish to purchase the ASPI Developer's Kit from Adaptec. To contact Adaptec, refer to the manufacturer listing in Appendix B.

For any serious work with SCSI, you will need a copy of the ANSI SCSI-2 specification document. Though we cover SCSI fundamentals in this book, and probe the depths of some programming issues, we can't duplicate all the details that the specification covers. Consider this book a supplement to the ANSI document, which is available from Global Engineering Documents. You'll find them listed in Appendix B.

Acknowledgments

This book would not have been possible without contributions from many people. Kathleen Tibbetts, formerly an editor at Addison-Wesley, had faith in the project from the beginning.

Pamela Thompson at Earle Associates and Lauren Uddenberg at Symbios Logic went above and beyond the call of duty to provide support and information about Symbios products.

Thanks go to Mike Berhan and Dan Polfer of Adaptec for reviewing the ASPI-related material. Thanks also to John Lohmeyer, chairman of the T10 Technical Committee, for his comments and critiques of the material covering the SCSI specifications.

Special thanks go to contributing authors Larry Martin and Gary Field. Larry shares his invaluable programming experience in the chapters on ASPI, Windows device support, and SCSI target mode. Gary, who maintains the SCSI FAQ for the *comp.periphs.scsi* newsgroup, shares his considerable knowledge of UNIX support for SCSI in a chapter devoted to the subject.

Most important, I wish to acknowledge the inspiration and encouragement that my wife, Mary, provided throughout this project.

About the Authors

Brian Sawert

Brian Sawert earned his physics degree from Northern Arizona University. He has worked with the Small Computer Systems Interface for several years, developing applications and drivers for SCSI devices ranging from optical drives to scanners. His publications include articles for *Dr. Dobb's Journal* and *Windows/DOS Developer's Journal*. An article entitled "The Advanced SCSI Programming Interface" explored SCSI programming using ASPI.

In real life Brian enjoys bike riding, collecting Jan and Dean records, and spending time with his wife, Mary, and their two pugs, Poco and Rocky.

Larry Martin

Larry Martin has been programming since the arrival of his first IBM PC in 1982. He used that marvelous machine to pay his way through college writing software for local businesses. Since then he has focused on the hardware-software interface, especially in embedded systems. Larry has been working with SCSI interfaces since his stint at Flagstaff Engineering in the late 1980s, where he wrote device drivers for adapter cards, scanners, and disk- and tape drives. He has also written target-mode code for different SCSI peripherals, and has even written a few ASPI-compliant drivers that make non-SCSI devices mimic their more popular counterparts. Larry's current focus is the emerging IEEE 1394 "FireWire" Serial Bus interface, and he is working with 3A International to develop 1394 test equipment that is useful to real-world programmers.

Larry's hobbies include skiing, scuba diving, and turning red in the face while cursing at inaccurate data sheets.

Gary Field

Gary Field has a computer science degree from Northeastern University and has worked with device-level software since 1978. In 1985 he became involved with SCSI at Wang Laboratories on MS-DOS platforms and later led the development of an ANSI CAM subsystem for several UNIX platforms. He has also maintained the usenet *comp.periphs.scsi* FAQ list for several years. Since 1996 Gary has worked at Digital Equipment Corporation in their UNIX I/O development group.

In his home life, he is a scout leader and in spare moments enjoys ham radio, electronic tinkering, and photography, as well as camping, boating, and fishing with his wife and son.

Introduction

Programming SCSI peripherals is as much an art as a science. Many of the details are obscure or undocumented, forcing newcomers to learn the craft the way other artists do—through oral tradition passed down by other programmers. How do you handle a particular message? Why doesn't a certain command work the way you expect it to? Sometimes only a battle-scarred veteran of SCSI programming can provide an answer.

For those of you who have never worked with SCSI before, we hope this book can provide the same kind of advice and insight. You who have already experienced the joy of programming SCSI devices may find new information or a different slant on what you already know that can make you a more effective programmer.

Newcomers may wish to ease into the material, starting with the chapters that describe the SCSI specification and present an overview of how SCSI works. If you already are familiar with SCSI, or just impatient, skip ahead to chapters on specific topics like ASPI or SCRIPTS programming, or SCSI under UNIX. This book is meant to be a working reference as much as a textbook.

Once your appetite has been whetted, explore some of the other resources listed in Appendix B. With the growing popularity of SCSI, more information is available daily.

So ease in to the material or plunge in boldly, but enjoy the journey!

Chapter 1

An Overview of SCSI Technology

In the dark ages before SCSI, the world of computer peripherals was a confusing place. In particular, small computers came equipped with a bewildering assortment of interfaces and communications protocols for disk drives, printers, and other devices. The ST506 and ESDI interfaces fought for dominance in the disk drive market. Proprietary standards for parallel and serial interfaces caused widespread compatibility problems. Each new device introduced for the small computer market brought another support challenge for software developers.

The SCSI Solution

The *Small Computer System Interface* (SCSI) was an attempt to create a standard interface and communications protocol for computer peripherals. SCSI defined cabling requirements, electrical signal standards, a transaction protocol, and a common command set. The ideal represented by SCSI was that a single device interface could host a variety of peripherals from storage devices like disk- and tape drives to output devices like printers. The specification was broad enough to encompass a wide range of devices on the same bus, and also offered the prospect of device compatibility across different platforms and operating systems.

In practice, early SCSI devices failed to live up to this lofty ideal. In areas where the specification was vague or loosely defined, manufacturers

1

interpreted it differently. Early SCSI devices had a reputation for working only with certain host adapters. Combining different types or makes of devices on the same bus was an exercise reserved for only the most stubborn systems integrators with the time and expertise to make them work together.

SCSI-1

SCSI, also referred to as SCSI-1, was defined in the ANSI specification X3.131-1986 in 1986. This document, over 200 pages long, outlined a new interface on several levels. It spelled out cabling requirements and connectors, and electrical requirements for signal voltages, timing, and bus termination at the physical-transport level. Beyond the physical interface specification, it outlined a communications protocol for SCSI devices to employ. Last of all, it defined a set of mandatory and optional device commands.

Figure 1-1 shows a graphic representation of the Small Computer System Interface.

The SCSI-1 specification did not define a programming interface. Later standards for software layering, such as Adaptec's *Advanced SCSI Programming Interface* (ASPI) and the *Common Access Method* (CAM),

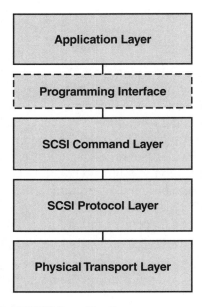

Figure 1-1. Elements of SCSI Specification

arose to fill this gap (represented by the dotted box in Figure 1-1). As with most de facto standards, the marketplace chose its favorite. CAM has been updated for use with SCSI-3, but generally is ignored in favor of ASPI in the PC market. CAM still finds support on many UNIX operating systems.

Many of the problems that arose in implementing SCSI centered on the physical and electrical components of the interface. Problems with cable lengths and signal termination were common. Different manufacturers used the same connector with different signal pinouts. In one case, Future Domain and Apple Computer both used cables with DB25 connectors. Because they were wired differently, using the wrong cable could damage a SCSI device.

The SCSI-1 specification left room for ambiguity in its definition of these layers. For instance, although the terminator power characteristics were defined, there was no requirement for which device would provide this. As a consequence, some SCSI host adapters supplied a TERMPWR signal, while others did not. Problems would appear when neither a host adapter nor any of the attached devices supplied terminator power.

Bus termination was a frequently misunderstood feature. Perhaps the specification was vague, or perhaps readers simply misinterpreted it. Whatever the reason, some of the most common questions in supporting SCSI and troubleshooting SCSI installations dealt with termination of devices in a SCSI chain.

At the command level, SCSI-1 left much open to interpretation. It defined a minimal command set, declaring some commands mandatory, some optional, and many vendor-specific. The mandatory commands dealt with device identification, status and error reporting, and error recovery. Most of the other commands fell under the optional or vendor-specific categories. While this made it easy for manufacturers to implement SCSI in their devices, the lack of standard command sets for different device types caused headaches for software developers. A programmer who wanted to support SCSI scanners in an application needed to know the command set for each scanner. If he wanted to use any of the optional commands, he had to know which devices supported them. SCSI had simplified things for hardware designers, but programmers were still waiting to see the benefits of a standard device interface.

The lack of a common command set wasn't an oversight on the part of the ANSI X3T9.2 committee. SCSI peripherals had appeared on the market even before the specification was approved. This created some pressure to declare the standard complete, rather than tie it up with further revisions. An interim working group developed a *Common Command Set*

(CCS), oriented toward disk drives. Command sets for many other classes of SCSI devices would not appear until the SCSI-2 specification.

SCSI-1 Features

Though it had its shortcomings, the SCSI standard brought features to small computers that were not available with other interfaces.

Intelligent Devices

Under the SCSI model, peripheral devices use intelligent onboard controllers. This moves the burden of command processing from the system processor to the device itself. Each device is responsible for error reporting and recovery. Commands for direct access devices, such as disk drives, use logical block addressing. The devices themselves map logical addresses to physical addresses, compensating for defective sectors or unusual geometries. Compare this to the old ST506 interface under DOS, which forced the operating system to keep track of bad sectors and could support only a limited range of disk drive configurations.

Multitasking I/O

SCSI-1 offered something new to small computers in its support for multitasking I/O. The disconnect/reconnect feature, especially effective for disk drive operations, gives devices the ability to disconnect from the bus during long operations, reconnecting when they are ready to complete them. When a disk drive receives a read request, it can disconnect while it locates and reads the data. During this time the bus is free for other devices or operations. When the device is ready to transfer its data, it reconnects to the initiator and completes the operation. Coupled with a multitasking operating system, this approach can drastically boost throughput.

Synchronous Data Transfer

The default data transfer method under SCSI is asynchronous, which relies on handshaking to acknowledge each byte transferred. This yields transfer speeds of about 1.5MB per second over the 8-bit-wide SCSI bus. SCSI-1 defined a synchronous transfer option that boosted the transfer rate to nearly 5MB per second. Perhaps slow by today's standards, it represented an improvement over the prevailing technology.

Multiple Device Types on a Single Interface

SCSI-1 defined an interface that supported up to eight devices in a chain configuration. System designers using SCSI-1 could connect up to seven peripherals to a single host adapter. In addition, these peripherals were not restricted to a single device type. A unique feature of SCSI is its ability to support disk drives, tape drives, scanners, and other devices on a common interface. In practice, this was difficult to achieve under SCSI-1 because of device incompatibilities and other factors.

The Birth of SCSI-2

As innovative as SCSI-1 was, it had its limitations. The standard allowed some exceptions in the way parity, messages, and commands were handled. Manufacturers who took advantage of these exceptions often found their products incompatible with others.

As with any standard in the computer industry, speed also was an issue. An 8-bit standard seemed out of date once the industry embraced a 16-bit architecture for personal computers. With the newer architecture, processor performance had also increased, so that even the 5MB per second synchronous transfer rates couldn't keep up with the newer CPU speeds.

By the time the SCSI-1 standard became official, improvements already had been proposed and implemented in the marketplace. These improvements were incorporated in the standard that became SCSI-2. It is important to note that devices billed as SCSI-2–compatible appeared before an official SCSI-2 standard existed. Many incompatibilities can be traced to these early implementations of unapproved features. As others have found out when working with new standards, *caveat implementor.*

New Features in SCSI-2

The updated specification for SCSI-2 addressed some of the shortcomings of SCSI-1, offered some improvements, and included some new features, including the following.

Fast SCSI

SCSI-2 improved synchronous transfer speeds with an optional fast transfer rate. This feature, known as Fast SCSI, raised the maximum synchronous data rate to 10 million transfers per second. The stricter timing requirements that make Fast SCSI possible also place greater demands on cabling and electrical requirements.

Two wiring alternatives have been available since the first SCSI specification. Single-ended wiring is intended for short runs, with a maximum cable length of 6 meters. Differential SCSI is designed for longer hauls, with a maximum length of 25 meters. In general, differential wiring preserves signal integrity and timing better, and is a better choice for fast transfer speeds. However, single-ended SCSI devices are more common than differential.

Wide SCSI

SCSI-2 introduced options for a 16-bit- and a 32-bit-wide data bus. Wide SCSI addressed the single byte transfer limitations of SCSI-1, instantly doubling or quadrupling transfer speeds. With the Wide SCSI option came new cable definitions to accommodate it. The old SCSI-1 cable was designated the A cable. A second cable, the B cable, provides additional signal lines that widen the data bus to 16 or 32 bits.

A consequence of having additional data lines is the ability to address more devices. Theoretically, a 16-bit bus can support 16 devices, and a 32-bit bus can support 32. However, electrical and other factors limit the actual number of devices a single bus can support. In practice, only 16-bit Wide SCSI seems to have penetrated the market—few manufacturers have implemented the 32-bit variation. This scarcity makes it safe to assume that the term "Wide SCSI" generally refers to the 16-bit version.

Fast Wide SCSI

What happens when you combine Fast SCSI with Wide SCSI? The SCSI-2 specification defined a Fast Wide SCSI option, boasting transfer speeds of 20 or 40MB per second, depending on the bus width. The same cabling restrictions apply as for Fast SCSI.

As is the case with Wide SCSI, 16-bit implementations of Fast Wide SCSI abound, but 32-bit Fast Wide SCSI is more of a paper standard than a working standard.

Queued I/O Processes

SCSI-2 added an option for two types of I/O process queuing: untagged and tagged. Untagged queuing permits a device to accept commands from an initiator while executing I/O processes from another. Tagged queuing gives targets the ability to accept a series of I/O processes from the same or different initiators. These are executed according to a queue management algorithm, or in a specified order.

Queuing should not be confused with command linking, which was supported in SCSI-1. With command linking, several commands are executed in sequence in a single I/O operation. A linked command sequence for a disk drive might include a `seek` operation followed by a `read` command. Linked commands are stored as a single entity in an I/O process queue.

New Command Sets

SCSI-2 defined command sets for devices that were not included in the original specification. Support for CD-ROM drives, scanners, optical media, medium changers, and communications devices were all spelled out in the SCSI-2 document. All command sets were extended and enhanced to reflect demand for more sophisticated featrues.

Improved SCSI-1 Features

Several years of experience with SCSI-1 had helped to expose both its strengths and its shortcomings. With this experience to guide them, the ANSI X3T9.2 task group proposed some incremental improvements in the standard. Several new low-level requirements were put into place.

Data Parity Required

SCSI-2 required the use of data parity. It was optional under SCSI-1.

Message Support Required

SCSI-2 devices were required to support messages as part of the transaction protocol. SCSI-1 made them optional, but the advanced features in SCSI-2 required a means of negotiation between initiators and targets.

SCSI-2 uses the `Identify` message to negotiate disconnect rights between an initiator and a target. Synchronous and wide data transfers, queue operations, and other features are negotiated through messages passed beween the initiator and target.

Terminator Power Provided by Initiator

SCSI-2 solved the issue of terminator power by mandating that the initiator provide it. It also outlined a method of active termination that is more effective than the passive termination scheme in common use.

Overall, the new specification closed loopholes in the original, enforced stricter compatibility requirements, and added support for newer devices and features.

SCSI-3 on the Horizon

The SCSI specification is dynamic, changing to reflect the needs of newer and faster computer peripherals. With SCSI-2 finalized in ANSI document X3.131-1994 in 1994, work began on the next revision almost immediately. Although the entire SCSI-3 specification has not yet been approved, SCSI-3 features and SCSI-3 compatible hardware already has appeared on the market.

Like the transition from SCSI-1 to SCSI-2, the dividing line between SCSI-3 and SCSI-2 isn't always clear. Some features of SCSI-3 seem to be extensions of SCSI-2 features that didn't emerge in time to become part of the older standard. Other features are brand new approaches to SCSI architecture that ensure the interface will be alive and healthy for years to come. Once again, improvements have focused on increasing transfer speeds, and also on extending the SCSI architecture. As with its predecessor, much of SCSI-3 is designed to maintain hardware and software compatibility with older standards.

Under SCSI-2, cabling was a confusing issue. Wide data paths were provided by an additional data cable that supplied the extra signal lines for 16-bit or 32-bit transfers. SCSI-3 proposes a single 16-bit cable for Wide SCSI implementations. This unofficial SCSI-3 feature already has been adopted by many peripheral manufacturers, and is much more common than the official SCSI-2 configuration.

Fast-20 and Fast-40 SCSI

SCSI-3 offers new Fast SCSI protocols. Fast-20, also known as Ultra SCSI, boosts the synchronous transfer rate to 20MB per second for 8-bit transfers, double the rate under SCSI-2. A Fast-40 protocol known as Ultra2 SCSI quadruples the rate to 40MB per second. The option exists, as in SCSI-2, to couple these fast protocols with a wide data bus. Wide Ultra SCSI and Wide Ultra2 SCSI can achieve rates of 40 and 80MB per second for 16-bit transfers. These higher rates require much tighter standards for bus timing and electrical parameters to maintain signal integrity. As with the older variety of Fast SCSI, they work more reliably using the differential SCSI alternative. In fact, Fast-40 requires the use of the new *Low Voltage Differential* (LVD) option. Many devices now offer multimode support that includes LVD, but to reach peak Fast-40 speeds requires that all connected devices support LVD. An added benefit of this differential option is that it can support more devices and longer cable lengths.

Table 1-1 compares the characteristics of the different parallel SCSI standards.

Table 1-1. Parallel SCSI Standards

Name	Transfer Speed	Data Width
Asynchronous SCSI	1.5MB/second	8 bits
Synchronous SCSI	5MB/second	8 bits
Fast SCSI	10MB/second	8 bits
Wide-16 SCSI	10MB/second	16 bits
Wide-32 SCSI	20MB/second	32 bits
Fast Wide-16 SCSI	20MB/second	16 bits
Fast Wide-32 SCSI	40MB/second	32 bits
Fast-20 (Ultra SCSI)	20MB/second	8 bits
Fast-40 (Ultra2 SCSI)	40MB/second	8 bits
Wide Ultra SCSI	40MB/second	16 bits
Wide Ultra2 SCSI	80MB/second	16 bits

Serial SCSI Standards

Though the 80MB per second rate offered by Wide Ultra2 SCSI represents an eightfold increase over the old standard, it pales in comparison to rates promised by a new set of standards defined in SCSI-3. Collectively, they are called the Serial SCSI standards. Unlike the current SCSI standard, which is limited to a parallel data interface, these three standards define different implementations of SCSI over a serial interface.

Several advantages of a serial architecture are apparent immediately. As parallel data busses become wider, cabling becomes more complex and unwieldy. In the worst case, a Wide SCSI installation would require a 50-pin and a 68-pin cable. The serial standards drastically reduce the number of conductors needed.

Serial data transfer offers other advantages. Longer cable lengths are possible with a serial connection. The cable length limit for a parallel SCSI connection using the differential alternative is about 25 meters. By comparison, the serial standards measure cable length over fiber optic media in kilometers.

Data integrity is improved, too. While the parallel interface relies on parity checking and handshaking, the serial standards all use a *Cyclic Redundancy Check* (CRC) to ensure reliable data transfers.

But the greatest improvement is in transfer speed. Draft specifications quote speeds of 100MB per second, with extensions that may double or quadruple that rate. Options for reserving bandwidth will increase the effective throughput even further.

The Serial SCSI standards comprise three separate standards, each with its own advantages: Fibre Channel, Serial Storage Architecture, and P1394.

Fibre Channel

The *Fibre Channel* (FC) standard was designed for flexibility. Despite the name, Fibre Channel supports both optical and copper media. Potentially, Fibre Channel SCSI could share the same cable with a fiber optic LAN or twisted pair telephone lines.

The protocol also defines different levels of service. Dedicated service reserves the entire bandwidth of the connection for the connected SCSI devices. A frame switched service level provides multiplexed service that may be shared with other protocols. Another level provides multiplexed service without confirming receipt of data packets.

Fibre Channel SCSI borrows many concepts from data networking. At its most complex, the standard defines a Fibre Channel switched fabric similar to a switched network, with simultaneously active connections. This topology could theoretically support millions of devices. A simpler topology call arbitrated loop allows up to 127 devices to communicate, two at a time. Fibre Channel promises to be the speed demon of the serial protocols, offering full duplex transfer speeds of 100MB per second or greater.

Serial Standard Architecture

Serial Standard Architecture (SSA) grew out of an IBM serial SCSI standard. Designed for twisted pair copper wiring, a fiber optic implementation is also in the works. Its great advantage lies in its support for full duplex communications and spatial reuse.

Like the Fibre Channel switched implementation, SSA permits multiple simultaneous connections over the same media. This design removes the limitation that only one initiator/target pair at a time can occupy the data bus.

P1394

P1394 is more commonly known by its Apple implementation, FireWire. Its design goals focused on simplicity and multimedia capabilities. It offers an isochronous transfer mode that can reserve bandwidth for timing sensitive transfers such as video or audio data. P1394 is not yet defined for optical media.

Layered Architecture

With the addition of the Serial SCSI standards, the SCSI specification is in danger of growing enormous and unwieldy. In this latest revision, the X3T10 Committee decided to break the standard into smaller units. Responsibility for some of the units passed to other committees, with the result that entire standard should be approved more quickly than in the past.

The X3 Committee itself also underwent some changes, becoming the *National Committee for Information Technology Standards* (NCITS). With the change in its parent organization, the X3T10 Committee became the T10 Technical Committee. Technically, NCITS and its committees are not part of the ANSI organization, although they develop standards that ANSI publishes.

The SCSI-3 standard adopts a layered model similar to the OSI model used in data communications. This structure helps to separate the hardware and software functions of the interface. Command sets and programming interfaces will be similar across different architectures, simplifying the programmer's task of porting from one to another.

Figure 1-2 shows the architecture of the SCSI-3 standard.

The standard defines three layers. The command layer includes new and extended command sets for SCSI devices. The protocol and physical layers include a parallel protocol and physical layer analogous to the SCSI-2 parallel model, and the new serial SCSI standards.

This model, called the *SCSI-3 Architecture Model* (SAM), defines not only the physical implementation of SCSI but also the transport mechanisms and protocols that accompany them. With all these new command sets, transports, and protocols comes an alphabet soup of acronyms to identify each one. A complete list appears in the Glossary in Appendix A.

Revisions to this model are already underway. *SCSI Parallel Interconnect-2* (SPI-2) will incorporate and replace the *SCSI-3 Interlocked Prototocol* (SIP), *SCSI-3 Parallel Interface* (SPI), and SCSI-3 Fast-20 and Fast-40. The Serial Bus Protocol will be divided into the *Serial Bus Protocol-2* (SBP-2) and *SCSI Transport via SBP-2* (STS). This change

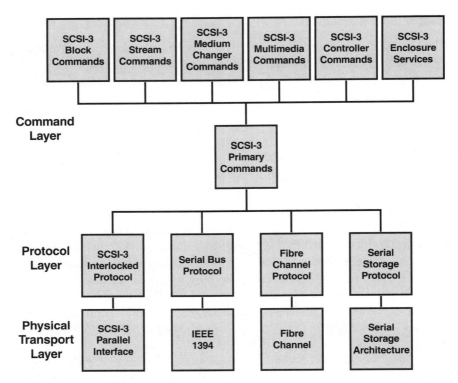

Figure 1-2. SCSI-3 Layered Architecture

allows for transport of non-SCSI command sets over IEEE 1394 hardware.

As mentioned earlier in this chapter, CAM offers access to the command sets, which are grouped by function. CAM has been updated for SCSI-3 and is now called CAM-3. It has not received wide support in the personal computer industry.

Plug and Play SCSI

With advances in PC architecture and operating systems, it was only a matter of time before the SCSI industry turned to self-configuring peripherals. An annex to the SCSI-3 draft standard defines *SCSI Configured AutoMagically* (SCAM). Host adapters using this protocol can dynamically assign SCSI ID numbers to devices on system startup, while still accommodating older SCSI hardware with fixed addresses. This feature is a cornerstone of Plug and Play (PnP) SCSI, a standard put forward by several SCSI manufacturers in conjunction with Microsoft.

Configuring SCSI devices manually, dealing with ID numbers, termination, and cabling requirements has long been considered an arcane craft. PnP SCSI takes over those responsibilities, assigning ID numbers at boot time through SCAM, and ensuring proper electrical termination and signal timing as devices are added to or removed from the SCSI bus.

The PnP standard defines two levels of service: Level 1 for basic Plug and Play operation, and Level 2 to support multiple initiators and ID assignments for hot-swapped SCSI devices. Plug and Play SCSI host adapters and peripherals are already on the market, though operating system support for SCAM lags behind. Software that assigns drive letters or boot devices based on a SCSI ID will have problems with devices that change their addresses. Even Microsoft, an early champion of the SCAM standard, has yet to built support for it into any operating system products.

Chapter 2

SCSI Fundamentals

All types of transactions, whether between humans or computer peripherals, rely on sets of rules or protocols to make them effective and efficient. As an example of chaotic interactions among humans, picture the floor of the New York Stock Exchange on a busy market day. At the other end of the spectrum, a debate on the floor of the U.S. Senate might serve as a model of orderly interactions, provided it's not an election year.

What's the difference? In the latter case, a strict set of rules guides the participants. Participants ask to be recognized by a chairman, who grants them permission to speak in turn. Parliamentary procedure and Robert's Rules of Order define the protocol for these transactions, just as the SCSI specification defines a protocol for data exchange among SCSI devices.

Perhaps the analogy is strained, but it does illustrate that SCSI transactions are orderly procedures with well-defined steps. Many programmers are confused by their first exposure to SCSI protocol, when they are confronted with complex phase diagrams. We'll get to those later, but first let's cover the basics.

SCSI Transactions: an Overview

When there is no activity on the SCSI bus, a bus-free condition exists. A SCSI device acting as initiator may claim control of the bus through a process called *arbitration*. It stakes its claim, checking for other devices also trying to gain control. If a device with a higher SCSI ID is competing for the bus, it has precedence—the lower numbered device must try again later.

Once the initiator has control, a target is selected for a transaction. If the target is present and ready to accept commands, it acknowledges its selection.

While the connection between initiator and target exists, the target controls the process by dictating transaction phases. In some instances, the initiator may request a particular phase, but the target controls the bus signals that determine it.

A message phase follows selection. The initiator signals to request this phase after selection, and the target responds. The messages that pass between initiator and target identify the devices to each other and negotiate parameters and ground rules for the transactions that follow.

Message phases may occur almost anywhere in the course of a SCSI transaction. The protocol uses messages to report errors, command status, and a variety of other information. It also uses them to send control information.

With the messages out of the way, the transaction moves into the command phase. This is where the initiator sends a block of data with command instructions and parameters to the target. Another message phase may follow if the target needs to report errors in the command block format or parameters.

Often a command may take some time to execute. This may be the case if the device has to rewind or reposition a mechanical element. If the initiator and target have negotiated disconnect privileges, the target will break the connection, freeing the initiator for other operations. When the target is ready to resume, it connects again with the initiator in a reselection phase. This is similar to the selection phase, with the target as the active device instead of the initiator.

Depending on the command issued, a data phase follows. The command determines the direction of data flow, whether the initiator sends or receives. The target sets the SCSI bus for transfer in the proper direction.

Messages may follow the data phase, but a status phase marks the end of command execution. The status code indicates the outcome of the command. If errors occurred, the status code indicates whether extended information, known as *sense data,* is available.

The final phase in a normal transaction is another message phase. The target sends a message to the initiator, telling it the command is complete and a status code has been sent. Once this message goes out, the target releases the data bus, returning it to a bus-free condition.

This is a simplified overview of a transaction. In the next chapter, we'll dig into the details of the different phases.

Chapter 3

SCSI Phases

A target and initiator move through several phases over the course of a SCSI transaction. How are these phases orchestrated, and what signals the transitions between them?

A SCSI transaction is similar to a courting ritual. When one of the parties in the relationship is ready to move on to the next phase, a signal is sent to the other. Thankfully, phases and signals in SCSI transactions are easier to decipher than their counterparts in human relations.

In a simple SCSI transaction, an initiator arbitrates for control of the bus. Once it gains control, it selects a target device to communicate with. The target responds, and the initiator exchanges messages with it to establish ground rules for the upcoming transaction. Disconnect privileges, data transfer width, and synchronous transfer timing are negotiated through messages. When these negotiations are complete, the initiator may send commands to the target, and data transfer may take place. On completion of a command, the target sends a status code to the initiator indicating the outcome. More messages may follow before the bus is released.

This process takes place in orderly transitions from one phase to another. Although the initiator begins the process, it is the target that controls the current bus phase. The initiator may request a change to a particular phase, but the target determines the transitions from one to another. What are these phases, and what do they represent?

SCSI Phases

The SCSI protocol defines eight distinct phases:

1. Bus Free phase
2. Arbitration phase
3. Selection phase
4. Reselection phase
5. Command phase
6. Data phase
7. Status phase
8. Message

These phases don't necessarily occur in the order listed above. As mentioned before, Message phases can occur almost anywhere. Support for Reselection depends on whether a target device has disconnect privileges. Data phases apply only to operations that transfer data.

Each of these phases is characterized by a different combination of signals on the SCSI bus, and a specific type of data exchanged. Six signals on the SCSI bus determine the state it is in, and the type and direction of data transfer. These signals are:

1. BSY (Busy)—a signal that indicates the bus is in use
2. SEL (Select)—a signal that indicates selection of a target or reselection of an initiator
3. C/D (Control/Data)—a signal that indicates control or data information
4. I/O (Input/Output)—a signal that indicates direction of data transfer relative to the initiator
5. MSG (Message)—a signal that indicates a Message phase
6. ATN (Attention)—a signal used by an initiator to request a Message phase

Bus Free

In Bus Free phase, there is no activity on the bus. No I/O processes are pending, no device has staked its claim, and the bus is up for grabs. None of the signals listed above are active.

Arbitration

In Arbitration phase, an initiator negotiates for control of the bus. It asserts the BSY signal, indicating that the bus is in use, and drives the data line corresponding to its SCSI ID. For an 8-bit data bus, the data lines are numbered DB(0) through DB(7). An initiator with ID 7 would assert DB(7) true to stake its claim on the bus.

After a specified delay period, the initiator examines the bus to determine if another device is trying to claim it. How does it know? If another data line corresponding to another device ID is asserted, that device also is trying to gain control. The device with the highest ID wins the arbitration in that case. Generally, SCSI host adapters are assigned higher ID numbers to assure their success in arbitration.

Once the initiator gains control of the bus, it signals the end of arbitration by asserting the SEL signal to move to the Selection phase.

Selection

The initiator selects a target by asserting the SEL signal while the BSY signal is still true. It then asserts the data lines corresponding to its own SCSI ID and the ID of the target it is selecting. The I/O signal is negated to distinguish this phase from reselection.

The initiator also sets the ATN signal true to request a Message Out phase following Selection. This step, optional under SCSI-1, became mandatory with SCSI-2.

Last of all, the initiator releases the BSY signal.

The target determines that it is being selected when both the SEL signal and its ID bit are true, and the BSY and I/O signals are false. It responds by setting the BSY signal true within a specified period of time. The initiator then confirms its selection by releasing the SEL signal.

Reselection

If a target has disconnected from the bus while processing a command, it reestablishes the connection by switching to Reselection phase. This is the mirror image of Selection, but the target takes the active role in arbitration and setting the bus signals instead of the initiator. In Reselection, the target also asserts the I/O signal along with the SEL signal. The initiator responds to reselection by asserting the BSY signal. Once the target responds by also asserting the BSY signal and releasing the SEL line, the initiator then releases the BSY signal, and the connection resumes.

Message Out

Because the initiator raised the ATN signal during Selection, the target next changes to the Message Out phase. It does this by asserting the MSG and C/D signals, and negating the I/O signal. Under SCSI-2 it became mandatory for the Message Out phase to follow device selection.

Only a few messages are valid in this initial Message Out phase. Under normal conditions, the initiator will send an `Identify` message. This message establishes a connection between the initiator and a logical unit within the target device. This connection is referred to as an I_T_L nexus. In devices that support optional target routines instead of logical units, an I_T_R nexus may be established. Support for target routines, although present in SCSI-2, has been phased out in SCSI-3.

Other messages may follow the `Identify` message. Requests for tagged queuing occur here, as well as synchronous or wide data transfer requests.

Chapter 4 discusses SCSI messages in more depth.

Command

When the Message Out phase ends, the target moves to Command phase. It signals this phase by raising the C/D line and negating the I/O and MSG lines. This tells the initiator that the target is ready to receive a *Command Descriptor Block* (CDB).

The size of the CDB varies according to which group the command belongs to. The SCSI-2 specification defines eight different command groups called, conveniently enough, Group 0 through Group 7. Commands defined in the SCSI specification fall into Groups 0, 1, 2, and 5. Groups 3 and 4 are reserved, and Groups 6 and 7 are set aside for vendor-specific commands.

The group code tells the target how many bytes to expect in the CDB. Once it has received the entire block, several things may happen.

If there is an error in the size or format of the CDB, the target may switch to Message In phase to report the error. If the command requires data transfer, the target changes to Data Out or Data In, depending on the command issued. If no data transfer is required, the target changes to Status phase and reports the outcome of the command by sending a status byte to the initiator.

The sections below cover these three possibilities.

Data In and Data Out

If a SCSI command requires data transfer when it is ready to begin sending or receiving data, the target participating in the transfer will set the bus state to Data In or Data Out. In the simplest case, the target remains connected to the initiator between the Command and Data phases. In more complex cases, the target may disconnect, then reconnect with the initiator when the data is ready. This requires that the initiator has granted disconnect privileges in the `Identify` message it sent the target after Selection.

For example, a disk drive may disconnect while it seeks and reads a requested sector. This frees the initiator for other transactions while the target is occupied.

The target signals Data phase by negating the C/D and MSG lines. It raises or lowers the I/O line depending on the direction of data transfer relative to the initiator. It asserts I/O to indicate a Data In phase, and negates it for a Data Out phase.

In the asynchronous model the initiator and target pace their data transfer with a series of REQ/ACK handshakes. If they negotiated a synchronous transfer, the timing between data bytes and the number of REQ pulses that can be sent in advance have already been established. In either case, the number of REQ and ACK pulses must be equal.

Status

When the command and any associated data transfer are complete the target switches to Status phase. It asserts the C/D and I/O signals and negates the MSG signal. A Status phase follows the completion of each command unless it terminates abnormally. This occurs if a message causes a process to abort, if a device resets or disconnects unexpectedly, or if the bus resets.

The status code is a single byte that indicates the success or failure of a command. It may show that a target is busy or reserved by another initiator. It may indicate the success of an intermediate command in a series. It may also alert the initiator that extended information known as sense data is available.

Refer to Chapter 6, on status codes and sense data, for more detail.

Message In

The final phase in a SCSI transaction is the Message In phase. The target asserts the C/D and MSG lines to signal a Message phase, and asserts the I/O line to indicate that the message is inbound toward the initiator.

Most often, the target will send a `Command Complete` message to show that it is done processing the command and has sent a status byte. It may also send messages to indicate error conditions or to alert the initiator before it disconnects from the bus while processing.

Phase Sequence

The flow from one phase to another is strictly defined, but can be complex. The description above covered a typical transaction in somewhat simplified form. In reality, once an initiator selects a target the phase sequence can follow a number of paths

Figure 3-1 illustrates the possible transitions between phases.

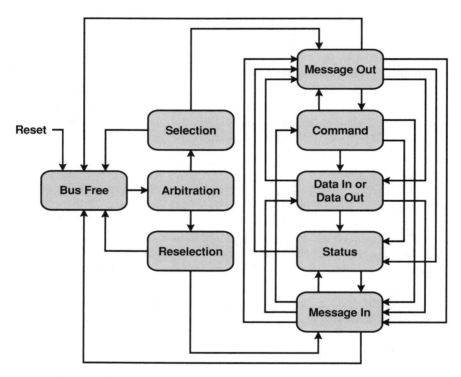

Figure 3-1. SCSI Phase Transitions

Chapter 4

SCSI Messages

SCSI transactions are complicated affairs. Designed into the SCSI proto-col, however, is a messaging system that helps keep things on track. This message system handles the details of interface management by providing a mechanism for error reporting and recovery, negotiating data transfer parameters, managing the process queue, and other functions.

Message phases can occur at almost any time after device selection. An initiator sends an `Identify` message to a target to establish an I_T_L nexus and indicate disconnect privileges. It may also send messages to negotiate synchronous or wide data transfers. If the target supports tagged queuing, an initiator sends messages to manage the queue.

A target may send a message to an initiator announcing its intent to disconnect from the bus. It precedes this message with a message request-ing that the initiator save pointers to the command, data, and status information for the current process.

A target also informs an initiator of the outcome of a command using messages. It may send a `Command Complete` message to tell the initiator that a process is finished. Or it may send a `Linked Command Complete` message to report that an intermediate command in a series of linked commands has completed.

Both initiators and targets may indicate errors through messages. The `Message Reject` message indicates that a preceding message is not implemented or is not appropriate.

The target controls the state of the data bus, and can change to Message In phase whenever it needs to send a message to the initiator. The initiator, on the other hand, cannot force a Message Out phase when it needs to communicate with the target. Instead, it raises the ATN signal to request that the target change to Message Out phase.

Message Types

Most messages consist of only one or two bytes. Extended messages contain three or more bytes, and may include arguments. The SCSI specification makes support for some messages mandatory, and others optional.

Table 4-1 lists the mandatory messages for initiators and targets.

Table 4-1. Mandatory SCSI Messages

Message Code	Message Name	Supported By
00H	Command Complete	Target and Initiator
05H	Initiator Detected Error	Target and Initiator
06H	Abort	Target
07H	Message Reject	Target and Initiator
08H	No Operation	Target and Initiator
09H	Message Parity Error	Target and Initiator
0CH	Bus Device Reset	Target
80H - FFH	Identify	Target and Initiator

Message code 00H, Command Complete, is the workhorse of the SCSI message set. Under normal conditions the target sends this message at the conclusion of a SCSI transaction. Message codes 02H through 1FH are single-byte messages. Message codes 20H through 2FH are 2-byte messages, with a single argument byte following the message code.

The Identify Message

The Identify message is a single byte, with bit encoded options. Because it is a mandatory message, let's examine it more closely.

The Identify message is sent by either an initiator or a target, usually after the Selection phase. This message establishes an I_T_L or I_T_R

Table 4-2. Identify Message

Bit 7	Bit 6	Bit 5	Bits 3-4	Bits 0-2
Identify	DiscPriv	LUNTAR	Reserved	LUNTRN

nexus by identifying a logical unit or target routine in the LUNTRN field. If the LUNTAR bit is set, LUNTRN specifies a logical unit number. The Disc-Priv bit indicates that the initiator has granted disconnect privileges to the target. This bit is undefined when a target sends this message.

Extended Messages

A message code of 01H indicates an extended message. Table 4-3 shows the general structure of an extended message.

Table 4-3. Extended Message

Byte #	Field Description
0	Extended message flag (01H)
1	Extended message length (n)
2	Extended message code
3 - (n+1)	Optional arguments

The second byte of an extended message is the length of the extended message code and any arguments. A value of 0 here indicates a length of 256 bytes.

Only three extended messages are defined under SCSI-2. Two of these, Synchronous Data Transfer Request and Wide Data Transfer Request, deserve a closer look.

Synchronous Data Transfer Request

The Synchronous Data Transfer Request message is sent by an initiator or a target to negotiate timing for synchronous data transfer. Under SCSI-2, the timing limits expanded to accommodate Fast SCSI.

Table 4-4 shows the structure of the Synchronous Data Transfer Request message.

Table 4-4. Synchronous Data Transfer Request

Byte #	Field Description
0	Extended message flag (01H)
1	Extended message length (03H)
2	`Synchronous Data Transfer Request` code (01H)
3	Transfer period factor
4	REQ/ACK offset

In setting up a synchronous transfer, two pieces of information are crucial. The transfer period factor is one-fourth the value of the transfer period. The transfer period is defined as the time between leading edges of successive REQ pulses. This is the time, measured in nanoseconds, that a data byte or word will remain on the bus.

A synchronous transfer permits the number of REQ pulses to lead the number of ACK pulses by the number given in the REQ/ACK offset. During asynchronous transfer, single REQ and ACK pulses alternate as data is sent. In synchronous transfer, a series of REQ pulses is acknowledged with a corresponding series of ACK pulses. The number of REQ and ACK pulses is equal, but the REQ pulse count may lead by the REQ/ACK offset before the ACK pulses are sent. This offset effectively determines the size of the data block transferred during a synchronous burst. A value of 0 in this field is equivalent to asynchronous transfer. A value of FFH indicates an unlimited offset.

The originating device sends the `Synchronous Data Transfer Request`. If the responding device agrees to the parameters, it returns the identical message. Otherwise, it will set the transfer period factor and REQ/ACK offset to values it can support.

Either device is free to send a `Message Reject` message in response to a synchronous request. In that case, the devices fall back to asynchronous transfer. Once they have negotiated synchronous parameters, they stay in effect until a device or bus reset, or until one of the participating devices renegotiates.

Wide Data Transfer Request

With the advent of Wide SCSI came the `Wide Data Transfer Request` message. This message sets the transfer width for devices that support 16-bit or 32-bit data paths.

Table 4-5 shows the structure of the `Wide Data Transfer Request` message.

Table 4-5. Wide Data Transfer Request

Byte #	Field Description
0	Extended message flag (01H)
1	Extended message length (02H)
3	`Wide Data Transfer Request` code (03H)
4	Data transfer width exponent

The transfer width in bytes is equal to 2 raised to the transfer width exponent. Exponent values of 0, 1, and 2 yield transfer widths of 8 bits, 16 bits, and 32 bits. As you may have guessed, values above 2 are not defined.

The procedure for negotiating transfer width is the same as for synchronous transfer negotiation. The originating device sends the message with the exponent set to a value it supports. The responding device may accept or reject that value. If negotiation fails, both devices fall back to narrow 8-bit data transfer. The negotiated value stays in effect until a device or bus reset, or until a renegotiation.

Other Common Messages

The SCSI specification defines other messages besides the `Command Complete`, `Identify`, and `Extended` messages. The remainder fall into 1-byte and 2-byte message families. Message codes 02H through 1FH correspond to 1-byte messages. The 2-byte messages are numbered 20H through 2FH.

We'll cover the more useful or interesting of these in the rest of this chapter. For a complete list, refer to the SCSI-2 specification document.

No Operation

A device may send a `No Operation` message (08H) when a message is required (but no other message is valid).

Abort

An initiator sends the Abort message (06H) to a target to clear any active I/O processes for an I_T_L or I_T_R nexus. This does not affect processes for other logical units or routines on the target.

Bus Device Reset

It's tempting for programmers to send Bus Device Reset messages (0CH) to clear error conditions, but this is a drastic measure. This message tells a target to clear all I/O processes and forces a hard reset of the device. It also creates a Unit Attention condition that must be dealt with.

Disconnect

A target needs a way to notify an initiator that it intends to disconnect while an I/O process is underway. The Disconnect message (04H) provides that. An initiator can also send this message to instruct a target to send a Disconnect message back.

A target may precede a Disconnect message with a Save Data Pointers message (02H), instructing the initiator to save the current data buffer offset. On reconnecting, a Restore Pointers message (03H) tells the initiator to resume data transfer from the previous offset.

Ignore Wide Residue

What happens in wide data transfers if an odd number of bytes is requested? There is a 2-byte message that deals with this situation. A target sends the Ignore Wide Residue message to indicate how many bytes in a wide data transfer to discard.

Table 4-6 shows the structure of this message.

Table 4-6. Ignore Wide Residue Message

Byte #	Field Description
0	Message code (23H)
1	Ignore count

The Ignore count tells how many bytes of the previous wide data transfer to discard. Valid numbers are 1, 2, and 3. A target sends this message immediately following a Data In phase.

Queue Tag Messages

If a device supports tagged queuing, it must support queue tag messages. There are five messages for managing queue operations. Two of them, `Abort Tag` (0DH) and `Clear Queue` (0EH), are single-byte messages. The `Abort Tag` message aborts the current I/O process without affecting other processes in the queue. `Clear Queue` clears all queued I/O processes and aborts the active process.

The other tag messages, `Simple Queue Tag`, `Head of Queue Tag`, and `Ordered Queue Tag`, are 2-byte messages that tell a target how to queue an I/O process for execution.

Table 4-7 shows the general structure of the 2-byte queue tag messages.

Table 4-7. Queue Tag Message

Byte #	Field Description
0	Queue tag message code (20H - 22H)
1	Queue tag (00H - FFH)

The `Queue tag` field contains an identifier that establishes an I_T_L_Q nexus. It uniquely identifies a process queued for a logical unit in a target.

An initiator sends a queue tag message to a target immediately following an `Identify` message, in the same Message Out phase. The target may reject this message if it does not support tagged queuing. A target also may send this message when it reconnects to continue a tagged I/O process.

Tagged command queuing should not be confused with linked commands. Linked commands are executed as a single I/O process.

Queue tag messages come in three varieties.

Simple Queue Tag

A `Simple Queue Tag` (20H) tells the target to execute a command according to a preset queue management algorithm. Restrictions on queue algorithms are specified in a command to the target device.

Head of Queue Tag

A `Head of Queue Tag` (21H) tells the target to place a command at the head of its command queue. It has no effect on the active I/O process.

Ordered Queue Tag

The Ordered Queue Tag (22H) tells the target to execute a command in the order received. This simply places it in the queue after any other pending commands.

Chapter 5

SCSI Commands

It used to be that the hardest part of supporting SCSI peripherals was finding documentation on the command set supported by a particular device. The SCSI-1 specification defined a minimal set of mandatory commands for querying device information and reporting errors. Almost everything else fell under the ominous category of "vendor-specific" commands.

The SCSI-2 specification does an admirable job of spelling out the command sets supported by different classes and types of devices. The increased length of the document over its predecessor is due largely to the commands that it adds and the painstaking detail in which it describes them. It may make the document cumbersome to work with, but having standard command sets makes a programmer's job much simpler.

This chapter gives an overview of SCSI command sets, how to use them, and what kind of data they return. It does not attempt to condense in a few pages what the SCSI document requires several hundred pages to present. For a complete reference to command sets for different device types, the SCSI specification is still the best place to turn.

Command Structure

SCSI commands and parameters are packaged in structures called *Command Descriptor Blocks,* or CDBs. As was the case with messages, different command groups correspond to command descriptors of different lengths. A Group 0 CDB is 6 bytes long. A CDB from Group 1 or 2 is

10 bytes long, and a Group 5 CDB occupies 12 bytes. The other groups are reserved for future use, or vendor-specific commands.

Operation Codes

The first byte of a CDB contains an operation code that describes the command. The 3 high bits of this code indicate the command group with possible values ranging from 0 to 7. The lower 5 bits contain the command code.

Table 5-1 shows the structure of the operation code.

Table 5-1. Operation Code

Bits 5–7	Bits 0–4
Group code	Command code

Logical Unit Number

The second field in a Command Descriptor Block contains a Logical Unit Number (LUN) in the upper 3 bits. Depending on the command group, the lower 5 bits may be reserved or contain part of the following field.

Table 5-2. Logical Unit Number

Bits 5–7	Bits 0–4
Logical Unit Number	Reserved or other data

Command Parameters

The fields that follow the Logical Unit Number generally contain command parameters. They may contain logical block addresses for direct access devices, transfer lengths for commands that transfer data, or other values related to specific commands or device types.

Control Field

The last field in every command descriptor is the `Control` field. This byte contains contains bit flags used in linked command operations. The `Link` flag indicates whether this CDB is part of a linked series of commands. The `Flag` bit determines the status code that the target returns on successful completion of a linked command. We'll look more closely at command linking later in this chapter.

Table 5-3 shows the structure of the `Control` field.

Table 5-3. Control Field

Bits 6–7	Bits 2–5	Bit 1	Bit 0
Vendor-specific	Reserved	Flag	Link

Parameter Lists

Some commands require parameter lists to follow the Command Descriptor Block. If this is the case, one of the parameter fields in the CDB may indicate the length of the data to follow.

Byte Order

It is important to note that values in multibyte fields are specified in big-endian order. That is, the most significant byte appears first, and the least significant byte appears last. This causes some confusion for programmers on Intel platforms, where numbers are stored in little-endian order with the lowest byte first.

Mandatory SCSI Commands

The SCSI specification defines both mandatory and optional commands that apply to all devices. Each device type also has its own set of commands, some mandatory, others optional. We'll start by looking at the commands that apply to all device types.

There are four mandatory commands that all devices must support. Table 5-4 lists these commands.

Table 5-4. Mandatory SCSI Commands

Code	Command Name
00H	Test Unit Ready
03H	Request Sense
12H	Inquiry
1DH	Send Diagnostic

These commands all deal with device identification, status, and error reporting. Many of the optional commands perform functions related to device configuration and reporting.

Test Unit Ready

The simplest of the mandatory commands, `Test Unit Ready`, simply reports whether a device is ready to execute commands. Table 5-5 shows the CDB for this command.

Table 5-5. Test Unit Ready

Byte #	Bit 7	Bit 6	Bit 5	Bit 4	Bit 3	Bit 2	Bit 1	Bit 0
0	Operation code (00H)							
1	Logical Unit Number			Reserved				
2	Reserved							
3	Reserved							
4	Reserved							
5	Control field							

This is an uncomplicated command structure. The `Control` field is laid out as described previously, though there is little use for the `Link` field with this command.

`Test Unit Ready` returns a status code of `Good` if the device is ready. It returns `Check Condition` if the device is not ready. In this case, sense information is available with more details. Interpreting status and sense information is an art in itself, which we explore in Chapter 6.

Inquiry

The `Inquiry` command causes a SCSI device to send information that identifies its manufacturer, model information, and supported features. The CDB for the `Inquiry` command looks like this.

Table 5-6. Inquiry

Byte #	Bit 7	Bit 6	Bit 5	Bit 4	Bit 3	Bit 2	Bit 1	Bit 0
0	Operation code (12H)							
1	Logical Unit Number			Reserved				EVPD

(Continued)

Table 5-6. Inquiry *(Continued)*

Byte #	Bit 7	Bit 6	Bit 5	Bit 4	Bit 3	Bit 2	Bit 1	Bit 0
2	Page code							
3	Reserved							
4	Allocation length							
5	Control field							

The EVPD flag tells the target device to return vital product data instead of the standard inquiry information. The Page code field specifies which vital product data to return. Support for the EVPD flag is optional. The Allocation length tells the target how much space is allocated for the returned data.

The information produced by a standard query command is returned in the format shown in Table 5-7.

Table 5-7. Inquiry Data Structure

Byte #	Bit 7	Bit 6	Bit 5	Bit 4	Bit 3	Bit 2	Bit 1	Bit 0
0	Peripheral qualifier			Device type code				
1	RMB	Device type modifier						
2	ISO version		ECMA version			ANSI approved version		
3	AENC	TrmIOP	Reserved		Response data format			
4	Additional data length							
5	Reserved							
6	Reserved							
7	RelAdr	WBus32	WBus16	Sync	Linked	Reserved	CmdQue	SftRe
8–15	Vendor identification string							
16–31	Product identification string							
32–35	Product revision level string							
36–55	Vendor-specific information string							
56–95	Reserved							
96–end	Vendor-specific data							

The inquiry data contains valuable nuggets of information about a device. To begin with, the Peripheral qualifier field tells whether the device is actually connected to the logical unit queried. The `Device type` field indicates the type of device at this address. The SCSI specification lists several device type codes.

Table 5-8. Peripheral Device Type Codes

Code	Device Description
00H	Direct access device (disk drive)
01H	Sequential access device (tape drive)
02H	Printer device
03H	Processor device
04H	Write-once device (WORM drive)
05H	CD-ROM device
06H	Scanner device
07H	Optical memory device (optical disk drive)
08H	Medium changer device (jukebox)
0AH–0BH	Graphic prepress device
1FH	Unknown device type

If there is no device connected to the specified target and LUN, the first byte in the inquiry data is set to 07FH, corresponding to a peripheral qualifier of 03H and a device type of 01FH.

The `RMB` flag indicates whether this device supports removable media. The `device type modifier` is only defined for backward compatibility with the SCSI-1 specification.

The third byte contains information about this device's compliance with different standards. Probably the most useful of these is the ANSI version field, which tells what version of the SCSI standard is supported.

The `AENC` and `TrmIOP` flags show support for asynchronous event notification and the `Terminate I/O Process` message. The `Response data format` field indicates whether the inquiry data structure conforms to SCSI-1, SCSI-2, or an intermediate standard. A value of 02H here indicates conformance to SCSI-2.

The `Additional data length` field tells how much data follows the standard inquiry data header. Note that this shows how much data is available, not how much actually was transferred.

Interesting things happen in byte number 7. A series of bit flags show what capabilities this device supports. In order of appearance, they show support for relative addressing (RelAdr), 32-bit Wide SCSI (WBus32), 16-bit Wide SCSI (WBus16), synchronous data transfer (Sync), command linking (Link), command queuing (CmdQue), and soft reset (SftRe).

The following three fields contain vendor and product information. These are ASCII strings padded with blanks to the width of their fields. The remaining fields are reserved or contain vendor-specific information.

Example: Iomega Zip Drive

Let's look at an example of inquiry data returned by a peripheral device. The device in question is an Iomega Zip drive. This drive is a SCSI direct access device with removable media. The data returned from an `Inquiry` command is shown in Table 5-9.

Table 5-9. Iomega Zip Drive Inquiry Data

Byte #	Bit 7	Bit 6	Bit 5	Bit 4	Bit 3	Bit 2	Bit 1	Bit 0
0	Peripheral qualifier (0)			Device type code (0)				
1	RMB (1)	Device type modifier (0)						
2	ISO version (0)		ECMA version (0)			ANSI approved version (2)		
3	AENC (0)	TrmIOP (0)	Reserved		Response data format (2)			
4	Additional data length (117)							
5	Reserved							
6	Reserved							
7	RelAdr (0)	WBus32 (0)	WBus16 (0)	Sync (0)	Linked (0)	Reserved	CmdQue (0)	SftRe (0)
8–15	Vendor identification string ("IOMEGA")							
16–31	Product identification string ("ZIP 100")							
32–35	Product revision level string ("N.38")							
36–55	Vendor-specific information string ("05/09/96")							
56–95	Reserved							
96–end	Vendor-specific data ("(c) Copyright IOMEGA 1995")							

The inquiry data shows that, indeed, this is a direct access device with removable media. It conforms to the ANSI standard for SCSI-2, and the data format also conforms to SCSI-2. It does not support 32-bit or 16-bit Wide SCSI, synchronous data transfer, linked commands, or command queuing.

The Vendor and Product identification fields confirm the make and model, and the revision string reveals the product revision level. The vendor-specific fields contain a manufacture date and a copyright notice.

An inquiry with the EVPD flag set and a page code of 00H should return a list of vital product information code pages the drive supports. However, the command fails with error codes indicating an illegal request. This device does not support the vital product data feature.

Optional Commands

Other commands defined for all device types are optional. Table 5-10 lists these commands.

Table 5-10. Optional SCSI Commands

Code	Command Name
18H	Copy
1CH	Receive Diagnostic Results
39H	Compare
3AH	Copy and Verify
3BH	Write Buffer
3CH	Read Buffer
40H	Change Definition
4CH	Log Select
4DH	Log Sense

The Copy, Copy and Verify, and Compare commands provide a means to copy and compare data between logical units on a target device. Parameters for these commands vary between device types, but specify source and destination addresses and transfer lengths.

The Log Sense and Log Select commands provide a mechanism for managing statistical information for target devices. The SCSI specification defines page code parameters for logging threshold and cumulative values, but does not dictate the type of data logged.

The Read Buffer and Write Buffer are used to test buffer memory on a device. In addition to this diagnostic function, they can reveal how much memory a particular device has.

The `Change Definition` command, where supported, permits an initiator to change the operating mode of a target. The initiator may request that the target adopt a SCSI-1, SCSI-2, or Common Command Set definition for compatibility.

Device Type–Specific Commands

There are four commands defined for all devices, but support is mandatory only for certain types. The `Mode Sense` and `Mode Select` commands come in 6-byte and 10-byte variations.

Table 5-11. Device Type–Specific SCSI Commands

Code	Command Name
15H	Mode Select (6-byte)
1AH	Mode Sense (6-byte)
55H	Mode Select (10-byte)
5AH	Mode Sense (10-byte)

These commands let an initiator read or set a wide range of device parameters. Parameters are organized by pages, identified by page codes. Many of the page codes are device-specific, while some pertain to common SCSI parameters like disconnect control and command queue algorithms.

Mode Select

The `Mode Select` command lets an initiator set operational parameters for a target or logical unit on a target. The CDB for the 6-byte `Mode Select` command is shown in Table 5-12.

Table 5-12. Mode Select (6-byte)

Byte #	Bit 7	Bit 6	Bit 5	Bit 4	Bit 3	Bit 2	Bit 1	Bit 0
0	Operation code (15H)							
1	Logical Unit Number			PF	Reserved			SP
2	Reserved							
3	Reserved							
4	Parameter list length							
5	Control field							

The `PF` flag specifies the page format of the parameter list. This flag should be set to indicate the pages conforming to the SCSI-2 specification. Clearing this flag indicates that the page formats are vendor-specific as in SCSI-1.

The `SP` flag requests that the target save pages to memory. The actual pages saved vary, but can be queried through the `Mode Sense` command.

The `Parameter list length` specifies the total length of all the mode pages and information that follows. We'll examine the actual format of the returned data when we look at the `Mode Sense` command.

Mode Sense

The `Mode Sense` command requests information describing a target's operational parameters. This command can query default parameters, current parameters, or those that can be changed using the `Mode Select` command.

The CDB for the 6-byte `Mode Sense` command is shown in Table 5-13.

Table 5-13. Mode Sense (6-byte)

Byte #	Bit 7	Bit 6	Bit 5	Bit 4	Bit 3	Bit 2	Bit 1	Bit 0
0	Operation code (1AH)							
1	Logical Unit Number			Reserved	DBD	Reserved		
2	PC		Page code					
3	Reserved							
4	Allocation length							
5	Control field							

The `DBD` flag tells the target to disable block descriptors in the returned data (block descriptors and data format are discussed below). The `PC` value specifies the type of parameters requested. It ranges from 0 to 3 for current values, changeable values, default values, and saved values.

Probably the most important field is the `Page code`. The value specifies which set of parameters to return. A value of 3FH in this field instructs the target to return all available mode pages.

What kind of information does `Mode Sense` return? The SCSI specification defines mode pages for specific device types. For example, direct access devices can return information on medium types and disk geometries, caching parameters, error recovery, and a wide range of other operational details.

Mode Sense Data Format

Devices that return mode information in page format follow a data structure outlined in the SCSI document. A mode parameter header leads the data, followed by block descriptors and mode pages. The header varies with the 6-byte and 10-byte mode commands. The header for the 6-byte `Mode Sense` command is shown below.

Table 5-14. Mode Parameter Header (6-byte)

Byte #	Bit 7	Bit 6	Bit 5	Bit 4	Bit 3	Bit 2	Bit 1	Bit 0
0	Mode data length							
1	Medium type							
2	Device-specific parameter							
3	Block descriptor length							

The `Mode data length` gives the total length of the remaining data. The `Medium type` code varies with device type, but generally describes medium density or format. The `Block descriptor length` gives the total length of the block descriptors that follow, at 8 bytes each.

Block descriptors give more specific information about the current or default medium supported by a device.

Table 5-15. Mode Parameter Block Descriptor

Byte #	Bit 7	Bit 6	Bit 5	Bit 4	Bit 3	Bit 2	Bit 1	Bit 0
0	Density code							
1–3	Number of blocks							
4	Reserved							
5–6	Block length							

Once again, the `Density code` varies among device types. The `Number of blocks` indicates how many blocks the length pertains to. It is set to 0 if the block length applies to the entire medium.

A list of mode pages follows the block descriptors. Table 5-16 shows the general layout of a mode page.

The `PS` flag shows whether a mode page can be saved. The `Page code` identifies the information returned. Some codes apply to all device types,

Table 5-16. Mode Page Format

Byte #	Bit 7	Bit 6	Bit 5	Bit 4	Bit 3	Bit 2	Bit 1	Bit 0
0	PS	Reserved	Page code					
1	Page length							
2–end	Mode parameters							

while others are device-specific. The `Page length` is the length of the mode parameters in the remainder of the page.

Example: Iomega Zip Drive

Let's revisit the Iomega Zip drive for a simple example of mode page information. We'll use the 6-byte `Mode Sense` command to query the drive for default information, requesting all available mode pages. The CDB looks like this:

Table 5-17. Iomega Zip Drive Mode Sense

Byte #	Bit 7	Bit 6	Bit 5	Bit 4	Bit 3	Bit 2	Bit 1	Bit 0
0	Operation code (1AH)							
1	Logical Unit Number (0)			Reserved	DBD (1)	Reserved		
2	PC (2)		Page code (3FH)					
3	Reserved							
4	Allocation length							
5	Control field							

The command returns the data shown in Table 5-18.

Table 5-18. Zip Drive Mode Parameter Header

Byte #	Bit 7	Bit 6	Bit 5	Bit 4	Bit 3	Bit 2	Bit 1	Bit 0
0	Mode data length (25H)							
1	Medium type (0)							
2	Device-specific parameter (0)							
3	Block descriptor length (8)							

What does it mean? The `Data length` tells us that 37 bytes follow. The 0 in the `Medium type` field tells us the information is for the default medium type. The `block descriptor length` tells us that a single 8-byte block descriptor follows.

For the Zip drive, a direct access device, the device-specific parameter consists of coded bit fields.

Table 5-19. Zip Drive Device-Specific Parameter

Bit 7	Bits 5–6	Bit 4	Bits 0–3
WP	Reserved	DPO/ FUA	Reserved

The `WP` flag indicates whether the medium is write-protected. The `DPO/ FUA` flag indicates whether the unit supports certain caching options for read requests.

A block descriptor follows the header (Table 5-20).

Table 5-20. Zip Drive Block Descriptor

Byte #	Bit 7	Bit 6	Bit 5	Bit 4	Bit 3	Bit 2	Bit 1	Bit 0
0	Density code (0)							
1–3	Number of blocks (0)							
4	Reserved							
5–6	Block length (200H)							

The `Density code` is not defined for direct access devices, so it contains no useful information. Because the `Number of blocks` field is 0, we know that the information in this descriptor applies to all the remaining blocks on the medium.

The `Block length` is 512 bytes, according to this descriptor. This field appears in big-endian order, as 20H 00H in bytes 5 and 6. A common pitfall in SCSI programming on Intel platforms is forgetting to correct byte order when reading data fields.

Three mode pages follow the descriptor. The first is an error recovery page (01H), followed by a disconnect-reconnect page (02H) and a vendor-specific page (2FH). Let's look at the error recovery page.

Table 5-21. Zip Drive Error Recovery Mode Page

Byte #	Bit 7	Bit 6	Bit 5	Bit 4	Bit 3	Bit 2	Bit 1	Bit 0
0	PS (0)	Reserved	Page code (01H)					
1	Page length (6)							
2	AWRE (1)	ARRE (1)	TB (0)	RC (0)	EER (1)	PER (0)	DTE (0)	DCR (0)
3	Read retry count (0)							
4	Correction span (0)							
5	Head offset count (0)							
6	Data strobe offset count (0)							
7	Reserved							

The PS field value of 0 tells us this page cannot be saved in nonvolatile memory. The Zip drive does not support saved pages, and a Mode Sense query requesting saved pages will return an error.

The normal page length for error recovery data is 10 bytes. Here, the length is only 6 bytes.

The third byte in this page contains an assortment of bit flags for error recovery options. Automatic read and write reallocation (AWRE and ARRE) is supported for defective data blocks. The Enable Early Recovery (EER) flag indicates that the device will use the most expedient error recovery method available. The other fields tell us that this device does not report recovered errors, terminate a data phase when an error occurs, or use error correction codes for recovery.

From a programmer's perspective, this is important information. Knowing how a device deals with errors drives the kinds of error handling code you build into your software.

Reading and Writing

We'll close this chapter with a look at the workhorse functions of the SCSI command set—the Read and Write commands. These commands vary with device type, so we'll examine how to use them with direct access devices.

As with other commands, Read and Write come in 6-byte and 10-byte versions corresponding to their Group 0 and Group 2 implementations. The 10-byte versions allow for larger numbers in addresses and transfer lengths specified in the Command Descriptor Blocks. They also contain extra fields that dictate cache handling and relative addressing.

Direct-access `Read` and `Write` commands are block oriented. They begin at a logical block address, with transfer lengths given by a block count. You need the block length as reported by `Mode Sense` or other commands to determine the number of bytes in a data transfer.

Read

The 6-byte `Read` command has a simple structure. Its fields identify the first logical block to read, and the number of blocks to transfer. Table 5-22 shows the CDB for the `Read` command.

Table 5-22. Read (6-byte)

Byte #	Bit 7	Bit 6	Bit 5	Bit 4	Bit 3	Bit 2	Bit 1	Bit 0
0	Operation code (08H)							
1	Logical unit number			Logical block address				
2	Logical block address (continued)							
3	Logical block address (continued)							
4	Transfer length							
5	Control field							

The `Logical block address` is spread across three fields, with the *Most Significant Byte* (MSB) appearing first. `Transfer length` occupies a single byte.

Write

The CDB for the `Write` command is nearly identical to that of the `Read` command. Only the operation code is different.

Table 5-23. Write (6-byte)

Byte #	Bit 7	Bit 6	Bit 5	Bit 4	Bit 3	Bit 2	Bit 1	Bit 0
0	Operation code (0AH)							
1	Logical unit number			Logical block address				
2	Logical block address (continued)							
3	Logical block address (continued)							
4	Transfer length							
5	Control field							

Other Commands

We've barely touched on all the commands supported by the different SCSI device types. The SCSI-2 specification document contains the complete list for those who wish to experiment.

Chapter 6

Status, Sense, and Errors

In a perfect world, there would be no need to receive feedback from SCSI devices. They always would be ready to communicate, every command would execute successfully, and programming SCSI peripherals would be a simple exercise. In reality, commands execute completely, partially, or not at all. Devices wait patiently offline because they are out of paper, and operations fail because a tape cartridge is write-protected. Even if everything else works perfectly, errors in the SCSI bus may prevent communications.

The SCSI specification is a comprehensive document that deals with many different types of devices. Each device type has its own collection of things that can go wrong, of errors to report, of changes in conditions that affect how the device responds to commands. If error handling under SCSI seems complicated or confusing, this is why.

The authors of the SCSI document did an admirable job of unifying support for different device types. They defined different levels of feedback in the specification. On a gross level, a status code reports the results of commands sent to devices. On a finer level, a detailed set of sense information pinpoints where errors occur.

Status

Every command phase that ends normally is followed by a status phase. In the status phase, a target sends a single byte back to the initiator that indicates the outcome of the command. Table 6-1 shows the structure of the status byte.

Table 6-1. Status Byte

Bits 6–7	Bits 1–5	Bit 0
Reserved	Status code	Reserved

The status byte can be cumbersome to work with, since the lowest bit is reserved. It is easy to forget that the actual status code starts with bit number one.

Status Codes

Only nine status codes are defined under the SCSI-2 specification. All others are reserved.

Table 6-2. Status Codes

Status Code	Description
00H	Good
01H	Check Condition
02H	Condition Met
04H	Busy
08H	Intermediate
0AH	Intermediate—Condition Met
0CH	Reservation Conflict
11H	Command Terminated
14H	Queue Full

Targets return the Good status on successful completion of a command. Some data search or prefetch commands return Condition Met instead.

The `Busy` status indicates that a device is engaged in another process or otherwise unable to accept a command until later. `Reservation Conflict` occurs when trying to access a device reserved by another initiator. If a device supports tagged command queuing, it may return `Queue Full` to indicate that its command queue cannot accept any more entries.

Some of the status codes pertain to linked commands. `Intermediate` and `Intermediate–Condition Met` are returned after each linked command where `Good` or `Condition Met` would normally apply.

The most interesting status code is `Check Condition`. This code, along with `Command Terminated`, indicates that a *contingent allegiance condition* exists. A contingent allegiance condition occurs when a target has extended error information, known as sense data, available. It preserves this data until the initiator retrieves it or another action clears the contingent allegiance condition. If the device can only maintain sense data for a single initiator, it will return a `Busy` status to other devices that attempt to access it.

Sense Data

Sense data contains detailed information about error conditions. It is organized into major categories called *sense keys* and subcategories called *additional sense codes* (ASC) and *additional sense code qualifiers* (ASCQ). The combination of these pices of data can convey finely detailed information about error conditions.

Before interpreting these numbers, we must retrieve them. The `Request Sense` command performs this function. `Request Sense` is a mandatory command for all device types. Table 6-3 shows the CDB for this command.

Table 6-3. Request Sense

Byte #	Bit 7	Bit 6	Bit 5	Bit 4	Bit 3	Bit 2	Bit 1	Bit 0
0	Operation code (03H)							
1	Logical Unit Number			Reserved				
2	Reserved							
3	Reserved							
4	Allocation length							
5	Control field							

The `Allocation length` tells the target how much sense data to return.

The data returned by this command follows a form defined by the SCSI specification. The form is the same for all devices, but some fields pertain only to certain types. It is also legal for a target to use a vendor-specific format for sense data.

Table 6-4. Sense Data Format

Byte #	Bit 7	Bit 6	Bit 5	Bit 4	Bit 3	Bit 2	Bit 1	Bit 0
0	Valid	Error code (70H or 71H)						
1	Segment number							
2	Filemark	EOM	ILI		Reserved	Sense key		
3–6	Information							
7	Additional sense length							
8–11	Command-specific information							
12	Additional sense code (ASC)							
13	Additional sense code qualifier (ASCQ)							
14	Field replaceable unit code							
15	SKSV	Sense key-specific						
16–17	Sense key-specific (continued)							
18–end	Additional sense data							

This data conveys a plethora of information about errors that have occurred. The `Valid` bit indicates that the following data conforms to the structure defined above. Only two `Error codes` are defined: 70H for current errors, and 71H for deferred errors. Support for deferred errors is optional. The segment number, `Filemark`, and `End of Medium` (EOM) fields apply to specific commands or device types.

If the `Incorrect Length Indicator` (ILI) is set, the amount of data a command requested did not match the amount available from the target. The `Information` field contains the difference in blocks for direct access or tape devices, or bytes for devices like scanners that are not block oriented.

The `Information` field may contain different data depending on the command or device type it pertains to. The same applies to the `Command-specific information` field.

Sense Key

The Sense Key reveals the broad category under which the reported error falls. These categories report hardware errors, write protect errors, illegal requests, and an assortment of other conditions. The SCSI specification defines the following sense keys. Other values are reserved.

Table 6-5. Sense Keys

Sense Key	Description
00H	No Sense
01H	Recovered Error
02H	Not Ready
03H	Medium Error
04H	Hardware Error
05H	Illegal Request
06H	Unit Attention
07H	Data Protect
08H	Blank Check
09H	Vendor-specific
0AH	Copy Aborted
0BH	Aborted Command
0CH	Equal
0DH	Volume Overflow
0EH	Miscompare

Some of these require further explanation. For instance, the Illegal Request key indicates that a CDB contained an invalid field or parameter. If this occurs, the Sense Key Specific Value (SKSV) flag is set in the sense data, and the sense key–specific fields contain pointers to the offending values in the CDB or parameters. This information comes in handy when debugging SCSI software.

For Recovered Error, Hardware Error, and Medium Error, the sense key–specific field contains a retry count if the SKSV flag is set.

Unit Attention

The Unit Attention key applies when something occurs that may change a device's operating parameters. A reset or power cycle, a medium change, or a change in mode parameters can all trigger a unit attention condition. In this condition the device will only respond to Inquiry and Request Sense commands, returning a Check Condition status for other commands. In this state, only a Request Sense command will clear the unit attention condition. If a contingent allegiance also exists, any command from the initiator will clear the unit attention condition.

A device enters this state on power up, which means that the first command issued may return a Check Condition status. This can be particularly troublesome for programmers unfamiliar with the ways of SCSI.

Additional Sense Codes

In many cases the sense key alone provides enough information for error recovery. When it does not, the ASC and ASCQ provide the missing details. The ASC gives additional information about the source of the error, and the ASCQ gives more specific details. Together the ASC and ASCQ pinpoint exactly what errors occur in SCSI operations. Some of these errors apply only to particular device types.

The complete list of ASC and ASCQ assignments occupies several pages of the SCSI document. A browse through this list will give you an idea of the kinds of errors your software may need to handle.

Example: Iomega Zip Drive

Let's look once again at the Iomega Zip drive for an example of sense data. We'll force a Unit Attention condition by changing the disk, and examine the result of a Request Sense command.

Table 6-6. Iomega Zip Drive Sense Data

Byte #	Bit 7	Bit 6	Bit 5	Bit 4	Bit 3	Bit 2	Bit 1	Bit 0
0	Valid (0)	Error code (70H)						
1	Segment number (0)							
2	Filemark (0)	EOM (0)	ILI (0)	Reserved	Sense key (06H)			
3–6	Information (0)							

(Continued)

Table 6-6. Iomega Zip Drive Sense Data *(Continued)*

Byte #	Bit 7	Bit 6	Bit 5	Bit 4	Bit 3	Bit 2	Bit 1	Bit 0
7	Additional sense length (17)							
8–11	Command-specific information (0)							
12	Additional sense code (ASC) (28H)							
13	Additional sense code qualifier (ASCQ) (0)							
14	Field replaceable unit code (0)							
15	SKSV (0)	Sense key–specific (0)						
16–17	Sense key–specific (continued) (0)							
18–end	Additional sense data (FFH, FEH, 01H, 02H, 1CH, 0, 0)							

The sense key corresponds to `Unit Attention`, which is what we would expect. The ASC and ASCQ point to a message, "Not ready to ready transition, medium may have changed." This indicates that a device that was unavailable is now online, which is what we would expect.

Some curious things to note are that the `Valid` flag is not set, and the `Additional sense` data field seems to contain vendor-specific data. This is a good reminder that not all SCSI devices conform completely to the standard. When working with a particular device, information from the manufacturer can be critical.

Chapter 7

ASPI: The Advanced SCSI Programming Interface

In the early days of SCSI most software developers hard-coded support for SCSI adapter cards directly into their applications. Adding support for a new SCSI adapter or chipset was a tedious and error-prone task, typically undertaken by programmers whose primary focus was (properly) on the application itself rather than on the SCSI interface code. Therefore applications tended to require specific combinations of host adapter and peripheral devices, often those matching the system of the programmer responsible for the SCSI interface code. Because the code was tied so closely to specific devices and adapters, constant maintenance upgrades were required to keep pace with changing hardware.

The challenges involved in developing SCSI code generally break down into two areas: generating the proper SCSI commands for the various peripheral (target) devices, and interfacing with the SCSI host adapter to send these commands to the devices. As described in Chapter 1, the first issue was addressed by the CCS and SCSI-2 improvements to the SCSI standards. These improvements helped device manufacturers implement a common set of commands appropriate to the type of their device, which in turn allowed programmers to write generic code for a given device type and have a reasonable expectation that their code would work with most other devices of that type. The second issue was addressed by the definition of standard programming interfaces that pass commands to devices, regardless of the particular host adapter being used. We'll be describing one of the most popular of these interfaces for PC platforms, the Advanced SCSI Programming Interface, in this chapter.

What Is ASPI?

The *Advanced SCSI Programming Interface* (ASPI) was developed by Adaptec, a leading manufacturer of host adapter cards. Adaptec published their Adaptec SCSI Programming Interface, renamed it, and encouraged other manufacturers to support it. ASPI was defined and available on most PC-based operating systems including DOS, Windows, OS/2, and Novell Netware, and was immediately supported by Adaptec's own popular line of SCSI host adapters. As programmers began to embrace ASPI, most other SCSI host adapter manufacturers introduced ASPI-compliant interfaces to their hardware, especially for the MS-DOS operating system. ASPI soon became a standard for PC-based SCSI programming and helped open the way to the widespread acceptance of SCSI devices on the PC platforms.

ASPI's success is due partly to its relative simplicity. It forgoes some SCSI features, such as tagged queueing and asynchronous event notification, in favor of a simpler interface model and easier implementation (as do many peripherals and operating systems). In addition, ASPI is primarily focused on the application viewpoint and handles only initiator, or host adapter, requests. This means that ASPI can send commands to a SCSI device, but it is not designed to deal with commands received from another initiator (host adapter). Most PC-based applications are interested in controlling peripheral devices, so the lack of this target mode support hasn't been a significant handicap for ASPI.

Why Should I Use ASPI?

Let's take a look at what ASPI actually does for a programmer. First, it insulates you from the hardware interface of SCSI host adapters. In theory (and largely in practice) you can write code using one ASPI manager and host adapter, and that code will run with any other host adapter supported by a compliant ASPI manager. All of the hardware-specific interface code is handled by the ASPI manager itself. Each different SCSI host adapter design has a corresponding ASPI manager, often developed by the manufacturer itself.

In addition to providing hardware independence, ASPI also provides a great deal of operating system independence. Application programmers using ASPI typically don't need to worry about interrupt handlers and other operating system specific details related to device driver programming. Page locking and swapping are still a concern under older operating systems like Windows 3.1 or DOS, but much less a concern under Windows 95 and NT. Aside from small details like this, ASPI interface itself is quite consistent across all operating system platforms, though the implementation details differ. From an application programmer's perspective the major difference in ASPI under different operating systems is the mechanism used to connect to the ASPI manager itself. On MS-DOS systems, for example, ASPI usually is implemented as a device driver loaded via the CONFIG.SYS file, while under Windows ASPI is implemented as a *Dynamic Link Library* (DLL). There are also small differences in the alignment and order of fields within structures passed to the ASPI manager on 16-bit versus 32-bit implementations. The examples that follow use the ASPI for Win32 structures and definitions, which are used on Windows 95 and Windows NT systems. If you are using ASPI on another platform, make sure you are using the structure definitions appropriate for that system.

ASPI Concepts

The next few sections describe some important ASPI concepts to explore before looking at the ASPI commands and structures themselves. These concepts include device addressing, issuing SCSI commands and waiting for them to complete, and some adapter-specific details that you need to know. While reading this you may get the impression that ASPI is much more complicated than it really is. In practice, ASPI is very simple and easy to use, and we'll be providing plenty of examples and sample code just a bit later. For now, you should note that an ASPI manager has one main routine that you call to issue most ASPI commands. This routine takes a pointer to a structure that contains all of the information necessary to execute a given ASPI command. In the examples below this routine is called `SendASPI32Command()`, and we'll show you how to use it a bit later. Feel free to look ahead if you are curious about the commands or structures.

The latest revisions of the ASPI specification have added other routines to support Plug and Play SCSI and large buffers.

Adapter and Device Addressing

The SCSI specification identifies devices by a SCSI device ID, and by a *Logical Unit Number* (LUN) that may identify a particular subunit on a device. Typical SCSI device IDs range from 0 to 7, and LUNs also range from 0 to 7. Given these two pieces of information, any unit or subunit on a single SCSI bus can be uniquely identified. However, it is possible to connect two or more different SCSI host adapters to a single system, so the ASPI manager requires one more piece of information—the host adapter number. It may help to think of a host adapter as an I/O channel, since some host adapter cards can support more than a single channel.

Host adapters are numbered consecutively, starting at 0. The first (or only) host adapter ID will be 0, the second will be 1, and so on. So under ASPI, SCSI devices can be uniquely identified by a host adapter number, a SCSI ID, and a logical unit number. Every ASPI command dealing with a specific SCSI device contains these three pieces of information (HA:ID:LUN).

Issuing SCSI Commands

Now that we can address a SCSI device we usually want to issue commands making it do something useful. This involves four basic steps: building the command, sending it to the ASPI manager, waiting for the command to complete, and then interpreting any status or error codes returned by the ASPI manager.

All ASPI commands use a data structure called a *SCSI Request Block* (SRB). The first few fields of the SRB are common to all ASPI commands, but the remaining fields depend on the specific command being executed. Before sending the SRB to the ASPI manager, an application must initialize the SRB with data appropriate to the command being issued. After the SRB has completed it will contain any data and status codes returned by the ASPI manager or the target device.

Building the SCSI Request Block

The first step required to issue an ASPI command is initializing the SRB structure. For the most part, you simply fill in the required field values. We'll describe the fields later in this chapter, but right now let's take a quick look at a common example—sending a SCSI `Inquiry` command to a target device. The first thing you must do is allocate an SRB and specify which ASPI command it describes. We also allocate a small data buffer to receive the inquiry data from the device.

```
SRB_ExecSCSICmd srb;              // allocate the SRB
unsigned char   buf[128];         // allocate data buffer
memset(&srb,0,sizeof(srb));       // clear all fields
srb.SRB_Cmd = SC_EXEC_SCSI_CMD;   // specify ASPI command
```

Next, you must provide the address of the SCSI device that will receive the command. Assuming you know the host adapter number, SCSI ID, and logical unit number of the device, this is straightforward:

```
srb.SRB_HaId = HostAdapterNumber;
srb.SRB_Target = TargetScsiId;
srb.SRB_Lun = 0;
```

We also need to provide the SCSI *Command Descriptor Block* (CDB) itself. For our example of an `Inquiry` command, this is done as follows:

```
srb.SRB_CDBLen = 6;                   // Inquiry cmd is 6 bytes
srb.SRB_CDBByte[0] = 0x12;            // Inquiry cmd opcode
srb.SRB_CDBByte[1] = 0;              // LUN and page flags
srb.SRB_CDBByte[2] = 0;              // Inquiry Page code
srb.SRB_CDBByte[3] = 0;              // Reserved
srb.SRB_CDBByte[4] = sizeof(buf);    // Allocation length
srb.SRB_CDBByte[5] = 0;              // Control byte
```

Refer back to the description of the SCSI `Inquiry` command in Chapter 5 for a description of this CDB.

Next, since the `Inquiry` command returns data to us, we must tell the ASPI manager where to put the data. We also set the `SRB_DATA_IN` flag to tell the ASPI manager that we are expecting to receive data from the device. If we were sending data to the device we would set the `SRB_DATA_OUT` flag.

```
srb.SRB_BufLen = sizeof(buf);        // buffer length
srb.SRB_BufPointer = buf;            // address
srb.SRB_Flags |= SRB_DATA_IN;        // transfer direction
```

And finally we need to tell the ASPI manager how much sense data should be returned to us in the event of a SCSI check condition. The SRB_ExecSCSICmd structure contains a buffer for the sense data, but we still need to specify its size. This can be tricky—bugs in both Windows 95 and NT limit the practical size of the sense buffer to 14 bytes. It's common to use the defined value SENSE_LEN, which is set to 16 bytes.

```
srb.SRB_SenseLen = SENSE_LEN;
```

That's it. We're now ready to send the SRB to the ASPI manager. (If you peeked ahead at the SRB definitions, you may have noticed that we skipped the `SRB_PostProc` field. We'll cover that a bit later.)

Sending an SRB to the ASPI Manager

Once the SRB is properly initialized, you simply pass its address to the ASPI manager, and the ASPI manager will handle all phases of the actual SCSI command and data transfer. This is quite simple—you just call the ASPI manager's entry point, passing the address of the SRB as a parameter:

```
SendASPICommand((LPSRB) &srb);
```

ASPI makes the actual execution of the command as simple as issuing a function call. Well, almost that simple . . . in the interest of performance, the ASPI manager usually just places the SRB in a queue and returns to the caller immediately, before the command has even started. This allows your application to prepare the next command while the last one is still executing. The ASPI manager handles all of the details involved in executing the command in the background, and then updates a status field in the SRB when the command finally completes.

Waiting for an SRB to Complete

Since the ASPI manager may return before an SRB has been completed, your application must not deallocate the SRB or rely on any returned data until the SRB is finished. The simplest way to guarantee this is to simply sit in a loop, waiting for the SRB_Status field to indicate that the SRB has completed.

```
while (srb.SRB_Status == SS_PENDING)  // while still pending
    ;                                 // do nothing
```

Polling the status field is an inefficient way to wait for a command to complete. Under MS-DOS this isn't much of an issue because there is only one application running at any given time. On a multitasking operating system, however, polling wastes CPU time that could be better spent running other threads or applications. Fortunately ASPI provides another method of waiting, called *posting,* which is simply a callback to a routine that you specify in the SRB. When the ASPI manager finishes processing the SRB it will call your routine, passing the address of the SRB on the stack. This callback routine can inspect the SRB's status fields, and possibly execute another SRB immediately. The callback routine is called as soon as possible after the SRB completes, even from within the ASPI manager's interrupt handler in some implementations. Because of this, you should keep your callback routines short and simple. Also, because the callback might occur at interrupt time, you should not use any operating system services that aren't completely reentrant. This means that your callback routine is usually restricted to inspecting the just completed SRB, and possibly sending a new SRB to the ASPI manager for processing. This is an easy and efficient way to receive ASPI notifications, but under Win32 it requires the ASPI manager to create a background thread to manage the callback. There is another method you can use in this environment that we'll discuss later.

One common problem encountered when using callback routines involves the calling convention used by the ASPI manager. The ASPI managers for Windows 95 and Windows NT expect the callback routine to use the standard CDECL calling convention, which equates to the __stdcall calling convention for most Win32 compilers. Under Windows 3.x you should use the FAR PASCAL convention, just like most 16-bit Windows callbacks and entry points. Under MS-DOS things are a bit more complicated. The ASPI manager pushes the address of the just completed SRB onto the stack and then makes a FAR call to the callback routine, as follows:

```
push [SrbOffset]                 ; push offset of SRB
push [SrbSegment]                ; push segment of SRB
call dword ptr [SRB_PostProc]    ; call callback routine
add  sp,4                        ; clean up stack
```

This corresponds to the C language calling convention used by most MS-DOS compilers. However, the ASPI specification for MS-DOS also requires that the callback routine preserves the values of all registers. Therefore, a callback routine under MS-DOS might look like the following:

```
CallbackRoutine:
      push    bp
      mov     bp, sp
      pusha
      push    ds
      push    es
      les     bx, dword ptr [bp+6]

      ; Now ES:BX has the address of the SRB

      pop     es
      pop     ds
      popa
      pop     bp
      retf
```

Fortunately, most MS-DOS C compilers have implemented extensions allowing you to specify these requirements to the compiler automatically. Check your compiler documentation for details, but most will support the following:

```
void __cdecl __saveregs __loadds CallbackRoutine( SRB _far *p )
    {
    }
```

If you are using another programming language, or if your compiler doesn't support these extensions, you can write a small assembly language subroutine like the one above that simply translates the call into the format required by your compiler.

With that behind us, let's take a look at how you can use a callback routine under Windows 95 and NT. Our example will simply signal a Win32 EVENT object. This example is rather artificial, but it does show how to set up a callback.

The first thing we need to do is create the event object and the callback routine itself:

```
HANDLE EventHandle;

void CallbackRoutine( SRB *p )
    {
    SetEvent(Handle);
    }
```

Let's assume we've already initialized an SRB to execute a SCSI Inquiry command as shown earlier, and simply fill in the missing pieces and send it to the ASPI manager.

```
srb.PostProc = CallbackRoutine;
srb.Flags |= SRB_POSTING;
ResetEvent(EventHandle);
dwStatus = SendASPI32Command((LPSRB) &srb);
if (dwStatus == SS_PENDING)
    WaitForSingleObject(EventHandle,INFINITE);
```

We use the Windows 95/NT WaitForSingleObject() service to block our thread until the SRB completes. At that point the ASPI manager will call our callback routine, which will in turn signal the event that our thread is blocking on. The net result is the same as for polling, but we haven't wasted any processor time.

Callback routines are also very useful when controlling streaming devices like tape drives and CD-ROM recorders, where the media is constantly moving and you must issue the next `read` or `write` command within a very short period of time. If the next command is issued too late, the tape drive will need to reposition (costing time), or the CD-ROM recorder will run out of data to write (wasting the CD). One common means of dealing with this is to prepare SRBs and place them in a queue in the foreground, and then rely on a callback routine to send the next pending SRB to the ASPI manager in the background, as soon as the previous command completes. This provides a simple but very useful form of multitasking.

Callback routines can be intimidating and difficult to debug, so they aren't often used unless performance is a critical issue. Many applications still simply poll for completion, wasting CPU time. To make things easier for programmers, the ASPI implementations for Windows 95 and NT provide a third method for waiting, called *Event Notification*. Instead of specifying the address of a callback routine, you can provide the handle of a Win32 event object that will be signalled automatically when the command completes. After starting the SRB you can then simply wait for the event, and your thread won't hog CPU time. Modifying our example above:

```
srb.PostProc = EventHandle;
srb.Flags |= SRB_EVENT_NOTIFY;
ResetEvent(EventHandle);
dwStatus = SendASPI32Command((LPSRB) &srb);
if (dwStatus == SS_PENDING)
    WaitForSingleObject(EventHandle,INFINITE);
```

Note that callback routines and event notification are mutually exclusive. Never set both the `SRB_EVENT_NOTIFY` and `SRB_POSTING` bits in an `SRB_Flags` field. Given the choice between callbacks and event notification, the latter is simpler and more efficient.

Processing Returned Status Information

The final step in processing an SRB involves checking the returned status fields. For SCSI I/O commands, this can involve up to four separate fields: `SRB_Status`, `SRB_HaStat`, `SRB_TargStat`, and the `SRB_SenseArea` buffer. We describe the different values returned in these fields later in this chapter, in the ASPI Error and Status Codes section. Right now you should just remember that things can go wrong, and these fields will tell you what happened.

Another thing to note is that if you use callback functions or event notification, the status field is not necessarily valid until the SRB has finished executing. This means that you should not poll the status field for information until the callback has executed or the event has triggered.

Adapter-Specific Properties

The ASPI interface tries to manage most hardware-specific details for you, but some cards have data buffer alignment or maximum transfer size restrictions that must be accommodated by the application. For example, many PC-based SCSI adapters can transfer a maximum of 65,536 bytes of data with a single command. Applications must be able to recognize this limitation and make sure they stay within it. Unfortunately, the original ASPI specification did not provide a way to determine this information for specific adapter cards. A February 1994 addendum to the ASPI specification details a method of gathering hardware-specific information, but you must take care to determine if a specific ASPI manager supports this extension. The ASPI for Win32 specification (Windows 95 and Windows NT) redefines portions of the `Host Adapter Unique` field for standard sets of adapter-specific information, which simplifies the detection process but isn't necessarily compatible with older ASPI managers under other operating systems. See the description of the `Host Adapter Inquiry` command for additional information.

Connecting to the ASPI Manager

As mentioned earlier, the actual implementation of the ASPI manager varies between operating systems. MS-DOS and OS/2 ASPI managers are implemented as device drivers, while Windows ASPI managers are implemented as DLLs. Different Windows implementations may also use additional components (VxDs or device drivers) to handle low-level operating system and hardware interface functions. For the most part, the differences in the implementation are insignificant to the application programmer, except for the method of connecting to the ASPI manager. On Windows systems you simply link your application to the ASPI manager's import library (WINASPI.LIB or WNASPI32.LIB), and rely on the Windows dynamic link mechanism to make the connection. For MS-DOS and OS/2 systems you must open the device driver and issue an IOCTL call to get the address of the ASPI manager's entry point.

Don't worry if this sounds complicated. It's actually quite simple. On 16-bit Windows systems you can use the following code to connect to the ASPI manager:

Listing 7-1. Connecting to ASPI under 16-Bit Windows

```
WORD   AspiStatus;
BYTE   NumAdapters;

AspiStatus = GetASPISupportInfo();

switch (HIBYTE(AspiStatus))
    {
    case SS_COMP:
        /* ASPI is properly initialized and running */
        /* The low byte of the status contains the  */
        /* number of host adapters installed under  */
        /* ASPI.                                     */
        NumAdapters = LOBYTE(AspiStatus);
        break;

    case SS_ILLEGAL_MODE:
        /* ASPI is not supported on the currently running */
        /* Windows mode (real, standard, or enhanced)     */
        NumAdapters = 0;
        break;

    case SS_OLD_MANAGER:
        /* The installed MS-DOS ASPI manager does not  */
        /* support Windows. Some MS-DOS ASPI managers */
        /* may be used under Windows, but many do not  */
        /* support Virtual DMA Services, or are other- */
        /* wise incompatible with Windows.             */
        NumAdapters = 0;
        break;

    default:
        /* Something is not right, so don't even try */
        NumAdapters = 0;
    }
```

The most common problem here is forgetting to link the WINASPI.LIB import library into your application, so the linker complains that it can't find the `GetASPISupportInfo()` routine. The process is similar for 32-bit Windows systems, except you link to the WNASPI32.LIB import library, call the `GetASPI32SupportInfo()` routine, and you don't have to worry about compatible MS-DOS ASPI managers:

Listing 7-2. Connecting to ASPI under 32-Bit Windows

```
DWORD    AspiStatus;
BYTE     NumAdapters;

AspiStatus = GetASPI32SupportInfo();

switch (HIBYTE(LOWORD(AspiStatus)))
    {
    case SS_COMP:
        /* ASPI is properly initialized and running. */
        /* The low byte of the status contains the   */
        /* number of host adapters installed.        */
        NumAdapters = LOBYTE(AspiStatus);
        break;

    default:
        /* No ASPI manager is currently installed */
        NumAdapters = 0;
    }
```

These examples assume you are linking the WINASPI.LIB or WNASPI32.LIB import library to your application. If not, you can still use the ASPI manager, but you must explicitly load it with the `Windows LoadLibrary()` routine, and get the address of the `GetASPISupport-Info()` routine with the `GetProcAddress()` routine. This process is a bit more complicated, but it lets your program start even if the ASPI manager isn't installed, allowing you to provide the user with more specific information than the standard Windows "couldn't find a required DLL" message. You can dynamically load the Win32 ASPI manager as shown below:

Listing 7-3. Dynamically Loading ASPI under 16-Bit Windows

```
DWORD (*GetASPI32SupportInfo)();              /* ptr to function */
DWORD (*SendASPI32Command(LPSRB lpSrb);  /* ptr to function */
HANDLE  WnAspiHandle;
DWORD   AspiStatus;
BYTE    NumAdapters;

WnAspiHandle = LoadLibrary("WNASPI32.DLL");
if (WnAspiHandle)
```

(Continued)

Listing 7-3. (*Continued*)

```
{
GetASPI32SupportInfo = GetProcAddress("GetASPI32SupportInfo");
SendASPI32Command = GetProcAddress("SendASPI32Command");
if (GetASPI32SupportInfo && SendASPICommand)
    {
    AspiStatus = GetASPI32SupportInfo();
    switch (HIBYTE(LOWORD(AspiStatus)))
        {
        case SS_COMP:
            /* ASPI is initialized and running.   */
            /* The low byte of the status contains */
            /* the number of host adapters.        */
            NumAdapters = LOBYTE(AspiStatus);
            break;

        default:
            /* No ASPI manager is currently installed */
            NumAdapters = 0;
        }
    }
else
    {
        /* Cannot retrieve address of     */
        /* GetASPI32SupportInfo() or      */
        /* SendASPI32Command(). The ASPI */
        /* may not be properly installed. */
    }
}
else
    {
    /* Cannot load WNASPI32.DLL     */
    /* make sure it is properly installed. */
    }
```

On MS-DOS systems, you must first open the ASPI manager's device driver and get the address of the ASPI manager's entry point. This is done by the following code sample:

Listing 7-4. Initializing ASPI under MS-DOS

```
            .DATA
AspiEntryPoint      DD 0                ; address of entry point
AspiHandle          DW 0                ; file handle
AspiDriverName      DB "SCSIMGR$",0     ; name of ASPI device

            .CODE
GetAspiEntryPoint PROC
    push    ds                          ; save current data segment
    mov     ax,@DATA                    ; load local data segment
    mov     ds,ax
    lea     dx,AspiDriverName           ; load offset of driver name
    mov     ax,3D00h                    ; MS-DOS open file
    iny     21h                         ;
    jc      failed
    mov     [AspiHandle],ax             ; save file handle

    mov     bx,[AspiHandle]             ; load file handle
    lea     dx,AspiEntryPoint           ; address of buffer
    mov     cx,4                        ; length = 4 bytes
    mov     ax,4402h                    ; MS-DOS IOCTL read
    int     21h                         ;
    jc      failed

    mov     bx,[AspiHandle]             ; load file handle
    mov     ax,3E00h                    ; MS-DOS close file
    int     21h                         ;

    mov     ax,word ptr [AspiEntryPoint]    ; return the address
    mov     dx,word ptr [AspiEntryPoint+2]  ; of ASPI entry point
    pop     ds
    ret

failed:
    mov     ax,0                        ; return NULL for error
    mov     dx,0
    pop     ds
    ret
GetAspiEntryPoint ENDP
```

An application can then use the following sequence to connect to the ASPI manager:

Listing 7-5. Connecting to ASPI under MS-DOS

```
BYTE    NumAdapters;
WORD (FAR *SendASPICommand)(void FAR *pSrb);   /* ptr to function */

SendASPICommand = GetAspiEntryPoint();
if (SendASPICommand)
    {
    SRB_HA_Inquiry HostAdapterInfo;
    memset( &HostAdapterInfo, 0, sizeof(HostAdapterInfo) );
    HostAdapterInfo.SRB_Cmd = SC_HA_INQUIRY;
    HostAdapterInfo.SRB_HaId = 0;                 /* first host adapter */
    SendASPICommand( (LPSRB) &HostAdapterInfo );
    switch (HostAdapterInfo.SRB_Status)
        {
            NumAdapters = HostAdapterInfo.HA_Count;
            break;

        default:
            /* Something is wrong */
            NumAdapters = 0;
        }
    }
else
    {
    /* ASPI manager is not installed */
    NumAdapters = 0;
    }
```

The MS-DOS example above actually uses the ASPI manager to execute a `Host Adapter Inquiry` command to retrieve the number of host adapters installed. This was done to make the MS-DOS code mimic the behavior of the `Windows GetASPISupportInfo()` routine, which returns the number of host adapter installed (in the least significant byte of the return value).

ASPI Commands

As mentioned above, all requests to an ASPI manager are routed through a single `SendASPICommand()` function that takes a pointer to a generic *SCSI Request Block* (SRB) as its only parameter. The first few fields in an SRB are common to all ASPI commands. These fields include a command code, a host adapter number, a status field, and a field for various control flags. The remaining fields in an SRB are specific to the type of command,

and contain information and values that are appropriate to that command. The common SRB fields are:

```
BYTE     SRB_Cmd;
BYTE     SRB_Status;
BYTE     SRB_HaId;
BYTE     SRB_Flags;
DWORD    SRB_Hdr_Rsvd;
/* Command specific fields follow */
```

The `SRB_Cmd` field defines the ASPI command, and the format of any command-specific data. The `SRB_Status` field returns the status of the command, whether it is pending, completed, or encountered an error. The possible values returned in the `SRB_Status` field are described later in the ASPI Error and Status Codes section. The `SRB_HaId` field indicates which host adapter will process the request, and the `SRB_Flags` field contains any bit-flags that apply to the command.

The possible ASPI command values for the `SRB_Cmd` field are:

Table 7-1. ASPI Command Values

Value	Command	Description
0	SC_HA_INQUIRY	Retrieve information on the installed host adapter hardware, including the number of host adapters installed.
1	SC_GET_DEV_TYPE	Identify devices available on the SCSI bus.
2	SC_EXEC_SCSI_CMD	Execute a SCSI I/O command.
3	SC_ABORT_SRB	Request that a pending SRB be aborted.
4	SC_RESET_DEV	Sends a SCSI bus device reset to a particular target.
5	SC_SET_HA_INFO (Not valid on Windows 95 or NT)	Sets host adapter–specific information or operating parameters. (This command is specific to a particular host adapter/ASPI manager combination, and is not typically issued by application programmers.)
6	SC_GET_DISK_INFO (Not valid on Windows NT)	Retrieve information about a SCSI disk device's INT 13h drive and geometry mappings. (This command is available only under MS-DOS compatible operating systems that support the BIOS Int 13h services for disk drives.)

(Continued)

Table 7-1. ASPI Command Values *(Continued)*

Value	Command	Description
7	SC_RESCAN_SCSI_BUS	Rescan the SCSI bus attached to a given host adapter. This causes the ASPI manager to note any newly attached or removed devices and update its internal tables accordingly. (This command is available only under the ASPI for Win32 implementation in Windows 95 and NT.)
8	SC_GETSET_TIMEOUTS	Set or retrieve SCSI command timeout values for a given target device. (This command is available only under the ASPI for Win32 implementation in Windows 95 and NT.)

The `SC_HA_INQUIRY` and `SC_GET_DEV_TYPE` commands are used to obtain information about the installed host adapters and SCSI devices. These are typically used to determine which devices are available on a system. The `SC_EXEC_SCSI_CMD` command is used for all SCSI transactions, and is the most frequently used command. The `SC_ABORT_SRB` and `SC_RESET_DEV` commands are used when trying to recover from timeout and error conditions. The `SC_SET_HA_INFO` and `SC_GET_DISK_INFO` commands aren't typically used by application programmers, so they aren't discussed further.

Host Adapter Inquiry (SC_HA_INQUIRY)

The `Host Adapter Inquiry` command is used to retrieve information about an installed SCSI host adapter and the ASPI manager itself. Your first few calls to the ASPI manager should be `Host Adapter Inquiry` commands to determine the number of installed SCSI host adapters and their capabilities. The adapter is specified by the 0-based number passed in the `SRB_HaId` field, and information is returned in the `HA_*` fields, as described below:

Listing 7-6. Host Adapter Inquiry SRB

```
typedef struct {
    BYTE      SRB_Cmd;                // command code = SC_HA_INQUIRY
    BYTE      SRB_Status;             // command status byte
    BYTE      SRB_HaId;               // host adapter number (0 - N)
    BYTE      SRB_Flags;              // request flags, should be 0
```
(Continued)

Listing 7-6. (*Continued*)

```
DWORD     SRB_Hdr_Rsvd;           // reserved, must be 0
BYTE      HA_Count;               // total number of host adapters
BYTE      HA_SCSI_ID;             // SCSI ID of the specified host adapter
BYTE      HA_ManagerId[16];       // ASCII string describing ASPI manager
BYTE      HA_Identifier[16];      // ASCII string describing host adapter
BYTE      HA_Unique[16];          // host adapter unique parameters
BYTE      HA_Rsvd1;               // reserved
} SRB_HAInquiry;
```

The first `Host Adapter Inquiry` command you issue should specify host adapter number (SRB_HaId) of 0. This will retrieve information about the first SCSI host adapter, and it will also give you the total number of host adapters installed in the system. If there is more than one adapter present, you can issue additional `Host Adapter Inquiry` commands for the other host adapters.

Listing 7-7. Host Adapter Inquiry Call

```
SRB_HAInquiry HostAdapterInfo;

memset( &HostAdapterInfo, 0, sizeof(HostAdapterInfo) );

HostAdapterInfo.SRB_Cmd = SC_HA_INQUIRY;
HostAdapterInfo.SRB_HaId = 0;    /* first host adapter */

SendASPICommand( (LPSRB) &HostAdapterInfo );

switch (HostAdapterInfo.SRB_Status)
    {
    case SS_COMP:
        /* ASPI manager is installed and running */
        NumAdapters = HostAdapterInfo.HA_Count;
        break;
     default:
        /* Something is wrong */
        NumAdapters = 0;
    }
```

Let's take a closer look at the fields in this SRB structure:

Table 7-2. Host Adapter Inquiry Fields

Field	Description
SRB_Cmd	ASPI Command Code
	This field must contain `SC_HA_INQUIRY` to retrieve the information that follows.
SRB_Status	ASPI Command Status
	This field is used to hold the pending and completed ASPI command status. On return, this field will contain one of the following values:
	`SS_COMP`—completed without error
	`SS_INVALID_HA`—invalid host adapter number
	(Refer to the ASPI Error and Status Codes section for additional information about this field.)
SRB_HaId	Host Adapter Index
	This field specifies which installed host adapter will be queried by this command. A value of 0 indicates the first installed host adapter, 1 is the second, and so forth. Some host adapters support multiple SCSI busses, and in this case, the value specified by this field is actually a logical bus index rather than a physical host adapter index. If you specify an index that is out of range the `SRB_Status` field will return an `SS_INVALID_HA` status code. You can determine the total number of host adapters available under the ASPI manager by setting this field to 0 and looking at the value returned in the `HA_Count` field.
SRB_Flags	ASPI Command Flags
	No flags are valid for this command, and this field should be set to 0.
SRB_Hdr_Rsvd	This field is reserved and should be set to 0.
HA_Count	Host Adapter Count
	This field returns the total number of host adapters available under the ASPI manager. Some host adapters support multiple SCSI busses, and in this case the value returned is actually the total number of logical SCSI busses installed rather than the number of physical host adapter cards. In most cases this distinction is unimportant, since you can simply treat multiple SCSI busses on a single card as if they were actually on separate cards.
HA_SCSI_ID	Host Adapter SCSI ID
	This field returns the SCSI ID of the specified host adapter.

(Continued)

Table 7-2. Host Adapter Inquiry Fields *(Continued)*

Field	Description
HA_ManagerId	ASPI Manager Identifier String
	The ASPI manager returns an ASCII string in this field describing the ASPI manager. Typically this string describes the developer of the ASPI manager. (Note that this string may not be null terminated.)
HA_Identifier	Host Adapter Identifier String
	This field returns an ASCII string describing the specified host adapter. This string typically describes the adapter type or model number. (Note that this string may not be null terminated.)
HA_Unique	Host Adapter Unique Parameters
	This field returns a variety of information describing the specified host adapter's characteristics and requirements. See the text below for additional information.

The HA_Unique field was originally reserved for information specific to a particular ASPI manager implementation. Under Windows 95 and NT, portions of this field are used to return information about the capabilities of the host adapter.

Table 7-3. Host Adapter Unique Parameters

Byte #	Description
0–1	Buffer Alignment Mask
	This value specifies the host adapter's buffer alignment requirements.
	0 = no alignment requirements
	1 = word alignment
	3 = dword alignment
	7 = quadword alignment
	and so forth. The alignment of the buffer can be checked by ANDing the buffer address with this mask value. The buffer is properly aligned if the result is 0.
	You must make sure any data buffer that you send to the ASPI manager meets this alignment.

(Continued)

Table 7-3. Host Adapter Unique Parameters *(Continued)*

Byte #	Description
2	Adapter Unique Flags
	Bit 0—reserved
	Bit 1—residual byte count reporting is supported
	Bits 2–7—reserved
	If bit 1 is set, the specified adapter supports residual byte count reporting. This means that after a SCSI I/O transfer (via the `SC_EXEC_SCSI_CMD` command) the `SRB_BufLen` field can be updated to indicate the number of bytes remaining in a transfer. This can be useful in buffer underrun situations, since you can then determine how much data was actually transferred by the command. See the `SC_EXEC_SCSI_CMD` description for additional information.
3	Maximum SCSI Targets Supported
	This value indicates the maximum number of SCSI targets that are supported by the given adapter. If this value is 0, you should assume that there are a maximum of 8 targets.
4–7	Maximum Transfer Length
	This field specifies the maximum number of bytes that can be transferred by a single SCSI I/O command on the specified adapter. Byte 7 is the most significant byte.
8–15	Reserved

It is very important to use the `HA_Unique` information when it is available. Some host adapters and drivers have limitations on the maximum amount of data that can be transferred with a single SCSI command, and this limit is reflected in the `Maximum Transfer Length` field within the `HA_Unique` data. A 64K limitation is common on many PC-based host adapters, and this limit may be further reduced by the operating system you are using. Be aware that you may have to break up transfers into smaller chunks to accommodate such limitations.

The Buffer Alignment Mask is becoming more important on newer hardware platforms. In the never-ending quest for speed, many system bus and host adapter designs use sophisticated schemes to improve data transfer times when data is properly aligned. Many system memory caches and busses are optimized for 64-bit, 128-bit, or even larger data burst transfers. When your data buffers are aligned on these natural bus size boundaries, transfers can be blazingly fast. However, data that is not properly aligned often requires additional bus cycles to move across the bus, slowing things down considerably.

Get Device Type (SC_GET_DEV_TYPE)

The Get Device Type command is used to retrieve basic information about a specific target device attached to a host adapter. The adapter is specified by the 0-based number passed in the SRB_HaId field, the SCSI ID of the target device is specified in the SRB_Target field, and the target device's LUN is specified in the SRB_Lun field. If the specified logical unit exists on the target, its device type identifier will be returned in the SRB_DeviceType field. This command allows you to quickly determine if a specific target device is available.

Listing 7-8. Get Device Type SRB

```
typedef struct {
    BYTE     SRB_Cmd;               // command code = SC_GET_DEV_TYPE
    BYTE     SRB_Status;            // command status byte
    BYTE     SRB_HaId;              // host adapter number
    BYTE     SRB_Flags;             // request flags, should be 0
    DWORD    SRB_Hdr_Rsvd;          // reserved, must be 0
    BYTE     SRB_Target;            // SCSI ID of device (typically 0-7)
    BYTE     SRB_Lun;               // Logical Unit Number of device
    BYTE     SRB_DeviceType;        // returns the SCSI device type
    BYTE     SRB_Rsvd1;             // reserved for alignment
    } SRB_GDEVBlock;
```

You should use this command to determine whether a specific target/LUN device exists. Most ASPI managers will scan the SCSI bus when they are first loaded and save information about each device found on a system. The Get Device Type command typically uses this saved information, and doesn't actually have to query the device again (possibly timing out on target/LUN devices that aren't attached). Applications can issue the Get Device Type command in a loop, once for each adapter/target/LUN combination possible, to build a list of devices attached to your system.

Listing 7-9. Get Device Type Call

```
SRB_GDEVBlock srb;
int adapter, target;
for (adapter=0; adapter<NumAdapters; adapter++)
    {
    for (target=0; target<NumDevices; target++)
    /* use NumDevices from Host Adapter Inquiry */
```

(Continued)

Listing 7-9. (*Continued*)

```
{
memset(&srb,0,sizoef(srb));
srb.SRB_Cmd = SC_GET_DEV_TYPE;
srb.HaId = adapter;
srb.Target = target;
srb.Lun = 0;
SendASPI32Command((LPSRB)&srb);
if (srb.SRB_Status == SS_COMP)
    {
    /* We found a device, it's type is */
    /* in the srb.SRB_DeviceType field */
    }
else
    {
    /* The device doesn't exist, or is */
    /* not responding. */
    }
}
}
```

Let's look at the SRB fields for the SRB_GET_DEV_TYPE command in more detail:

Table 7-4. Get Device Type Fields

Field	Description
SRB_Cmd	ASPI Command Code
	This field must contain SC_GET_DEV_TYPE to retrieve the information that follows.
SRB_Status	ASPI Command Status
	This field is used to hold the pending and completed ASPI command status. On return, this field will contain one of the following values:
	SS_COMP—without error
	SS_INVALID_HA—host adapter number
	SS_NO_DEVICE—device not installed
	(Refer to the ASPI Error and Status Codes section for additional information about this field.)

(Continued)

Table 7-4. Get Device Type Fields *(Continued)*

Field	Description
SRB_HaId	Host Adapter Index
	This field specifies which installed host adapter will be queried by this command. A value of 0 indicates the first installed host adapter, 1 is the second, and so forth. See the description of the Host Adapter Inquiry command for additional information.
SRB_Flags	ASPI Command Flags
	No flags are valid for this command, and this field should be set to 0.
SRB_Hdr_Rsvd	This field is reserved and should be set to 0.
SRB_Target	Target Device SCSI ID
	This field specifies the SCSI ID of the device in question. Typical values are 0–7. Some host adapters allow more than eight target devices on a single bus, so be sure to check the information returned by the Host Adapter Inquiry command to determine the largest possible value for this field on each host adapter.
SRB_Lun	Target Device Logical Unit Number
	This field specifies the Logical Unit Number (LUN) of the device in question. Some SCSI peripherals gang several individual device units on a single SCSI ID. These subunits are identified by their LUN and this field is used to select one of them. If a device has only a single logical unit, set this field to 0.
SRB_DeviceType	Device Type ID
	This field returns the SCSI peripheral device type identifier for the specified target/LUN. This value is usually the same as the peripheral device type returned by the SCSI Inquiry command. You may want to issue an Inquiry command to be certain.
SRB_Rsvd1	Reserved for alignment.
	Set this field to 0.

Execute SCSI Command (SC_EXEC_SCSI_CMD)

The Execute SCSI Command command sends a SCSI I/O command to a target device. You provide a SCSI *Command Descriptor Block* (CDB) and a data buffer, and the ASPI manager will take care of the rest. All of the complexity of the SCSI bus is hidden behind this one ASPI command.

Listing 7-10. Execute SCSI Command SRB

```
typedef struct {
    BYTE    SRB_Cmd;             // command code = SC_EXEC_SCSI_CMD
    BYTE    SRB_Status;          // command status byte
    BYTE    SRB_HaId;            // host adapter number to query (0 - N)
    BYTE    SRB_Flags;           // request flags, see below
    DWORD   SRB_Hdr_Rsvd;        // reserved, must be 0
    BYTE    SRB_Target;          // SCSI ID of target (typically 0 - 7)
    BYTE    SRB_Lun;             // Logical Unit Number of  device
    WORD    SRB_Rsvd1;           // reserved for alignment
    DWORD   SRB_BufLen;          // Data buffer length
    BYTE    *SRB_BufPointer;     // Data buffer address
    BYTE    SRB_SenseLen;        // Sense buffer length
    BYTE    SRB_CDBLen;          // CDB length
    BYTE    SRB_HaStat;          // Host adapter status (returned)
    BYTE    SRB_TargStat;        // Target status (returned)
    void(*SRB_PostProc)(LPSRB);  // Post routine address
    BYTE    SRB_Rsvd2[20];       // reserved
    BYTE    SRB_CDBByte[16];     // SCSI CDB
    BYTE    SRB_SenseArea[16];   // Buffer for SCSI sense data
    } SRB_ExecSCSICmd;
```

Let's examine these fields in more detail:

Table 7-5. Execute SCSI Command Fields

Field	Description
SRB_Cmd	ASPI Command Code
	This field must contain SC_EXEC_SCSI_CMD to execute a SCSI I/O command.
SRB_Status	ASPI Command Status
	This field is used to hold the pending and completed ASPI command status. On return, this field will contain one of the following values:
	SS_PENDING—is still in progress
	SS_COMP—without error
	SS_INVALID_HA—host adapter number
	SS_ABORTED—was aborted
	SS_ERR—completed with an error

(Continued)

Table 7-5. Execute SCSI Command Fields *(Continued)*

Field	Description
SRB_Status *(Continued)*	SS_INVALID_SRB—SRB field or flag is invalid
	SS_INVALID_PATH_ID—the target ID or LUN is invalid
	SS_BUFFER_TOO_BIG—the ASPI manager cannot handle the specified data buffer length
	SS_BUFFER_ALIGN—the ASPI manager cannot handle the alignment of the specified data buffer address.
	SS_SECURITY_VIOLATION—the caller does not have the necessary security privileges to execute the SCSI I/O command on the specified device
	(Refer to the ASPI Error and Status Codes section for additional information about this field.)
SRB_HaId	Host Adapter Index
	This field specifies which installed host adapter will be accessed by this command. A value of 0 indicates the first installed host adapter, 1 is the second, and so forth. See the description of the Host Adapter Inquiry command for additional information.
SRB_Flags	ASPI Command Flags
	This field contains a set of bit flags that control the execution of this SRB. The flags valid for this command are:
	SRB_DIR_IN
	SRB_DIR_OUT
	(For data transfer commands, either SRB_DIR_IN or SRB_DIR_OUT must be set.)
	SRB_EVENT_NOTIFY
	SRB_POSTING
	SRB_ENABLE_RESIDUAL_COUNT
SRB_Hdr_Rsvd	This field is reserved and should be set to 0.
SRB_Target	Target Device SCSI ID
	This field specifies the SCSI ID of the device accessed by this command. Typical values are 0–7. Some host adapters allow more than eight target devices on a single bus, so be sure to check the information returned by the Host Adapter Inquiry command to determine the largest possible value for this field on each host adapter.

(Continued)

Table 7-5. Execute SCSI Command Fields *(Continued)*

Field	Description
SRB_LUN	Target Device Logical Unit Number
	This field specifies the Logical Unit Number (LUN) of the device accessed by this command. Some SCSI peripherals gang several individual device units on a single SCSI ID. These subunits are identified by their LUN and this field is used to select one of them. If a device has only a single logical unit, set this field to 0.
SRB_Rsvd1	Reserved for alignment.
	Set this field to 0 for compatibility with future ASPI versions.
SRB_BufLen	Data Buffer Length
	Set this field to the size of the data buffer used for the SCSI I/O command. For write commands, this is the number of data bytes that will be sent to the target device. For read commands, this is the maximum number of data bytes that will be read from the target device. If the SCSI I/O command does not involve a data transfer, set this field to 0. If residual byte count reporting is supported and enabled, this field returns the number of bytes NOT transferred by the SCSI I/O command. You can think of this field as a counter that is decremented once for every data byte transferred to/from the target device. If you try to read 100 bytes from a target device but the device only returns 10 bytes, this field will return with a value of 90 (if residual byte count reporting is supported and enabled).
SRB_BufPointer	Data Buffer Pointer
	Set this field to the address of the data buffer used for the SCSI I/O command. For write commands, data will be sent from this buffer to the target device. For read commands, data will be sent from the target device to this buffer.
SRB_SenseLen	Sense Data Length
	Set this field to the size of the SRB_SenseArea field available at the end of this structure. When a target device generates a check condition status, the ASPI manager automatically issues a Request Sense command and places the sense data in the SRB_SenseArea field. Most applications simply set the size to 14, with a 16-byte buffer allocated for alignment.

(Continued)

Table 7-5. Execute SCSI Command Fields *(Continued)*

Field	Description
SRB_CDBLen	CDB Length
	Set this field to the size of the CDB contained in the SRB_CDBByte[ ] field. This value will vary depending on the SCSI I/O command being issued, but typical values are 6, 10, and 12. The ASPI manager sends this many command bytes from the SRB_CDBByte[ ] field to the target device during the command phase of a SCSI transaction.
SRB_HaStat	Host Adapter Status
	This field returns a host adapter status value, which indicates any error conditions encountered by the host adapter during the execution of this SRB. Possible values are:
	HASTAT_OK
	HASTAT_SEL_TO
	HASTAT_DO_DU
	HASTAT_BUS_FREE
	HASTAT_PHASE_ERR
	HASTAT_TIMEOUT
	HASTAT_COMMAND_TIMEOUT
	HASTAT_MESSAGE_REJECT
	HASTAT_BUS_RESET
	HASTAT_PARITY_ERROR
	HASTAT_REQUEST_SENSE_FAILED
	(Refer to the ASPI Error and Status Codes section for additional information.)
SRB_TargStat	Target Status
	This field returns the status value sent by the target device at the end of a SCSI I/O command. The possible values returned in this field are defined in the SCSI specifications.
	0x00 Good
	0x02 Check Condition
	0x04 Condition Met
	0x08 Busy

(Continued)

Table 7-5. Execute SCSI Command Fields *(Continued)*

Field	Description
SRB_TargStat *(Continued)*	0x10 Intermediate
	0x14 Intermediate—Condition Met
	0x18 Reservation Conflict
	0x22 Command Terminated
	0x28 Task Set Full
	0x30 Auto Contingent Allegiance Active
	(Refer to the ASPI Error and Status Codes section for additional information.)
SRB_PostProc	Post Procedure
	Set this field to the address of your post procedure if you are using command posting, or to the handle of a Win32 event semaphore if you are using event notification. If you are using either of these, you must also set the appropriate bit flag in the SRB_Flags field (SRB_POSTING or SRB_EVENT_NOTIFICATION).
SRB_Rsvd2	Reserved; you should set this field to 0.
SRB_Rsvd3	Reserved; you should set this field to 0.
SRB_CDBByte	Command Descriptor Block
	This field contains the SCSI *Command Descriptor Block* (CDB) which is sent to the target device during the command phase of a SCSI transfer.
SRB_SenseArea	Sense Data Buffer
	When the target device returns a Check Condition status, the ASPI manager automatically retrieves the device's sense data and places it in this field. The sense data describes the error or exception that caused the Check Condition status. Refer to Chapter 6 for additional information.

Abort SRB (SC_ABORT_SRB)

The Abort SRB command is used to abort a pending SRB. You might need to use this if a command hasn't completed within a reasonable amount of time. Older versions of ASPI didn't enforce or support timeouts directly, but the latest Win32 implementations feature a Get/Set Timeout function.

The execution times of SCSI commands can vary widely. If you don't use the timeout function, your application is responsible for determining when a command has taken too long to complete. When you decide that enough is enough, you can issue the Abort SRB command to request that the ASPI manager gracefully stop the command and release any resources it may be using.

Listing 7-11. The SRB for the Abort SRB Command

```
typedef struct {
    BYTE     SRB_Cmd;              // command code = SC_ABORT_SRB
    BYTE     SRB_Status;           // command status byte
    BYTE     SRB_HaId;             // host adapter number
    BYTE     SRB_Flags;            // request flags, should be 0
    DWORD    SRB_Hdr_Rsvd;         // reserved, must be 0
    void *SRB_ToAbort;             // address of SRB to abort
    } SRB_Abort;
```

The SRB_HaId field must be set to the same host adapter number as specified in the SRB you wish to abort, and the SRB_ToAbort field must point to that SRB. This command will always complete before the ASPI manager returns to your application, although the SRB you are aborting might not complete until later. If the original SRB is successfully aborted, its SRB_Status field will eventually be set to SS_ABORTED. Note that you must still wait for the original SRB to complete. Be very careful not to deallocate or reuse it until its SRB_Status field is no longer SS_PENDING. Remember also that unless you are using polling, you should not check this field until the command is complete.

Listing 7-12. Abort SRB Call

```
HANDLE EventHandle;
SRB_ExecSCSICmd OriginalSrb;

/* Assume OriginalSrb has already been initialized */
OriginalSrb.PostProc = EventHandle;
OriginalSrb.Flags |= SRB_EVENT_NOTIFY;
ResetEvent(EventHandle)
SendASPI32Command((LPSRB)&OriginalSrb);
if (WaitForSingleObject(EventHandle,timeout) == WAIT_TIMEOUT)
    {
    SRB_Abort AbortSrb;
    AbortSrb.SRB_Cmd = SC_ABORT_SRB;
    AbortSrb.SRB_HaId = OriginalSrb.SRB_HaId;
```

(Continued)

Listing 7-12. (*Continued*)

```
AbortSrb.Flags = 0;
AbortSrb.Hdr_Rsvd = 0;
AbortSrb.SRB_ToAbort = &OriginalSrb;
SendASPI32Command((LPSRB) &AbortSrb);
if (AbortSrb.SRB_Status != SS_COMP)
    {
    /* Something is terribly wrong */
    }
else
    {
    while (OriginalSrb.SRB_Status == SS_PENDING)
        {
        /* Wait for OriginalSrb to complete. */
        /* You should have an additional */
        /* timeout here as a fail-safe in */
        /* case of catastrophic failure. */
        }
    }
}
```

Note that the above code is not guaranteed to work under Windows 95 and NT. Once a request has been passed to the miniport driver under these platforms, it cannot be aborted.

Table 7-6. Abort SRB Fields

Field	Description
SRB_Cmd	ASPI Command Code
	This field must contain SC_ABORT_SRB to execute the Abort SRB command.
SRB_Status	ASPI Command Status
	This field is used to hold the pending and completed ASPI command status. On return, this field will contain one of the following values:
	SS_COMP—completed without error
	SS_INVALID_HA—invalid host adapter number
	SS_INVALID_SRB—an SRB field or flag is invalid
	If this field returns SS_COMP, the ASPI manager will attempt to abort the specified SRB. If any other value is returned the ASPI manager will not attempt to abort the SRB.

(Continued)

Table 7-6. Abort SRB Fields *(Continued)*

Field	Description
SRB_HaId	Host Adapter Index
	This field must contain the same host adapter number that was specified in the SRB you wish to abort.
SRB_Flags	ASPI Command Flags
	No flags are valid for this command, and this field should be set to 0.
SRB_Hdr_Rsvd	This field is reserved and should be set to 0.
SRB_ToAbort	SRB To Abort
	This field contains the address of the SRB you wish to abort. This should be the same pointer passed to the SendASPI32Command() that started the original SRB.

Reset SCSI Device (SC_RESET_DEV)

The Reset SCSI Device command is used to send a SCSI Bus Device Reset message to a target device. This causes the target to abandon all I/O processes that may be pending and reset all of its operating parameters to their power-on values. Note that this command is specific to a particular device, and does not involve strobing the SCSI bus RST signal. Rather, the host adapter will try to send the Bus Device Reset message via a normal SCSI bus transaction. This command doesn't work properly under Windows 95 and NT at this time, but is supported to maintain compatibility with other ASPI implementations.

Listing 7-13. Reset SCSI Device SRB

```
typedef struct {
    BYTE     SRB_Cmd;              // command code = SC_RESET_DEV
    BYTE     SRB_Status;           // command status byte
    BYTE     SRB_HaId;             // host adapter number
    BYTE     SRB_Flags;            // request flags, should be 0
    DWORD    SRB_Hdr_Rsvd;         // reserved, must be 0
    BYTE     SRB_Target;
    BYTE     SRB_Lun;
    BYTE     SRB_Rsvd1[12];
    BYTE     SRB_HaStat;
    BYTE     SRB_TargStat;
    void(*SRB_PostProc)(LPSRB);
    BYTE     SRB_Rsvd2[36];
    } SRB_BusDeviceReset;
```

Note that the fields are very similar to those in the SRB_Exec-SCSICmd structure. They have the same meaning for the `Reset SCSI Device` command as they do for `Execute SCSI` command. The ASPI manager will typically queue this command and return an `SS_PENDING` status. You must wait for the SRB to complete, and you can specify a callback routine or event handle just like you would for an `Execute SCSI Command` sequence.

Listing 7-14. Reset SCSI Device Call

```
HANDLE EventHandle;
SRB_BusDeviceReset srb;
memset(&srb,0,sizeof(srb));
srb.SRB_Cmd = SC_RESET_DEV;
srb.SRB_HaId = HostAdapterNumber;
srb.SRB_Target = TargetScsiId;
srb.SRB_Lun = 0;
srb.PostProc = EventHandle;
srb.Flags = SRB_EVENT_NOTIFY;
ResetEvent(EventHandle);
dwStatus = SendASPI32Command((LPSRB) &srb);
if (dwStatus == SS_PENDING)
    WaitForSingleEvent(EventHandle,INFINITE);
```

Table 7-7. Reset SCSI Device Fields

Field	Description
SRB_Cmd	ASPI Command Code
	This field must contain SC_RESET_DEV to execute this command.
SRB_Status	ASPI Command Status
	This field is used to hold the pending and completed ASPI command status. On return, this field will contain one of the following values:
	SS_PENDING—request is still in progress
	SS_COMP—completed without error
	SS_INVALID_HA—invalid host adapter number
	SS_ABORTED—command was aborted
	SS_ERR—command completed with an error

(Continued)

Table 7-7. Reset SCSI Device Fields *(Continued)*

Field	Description
SRB_Status *(Cont.)*	`SS_INVALID_SRB`—an SRB field or flag is invalid
	`SS_INVALID_PATH_ID`—the target ID or LUN is invalid
	(Refer to the ASPI Error and Status Codes section for additional information about this field.)
SRB_HaId	Host Adapter Index
	This field specifies which installed host adapter will be accessed by this command. A value of 0 indicates the first installed host adapter, 1 is the second, and so forth. See the description of the `Host Adapter Inquiry` command for additional information.
SRB_Flags	ASPI Command Flags
	This field contains a set of bit flags that control the execution of this SRB. The valid flags for this field are:
	`SRB_EVENT_NOTIFY`
	`SRB_POSTING`
SRB_Hdr_Rsvd	This field is reserved and should be set to 0.
SRB_Target	Target Device SCSI ID
	This field specifies the SCSI ID of the device to be reset by this command.
SRB_Lun	Target Device Logical Unit Number
	This field is defined for this command, but it isn't really used. SCSI Bus Device Resets are performed on the target device itself, and encompass all logical units on the device.
SRB_Rsvd1	Reserved; you should set all bytes in this field to 0.
SRB_HaStat	Host Adapter Status
	This field returns a host adapter status value, which indicates any error conditions encountered by the host adapter during the execution of this SRB. (Refer to the ASPI Error and Status Codes section for additional information.)
SRB_TargStat	Target Status
	This field returns the status value sent by the target device at the end of a SCSI I/O command. (Refer to the ASPI Error and Status Codes section for additional information.)

(Continued)

Table 7-7. Reset SCSI Device Fields *(Continued)*

Field	Description
SRB_PostProc	Post Procedure
	Set this field to the address of your post procedure if you are using command posting, or to the handle of a Win32 event semaphore if you are using event notification. If you are using either of these, you must also set the appropriate bit flag in the SRB_Flags field (SRB_POSTING or SRB_EVENT_NOTIFICATION).
SRB_Rsvd2	This field is reserved and should be set to 0.
SRB_Rsvd3	Reserved; you should set all bytes in this field to 0.

Rescan SCSI Bus (SC_RESCAN_SCSI_BUS)

The Rescan SCSI Bus command causes the ASPI manager to check the specified host adapter's SCSI bus for any changes. Newly attached devices will be recognized and supported by the ASPI manager. This command is available only under the ASPI for Win32 implementation in Windows 95 and NT. Under Windows NT, the ASPI manager will detect new devices, but will not remove existing targets if they are disabled or exchanged. Under Windows 95, this command works with the plug and play services to add or remove devices. Therefore devices may not appear until several seconds after the rescan command is issued.

Listing 7-15. Rescan SCSI Bus SRB

```
typedef struct {
    BYTE     SRB_Cmd;          // command code = SC_RESCAN_SCSI_BUS
    BYTE     SRB_Status;       // command status byte
    BYTE     SRB_HaId;         // host adapter number
    BYTE     SRB_Flags;        // request flags, should be zero
    DWORD    SRB_Hdr_Rsvd;     // reserved, must be zero
    } SRB_RescanPort;
```

Listing 7-16. Rescan SCSI Bus Call

```
int adapter;
for (adapter=0; adapter<NumAdapters; adapter++)
    {
    SRB_RescanPort srb;
    memset(&srb,0,sizeof(srb));
```
(Continued)

Listing 7-16. (*Continued*)

```
    srb.SRB_Cmd = SC_RESCAN_SCSI_BUS;
    srb.SRB_HaId = adapter;
    SendASPI32Command((LPSRB) &srb);
    }
Sleep(10000L);        // Wait 10 seconds for devices to appear
// Now we can use SC_GET_DEVICE_TYPE to find any new devices
```

Table 7-8. Rescan SCSI Bus Fields

Field	Description
SRB_Cmd	ASPI Command Code
	This field must contain `SC_RESCAN_SCSI_BUS` to execute this command.
SRB_Status	ASPI Command Status
	This field is used to hold the pending and completed ASPI command status. On return, this field will contain one of the following values:
	`SS_COMP`—completed without error
	`SS_INVALID_HA`—invalid host adapter number
	`SS_INVALID_SRB`—an SRB field or flag is invalid
	(Refer to the ASPI Error and Status Codes section for additional information about this field.)
SRB_HaId	Host Adapter Index
	This field specifies which installed host adapter will be rescanned by this command. A value of 0 indicates the first installed host adapter, 1 is the second, and so forth. See the description of the `Host Adapter Inquiry` command for additional information.
SRB_Flags	ASPI Command Flags
	No flags are defined for this command, and this field should be set to 0.

Get/Set Timeouts (SC_GETSET_TIMEOUTS)

The `Get/Set Timeouts` command allows you to set or retrieve timeout values for SCSI commands sent to a particular device. This command is available only under the ASPI for Win32 implementation in Windows 95 and NT. Timeouts are specified in one-half second increments, with a maximum timeout value of 108000 (30 hours). The `SRB_Flags` field determines whether you are getting or setting the timeout value.

Listing 7-17. Get/Set Timeouts SRB

```
typedef struct {
    BYTE    SRB_Cmd;             // command code = SC_GETSET_TIMEOUTS
    BYTE    SRB_Status;          // command status byte
    BYTE    SRB_HaId;            // host adapter number, or 0xFF for all
    BYTE    SRB_Flags;           // SRB_DIR_IN or SRB_DIR_OUT
    DWORD   SRB_Hdr_Rsvd;        // reserved, must be zero
    BYTE    SRB_Target;          // target ID, or 0xFF for all
    BYTE    SRB_Lun;             // target LUN, or 0xFF for all
    DWORD   SRB_Timeout          // Timeout value, in 1/2 seconds
    } SRB_GetSetTimeouts;
```

Listing 7-18. Get/Set Timeouts Call

```
SRB_GetSetTimeouts srb;
DWORD old_timeout = 0;
memset(&srb,0,sizeof(srb));
srb.SRB_Cmd = SC_GETSET_TIMEOUTS;
srb.SRB_HaId = HostAdapterNumber;
srb.SRB_Target = TargetScsiId;
srb.SRB_Lun = 0;
srb.SRB_Flags = SRB_DIR_IN;      // retrieve current timeout
SendASPI32Command((LPSRB)&srb);
if (srb.SRB_Status == SS_COMP)
    old_timeout = SRB.Timeout;
srb.Flags = SRB_DIR_OUT;         // set new timeout value
srb.SRB_Timeout = 10;            // 5 seconds
SendASPI32Command((LPSRB)&srb);
```

Timeouts are specific both to the device and the application. One application can set different timeout values for different devices, and other applications can set other timeouts for the same devices. Once a timeout has been set, it applies to all subsequent SC_EXEC_SCSI_CMD commands sent to the ASPI manager.

You must be very careful when setting a timeout value for your application. When a SCSI command does timeout, the entire SCSI bus will be reset. Note that this is a real SCSI bus reset via the RST signal, not just a Reset Device message sent to the device. All pending SCSI commands and SRBs on every device attached to that bus will be aborted, not just the command that timed out. Therefore your timeouts should be long enough to not occur during normal operation. Also note that your SCSI commands can be interrupted by a timeout from another application's SRB.

Your application should be able to handle this condition, retrying the operation as necessary.

Table 7-9. Get/Set Timeout Fields

Field	Description
SRB_Cmd	ASPI Command Code
	This field must contain SC_GETSET_TIMEOUTS to execute this command.
SRB_Status	ASPI Command Status
	This field is used to hold the pending and completed ASPI command status. On return, this field will contain one of the following values:
	SS_COMP—completed without error
	SS_INVALID_HA—invalid host adapter number
	SS_INVALID_SRB—an SRB field or flag is invalid
	SS_INVALID_PATH_ID—the target ID or LUN is invalid
	(Refer to the ASPI Error and Status Codes section for additional information about this field.)
SRB_HaId	Host Adapter Index
	This field specifies which installed host adapter will be rescanned by this command. A value of 0 indicates the first installed host adapter, 1 is the second, and so forth. You may also specify a special *wildcard* value of 0xFF to indicate that the timeout applies to the specified target/LUN combination on all host adapters.
SRB_Flags	ASPI Command Flags
	This field specifies whether you are getting or setting the timeout value. Use SRB_DIR_IN to retrieve the current timeout value for a given device, or SRB_DIR_OUT to set a new timeout value. When setting a timeout, the SRB_HaId, SRB_Target, and SRB_Lun fields may contain wildcard values of 0xFF, which indicate that the timeout applies to all matching adapters, targets, or LUNs, respectively.
SRB_Hdr_Rsvd	This field is reserved and should be set to 0.
SRB_Target	Target Device SCSI ID
	This field specifies the SCSI ID of the device that the timeout value affects. If you are setting a timeout value, this field may be set to 0xFF, which indicates that the timeout applies to all SCSI devices with matching adapter and LUN numbers.

(Continued)

Table 7-9. Get/Set Timeout Fields *(Continued)*

Field	Description
SRB_Lun	Target Device Logical Unit Number
	This field specifies the Logical Unit Number (LUN) of the device that the timeout value affects. If you are setting a timeout value, this field may be set to 0xFF, which indicates that the timeout applies to all logical units on the device.
SRB_Timeout	Timeout Value
	This field returns or specifies the timeout value in one-half second increments. Its value can be 0–108000 (30 hours). A value of 0 is treated as a special case indicating the maximum timeout available. For compatibility with older applications, the default setting is the maximum allowed.

ASPI Error and Status Codes

If you look closely at the SRB_ExecSCSICmd structure you will see three separate status fields: SRB_Status, SRB_HaStat, and SRB_TargStat. Each of these contain status information pertaining to different stages during the execution of a SCSI I/O command. SRB_Status indicates the processing status of the SRB itself, including any errors in the SRB structure, fields, or execution. SRB_HaStat returns the status from the host adapter, describing any problems with the SCSI bus transfer. SRB_TargStat is the status returned by the target device, and describes any problems with the SCSI I/O command or its execution on the target device.

ASPI SRB Status (SRB_Status)

SRB_Status contains the processing status of the SRB. The values returned in this field are related to the processing of the SRB itself, and generally are independent of the host adapter and target device. For example, SRB_Status can indicate whether a command is still pending, completed, aborted, or invalid. One value, SS_ERR, indicates that the host adapter encountered a problem with a SCSI I/O command sent to the target device. In this case you must look at the SRB_HaStat and SRB_TargStat fields to determine the cause of the error. If the SRB_Status is SS_COMP, the values of SRB_HaStat and SRB_TargStat are not guaranteed to be valid. Do not rely on them for information about commands that complete normally.

During the execution of an SRB, the SRB_Status field will contain a value of SS_PENDING, indicating that the ASPI manager has not yet finished processing the SRB. When the SRB completes, the ASPI manager will write the completion status of the SRB into this field. The value written indicates whether the ASPI manager encountered any problems pertaining to the SRB itself.

SS_PENDING

This value indicates that the SRB has not yet completed. This status value is only returned for the SC_EXEC_SCSI_CMD and SC_RESET_DEV commands, and indicates that the SRB has been queued or started, but has not yet finished. Typically a host adapter will generate an interrupt when a SCSI I/O command completes, and the ASPI manager will trap that interrupt to complete its processing. This includes updating any relevant return fields in the SRB, and possibly retrieving SCSI sense data from the target device. Then the ASPI manager will set the SRB_Status field to another value indicating the completion status of the SRB.

SS_COMP

This value indicates that the SRB has completed without an error. You should know that some ASPI managers and host adapter drivers don't consider a data buffer underrun an error when reading data from the target device. This is because a data buffer underrun is a common condition when working with certain device types. For example, when reading a tape containing variable length blocks, you typically issue a SCSI read command with a data buffer big enough to hold the largest block you expect to encounter. If the actual tape block read is smaller, you may get a data buffer underrun indication (HASTAT_DO_DU) in the SRB_HaStatus field, and you will certainly get a check condition indication in the SRB_TargStat field. Again, these fields are not reliable for commands that complete successfully. The officially sanctioned way to check for data overruns and underruns it to enable residual byte reporting.

SS_ERR

This value indicates that the SRB had completed, but that an error or exception condition was encountered. There are several possible causes for this status being returned, and you must check the SRB_HaStat and SRB_TargStat fields to determine exactly what happened. Getting an SS_ERR status for an SRB doesn't necessarily mean that anything terrible happened. It often means simply that the target device returned a check condition status, which is a common indication for many device types.

See the description of the `SRB_TargStatus` check condition value for additional information.

SS_INVALID_CMD

This value is returned if the `SRB_Cmd` field contains a value that is not a valid ASPI command. If you see this status code, you are almost certainly not initializing the SRB correctly.

SS_INVALID_HA

This value is returned if the `SRB_HaId` field indicates a nonexistent host adapter number. Host adapters are numbered consecutively, starting with 0. You can determine the number of host adapters installed by issuing an `SC_HA_INQUIRY` command with the `SRB_HaId` field set to 0. Upon return, the `HA_Count` field will contain the number of host adapters available via the ASPI manager.

SS_NO_DEVICE

This value indicates that the SCSI ID specified in the `SRB_Target` field is not available on the host adapter's SCSI bus. This typically means that there is no target device at that SCSI ID number. Use the `SC_GET_DEVICE_TYPE` command to determine whether a particular SCSI ID is available on a given host adapter's SCSI bus.

SS_INVALID_SRB

This value indicates that the SRB contains an invalid value in one or more fields. If you see this status code, you should double-check your SRB initialization code. Setting mutually exclusive bit flags in the `SRB_Flags` field is one common cause of this error.

SS_FAILED_INIT

This value is returned if the ASPI manager failed to initialize properly. ASPI managers for some operating systems (Windows) will return this error if they are unable to attach to an underlying device driver required for proper operation. If you see this status code, you should check for problems with your ASPI manager installation.

SS_ASPI_IS_BUSY

This value is returned if the ASPI manager cannot accept the SRB for processing. This can happen if you start a large number of SRB requests and the ASPI manager runs out of space to queue them. Most applications have only one or two pending SRB requests, so this rarely is a problem. If you see this status code, you should pace your requests. One possible solution would be to maintain your own queue of SRB requests, and send them to the ASPI manager only as others complete.

SS_BUFFER_TOO_BIG

This value indicates that the host adapter could not handle the SRB because its data buffer was too large (`SRB_BufLen`). If you see this status code, you should break your data transfers into smaller chunks.

SS_BUFFER_ALIGN

This value indicates that the data buffer address in the `SRB_BufPointer` field was not properly aligned for the host adapter. Some host adapter require data buffers to be aligned on certain hardware-imposed boundaries. If you see this status code, you should change the alignment of your data buffer to the alignment value returned by the `SC_HA_INQUIRY` command.

SS_SECURITY_VIOLATION

This value indicates that you don't have permission to access the specified target device. This may happen if you try to issue commands to a SCSI hard disk that is controlled by the operating system.

SS_ABORTED

This value indicates that the SRB was aborted before it was able to complete normally. You may see this status if you issued an `SC_ABORT_SRB` command to abort the SRB, or if the SRB was aborted due to a SCSI bus reset. You should not rely on any other return fields, since they may not have been updated before the command was aborted.

SS_ABORT_FAIL

This value indicates that a `SC_ABORT_SRB` command failed.

SS_NO_ASPI

The ASPI Manager DLL is present, but it could not establish a link to a required device driver or VxD. You should reinstall the ASPI manager.

SS_ILLEGAL_MODE

You are trying to run ASPI for Win32 from the Win32s environment, which is not supported. You can only use the 16-bit ASPI for Windows components under Windows 3.x.

SS_MISMATCHED_COMPONENTS

The ASPI Manager DLL is present, but a required device driver or VxD has a version number that doesn't match. You should reinstall the ASPI manager.

SS_NO_ADAPTERS

This value can be returned by `GetASPI32SupportInfo()` if there are no SCSI host adapters installed on a system. Older versions of ASPI treated this as a fatal error and refused to load, but with Plug and Play it is possible that a SCSI PCMCIA adapter may be inserted at a later time.

SS_INSUFFICIENT RESOURCES

This value indicates that the ASPI manager cannot allocate enough system resources to initialize properly. This usually indicates that the system is low on memory.

Host Adapter Status (SRB_HaStat)

The `SRB_HaStat` field returns the host adapter status. The `SRB_HaStat` field is defined only for the `SC_EXEC_SCSI_CMD` and `SC_RESET_DEV` commands, since these are the only ASPI commands that actually use the host adapter to manipulate the SCSI bus. The value returned in the `SRB_HaStat` field tells you of any problems that occurred transferring a command or data to the target device. Problems here generally involve hardware issues or timeouts.

HASTAT_OK

This value indicates that the SCSI transaction completed normally. You must still check the `SRB_TargStat` field for possible target errors. The `HASTAT_OK` value simply means that the SCSI bus transfer was successful. The `SRB_TargStat` field contains the status of the SCSI command itself. For example, the host adapter will successfully transfer an invalid CDB to a target device, but the target will then reject it. In this case the `SRB_HaStat` field will contain `HASTAT_OK`, but the `SRB_TargStat` field will contain 0x02, indicating a check condition. Further examination of the sense data will show the exact cause of the problem.

HASTAT_SEL_TO

This value indicates that the target device didn't respond to a selection on the SCSI bus. This usually means that there is no device at the specified SCSI ID. It may also indicate a problem with the SCSI bus itself, such as missing or incorrect termination. In any case, there isn't much you can do about this from your application. If the device won't respond to a selection, it can't accept any SCSI commands, and you're stuck. You can try sending the ASPI manager a SC_RESET_DEV command, but this typically only sends a "device reset" message to the target device. Since the target isn't responding to the SCSI bus selection, it won't get the reset message. However, some ASPI managers will detect that a previously responding device has disappeared, and may issue a SCSI bus reset (via the RST signal) in an attempt to get the wayward device back online.

HASTAT_DO_DU

This value indicates that the actual length of the SCSI data transfer was larger than the length specified in the SRB_BufLen field. For example, the CDB for a write command may specify a length of 1024 bytes, but your data buffer length is 512 bytes. In this case, the target will ask the host adapter to transfer all 1024 bytes, but the host adapter only has 512 bytes to send. Most ASPI managers will alert you to this problem by returning HASTAT_DO_DU in the SRB_HaStat field. If you detect this condition, you should double-check your buffer length and CDB. You should also check the SRB_TargStat field, since there may have also been a check condition status for the SCSI command.

HASTAT_BUS_FREE

This value is returned if the target device unexpectedly disconnects from the SCSI bus. This might be due to a cabling or signal problem, and is most likely to occur during or just after selection. If the target encounters a problem with the SCSI bus or phase changes, it will typically abort the SCSI transaction and let go of the bus. This condition is detected by the host adapter and reported with the HASTAT_BUS_FREE status code. You can retry the command in hopes that this is a transient problem, but if you see the HASTAT_BUS_FREE error frequently, you should check your SCSI bus cabling and termination.

HASTAT_PHASE_ERR

This value is returned if the target device enters a SCSI bus phase that wasn't expected by the host adapter. This could be a transitory condition, or it may indicate an incompatibility between the host adapter and the target device. SCSI-2 defines the allowable bus phase transitions, so this shouldn't be a problem with newer adapters and target devices.

HASTAT_TIMEOUT

This value is returned if a transaction times out during processing. It indicates a timeout while waiting for a bus transaction, which may be due to a phase or protocol error. An ASPI manager or host adapter's device driver may implement their own timeout mechanism for SRBs, and this status code is used to reflect the timeout condition.

HASTAT_COMMAND_TIMEOUT

This value is returned if a host adapter detects that an SRB has expired. It may indicate a device error, or a phase or protocol error. This return value differs from the `HASTAT_TIMEOUT` value in that the `HASTAT_COMMAND_TIMEOUT` code usually indicates that the SCSI transaction has been started, but did not complete within a given length of time.

HASTAT_MESSAGE_REJECT

This value indicates that the target sent a `SCSI Message Reject` message code to the host adapter. This message code is sent to indicate that the target could not accept a message code sent by the host adapter, or that the message code is not implemented by the target. This status code may indicate an incompatibility between the host adapter and the target device.

HASTAT_BUS_RESET

This value indicates that a SCSI bus reset was detected.

HASTAT_PARITY_ERROR

This value is returned when a parity error is detected on the SCSI bus. This means that the command or data transferred may be corrupt. As usual, you should check your cabling and termination.

HASTAT_REQUEST_SENSE_FAILED

This value indicates that the ASPI manager or host adapter couldn't retrieve the target device's sense data after receiving a check condition status from the target. If you see this condition, you should ignore any data in the `SRB_SenseArea[ ]` field in the SRB.

Target Device Status (SRB_TargStat)

The `SRB_TargStat` field contains the SCSI status value returned by the target device during the final status phase of a SCSI command. These values are defined by the SCSI specification, rather than ASPI, but I'll discuss them here because they logically fit in with the other error and status codes described above. I'll only describe the values that are likely to be returned by an ASPI manager. If you encounter a value not described below, you should check the latest SCSI specification for details.

Table 7-10. Target Device Status Codes

Value	Description
0x00	Good
	This value is returned when there are no errors or exceptional conditions that require servicing.
0x02	Check Condition
	This value indicates that an auto contingent allegiance condition has occurred. In human terms, this means that something has happened that you should know about. You can find out exactly what happened by inspecting the sense data. When the ASPI manager detects a check condition, it will automatically retrieve the sense data from the target device, and copy it to the SRB_SenseArea[ ] field in the SRB. You should check the sense code, sense key, and the ASC/ASQ values in the sense data to determine the cause of the check condition. Note that a check condition isn't necessarily an error, but it does indicate something you should check.
0x08	Busy
	This status value indicates that the target device (actually the logical unit) is busy and cannot accept a command. This can happen if a previous SCSI command has started but not yet completed on the device. You can periodically reissue the command until the target accepts it.
0x18	Reservation Conflict
	This value is returned whenever the logical unit you tried to access has been reserved by another initiator. This should only happen if there are multiple initiators (host adapters) connected to the same SCSI bus. (SCSI defines the Reserve and Release commands to obtain and release exclusive access to a logical unit.) You should see this target status code only if another initiator has reserved the logical unit.

Additional ASPI for Win32 Functions

The ASPI for Win32 specification has recently been revised to extend support for large data buffers (greater than 64K) on a wider variety of host adapters. The ASPI for Win32 specification has always allowed for large data buffers, but many host adapters and drivers were not able to support them due to special buffer alignment and paging restrictions. (With the use of virtual memory and paging in Windows, user-allocated buffers are often too fragmented for many host adapters to use.) The new GetASPI32Buffer() and FreeASPI32Buffer() routines allow an application to allocate a data buffer that meets all necessary requirements for use by these host adapters. These routines are exported by the ASPI for Win32 DLL in the same manner as the GetASPI32SupportInfo() and SendASPI32Command() routines.

```
BOOL GetASPI32Buffer( ASPI32BUFF *p );
BOOL FreeASPI32Buffer( ASPI32BUFF *p );
```

They each take a pointer to a data structure that describes the allocated data buffer.

Listing 7-19. ASPI32BUFF Structure

```
typedef struct {
    LPBYTE   AB_BufPointer;      // Pointer to allocated data buffer
    DWORD    AB_BufLen;          // Length of data buffer (in bytes)
    DWORD    AB_ZeroFill;        // if 1, buffer will be zero-filled
    DWORD    AB_Reserved;        // Reserved, must be 0
    } ASPI32BUFF;
```

When allocating a buffer you fill in the AB_BufLen and AB_Zero-Fill fields, and pass the structure to the GetASPI32Buffer() routine. When releasing the data buffer you fill in the AB_BufPointer and AB_BufLen fields with the values returned by the allocation, and pass the structure to the FreeASPI32Buffer() routine.

There is a maximum buffer size of 512K. If the ASPI manager cannot allocate the requested amount, it will return FALSE. You should assume that this call may fail, and your application should be prepared to break transfers down into smaller chunks.

The ASPI for Win32 specification has one final function—TranslateASPI32Address()—which translates SCSI device addresses from Windows 95 DEVNODEs and ASPI adapter/unit/LUNs. This function is useful for determining the ASPI target address associated with Plug and Play events.

```
BOOL TranslateASPI32Address( DWORD *aspi_path, DWORD *devnode );
```

The first parameter is a pointer to a DWORD representing the ASPI device address. The least significant byte contains the LUN, the next byte contains the SCSI ID, and the third byte contains the host adapter number. Or in C terms, the expression `((adapter << 16) | (target << 8) | lun)`. The second parameter is a pointer to a DWORD that contains the Windows 95 DEVNODE ID that should be translated.

On return from the `TranslateASPI32Address()` routine, the DWORD specified by the first parameter will be updated with the ASPI address indicated by the Windows 95 DEVNODE ID. You can perform the opposite translation by specifying a valid ASPI address for the first parameter, and using a DEVNODE ID of zero for the second parameter. In this case the Windows 95 DEVNODE ID corresponding to the given ASPI address will be placed into the second parameter.

Chapter 8

Low-Level SCSI Programming with SCRIPTS

Programmers who worked with early SCSI protocol chips are fond of telling stories about how difficult it was. Like your grandfather's tales of trudging through blizzards to get to school, these stories illustrate the hardships the teller encountered, struggling with assembly language, manipulating registers and I/O ports, and building strict timing constraints into the code. Thankfully, we've come a long way since then. The tools now available for programming at the chip level make the old ones seem as primitive as stone knives.

As SCSI protocol chips and I/O controllers become more sophisticated, they also become easier to work with. Many have built-in processors, scripting engines that are programmed with a high-level language to handle the gritty details of SCSI protocol. In this chapter we'll examine one of the more popular and powerful of these, Symbios Logic's SCRIPTS language.

Symbios Logic is the successor to NCR Microelectronics, a pioneer maker of SCSI hardware. If you understand the fundamentals of the SCSI protocol (which you should if you've read this far), reading a SCRIPTS listing is simple.

Working with SCRIPTS

Programming at this low level is not appropriate for most application software. It requires access to hardware ports and physical memory addresses.

Most modern operating systems shield the hardware from poorly behaved programs. Direct access is reserved for device drivers or code running with greater privileges than normal applications.

The sample code we present in this chapter runs under DOS, which has no such restrictions. This will better illustrate how to use SCRIPTS by keeping system calls and overhead as simple as possible. If you're developing under Windows 95, you can boot up at a command prompt only, or exit and restart in MS-DOS mode. The code will not work from a DOS box within Windows.

When working with SCRIPTS you need to arm yourself with two important tools: the Programming Guide and the Software Development Kit (SDK) for your particular chipset. Both are available through Symbios Logic distributors.

The Programming Guide contains extensive documentation on the SCRIPTS language and the NASM compiler for SCRIPTS. It also lists chip registers and their functions, feature sets and capabilities, and lots of other information. The guide comes in different versions for different chipsets, so make sure you have the right one for your hardware.

The SDK comes on a disk that accompanies the Programming Guide. It consists of sample code, utilities, and the NASM compiler. The SDK is also available on the Symbios Logic ftp site, along with more sample code and utilities.

The sample code in this chapter uses utility routines found in the SDK. The target hardware is a Symbios Logic SYM8251S SCSI host adapter. This is a PCI adapter with Wide SCSI support. The code uses inline 80386 assembly code to access extended CPU registers for the PCI function calls. The SDK and the sample code require Borland C++ and Turbo Assembler because they support this type of inline code. If you are using a different compiler, you will need to break out the assembly code and build it separately.

An Overview of SCRIPTS

The philosophy behind SCRIPTS is simple: start with a SCSI controller core and support circuitry, then add a dedicated RISC processor for programming capability; create a programming language with high-level support for arbitration, phase management and comparison, interface control, and logical functions; and execute the compiled programs in the SCRIPTS engine, shifting the processing burden from the CPU.

The SCRIPTS processor is dedicated to SCSI operations. It functions independently of the operating system. This can be inconvenient when you need to pass it the address of a buffer. SCRIPTS deals only in physical memory addresses, rather than segmented or virtual addresses.

Symbios Logic provides the NASM compiler for SCRIPTS programs. The output from this program is a file containing C language arrays of long hexadecimal integers that represent SCRIPTS opcodes and constants. You include the file as a header in your C source code, which declares the arrays as global variables.

These arrays are small program units for SCSI operations. To execute them, you simply pass them to the SCRIPTS engine by writing the physical address of the array to a register on the chip. Some of the more advanced chips come equipped with onboard RAM for SCRIPTS storage. These chips can execute a SCRIPTS program without the overhead of fetching instructions from system memory.

SCRIPTS Instructions

The SCRIPTS language contains instructions for I/O, transfer of control, memory moves, and other functions. The I/O functions deal with fundamental SCSI operations. For instance,

```
SELECT ATN scsi_id, REL(do_reselect)
```

selects the target encoded in `scsi_id`, raising the ATN flag to request a Message Out phase afterward. If the initiator is selected or reselected by a target, execution jumps to the relative address `do_reselect`. It's a fairly simple one-line command for a complex operation.

`Move` instructions are common. Messages, commands, status, and data are all transferred between data buffers and the SCSI bus using some form of `move` command.

```
MOVE 1, msg_buf, WHEN MSG_OUT
MOVE FROM cmd_buf, WHEN CMD
MOVE FROM msgin_buf, WHEN MSG_IN
```

In the first instruction, the processor waits until it detects Message Out phase, then moves a single byte from `msg_buf` onto the SCSI bus. In the second, the processor waits for Command phase, then reads a table entry at `cmd_buf` for a byte count and buffer address. The last instruction waits for Message In phase, reads from the SCSI bus, and stores the data at the location pointed to by the table entry `msgin_buf`.

Some instructions transfer control to other parts of the script.

```
JUMP REL(handle_phase)
JUMP send_cmd
CALL get_data WHEN DATA_IN
```

The JUMP instructions transfer control to a specified location. The location may be relative to the current instruction, or an absolute location. The CALL instruction works as you might expect, executing a subroutine that returns control to the next instruction. It also supports relative or absolute addressing.

Some instructions perform specific SCSI operations.

```
SELECT FROM scsi_id, reselect_addr
WAIT RESELECT, select_addr
WAIT DISCONNECT
CLEAR ATN
```

The first instruction tries to select the device at `scsi_id`, jumping to `reselect_addr` if it is first reselected by another device. The second instruction is the opposite, telling the chip to wait for reselection, jumping to `select_addr` if it is first selected by another device. The third instruction waits until the device disconnects from the SCSI bus. The last simply clears the ATN flag.

Another set of instructions handles register operations.

```
LOAD SCNTL3 1, def_scntl3
STORE ISTAT 1, cur_istat
MOVE SCNTL3 | 0x08 TO SCNTL3
MOVE SWIDE TO SFBR
```

The LOAD and STORE instructions transfer data between registers and memory locations. The first example loads the SCNTL3 register with a single byte from `def_sctnl3`, while the second stores the contents of ISTAT in the buffer at `cur_istat`.

The MOVE command is useful for operations that read, modify, and write back the contents of a register. The third example illustrates setting bit 3 in the SCNTL3 register.

The last example illustrates a special case. Moves between registers are only valid if one of the registers is SFBR, the *SCSI First Byte Received* register. This register receives special treatment because of another purpose it serves—data comparisons in conditional instructions operate against the value stored in SFBR.

There are other variations of these register commands that move data, manipulate bits, or perform mathematical operations. They provide the only means to manipulate registers when a SCRIPTS program is running.

With a few exceptions, you cannot access the registers from your C code during SCRIPTS execution.

Logical Operators and Conditional Tests

Most of the SCRIPTS instructions support logical tests of SCSI phase, data, or other conditions.

```
JUMP address WHEN DATA_IN
JUMP address IF DATA_OUT
JUMP address IF ATN
JUMP address IF 0x01
JUMP address IF 0x0 MASK 0xFF
```

The WHEN operator waits until the given condition is true, but the IF operator performs an immediate comparison. You'll usually use WHEN to test for a SCSI phase. Conditions you can test for include SCSI phases, flags, and data values. The data comparisons test the contents of the SFBR register, which holds the first byte received in the most recent I/O operation. This may be a message byte, an opcode in a Command Descriptor Block, or the first byte of a data block. The MASK operator lets you apply a filter to the data before comparison.

We've used the JUMP operator to illustrate logical tests, but most of the control instructions and many of the move instructions also support them. For example:

```
MOVE FROM data_buf, WHEN DATA_IN
CALL address WHEN DATA_OUT
INT err_bad_phase IF NOT MESSAGE_OUT
```

Embedding SCRIPTS in C Code

What happens after you've compiled your SCRIPTS code and created an output file? Somehow, you have to tell the SCRIPTS engine to execute it, and tell it where the code is.

The NASM output file contains a DWORD array with the compiled SCRIPTS code. By default, it calls this array SCRIPT, and it looks something like this.

```
ULONG   SCRIPT[] = {
    (array of DWORD values...)
};
```

Executing this code is simple. The Symbios Logic chip has a *DMA SCRIPTS Pointer* (DSP) register. When you set this register to the physical address of your SCRIPTS code, it begins execution. There's only one small catch—the address must be DWORD aligned.

That's fairly easy to do in your C code. Just allocate a buffer slightly larger than your SCRIPTS array, find the first DWORD aligned address in the buffer, and copy the array to the new address.

Listing 8-1. SCRIPTS Code Alignment

```
DWORD *my_script;              // pointer to script

DWORD *alloc_script(WORD size)
{
   BYTE *ptr;                  // temporary pointer
   WORD seg, off;             // pointer parts
   DWORD *newptr = NULL;

   ptr = malloc(size + 4);

   if (ptr) {
   // allocated script memory
   // DWORD align the buffer
      seg = FP_SEG(ptr);
      off = FP_OFF(ptr);
      off += (4 - (off & 0x03));
      newptr = (DWORD *) MK_FP(seg, off);
   }

   return newptr;
}


my_script = alloc_script(sizeof(SCRIPT));

if (my_script != NULL) {
// allocated script memory
// copy script array
   memcpy(my_script, SCRIPT, sizeof(SCRIPT));
}
```

To pass this new address to the SCRIPTS engine, write to the DSP register.

```
IOWrite32(io_base + DSP, getPhysAddr(my_script));
```

Changing Run-Time Parameters

SCRIPTS is a self-contained language. It runs on a dedicated processor and the only access to system resources is through the memory bus and the interrupt controller. You cannot pass arguments to a SCRIPTS routine, or call it as you would a normal C function. Once a SCRIPTS program is compiled it resides in memory, a discrete unit of code embedded in your data segment. How do you communicate with it? How do you direct its operation?

Patching

The output file that NASM generates contains, in addition to the compiled SCRIPTS array, several other components. NASM also lists information about absolute values, entry points, addresses, and other named elements. For instance, you might declare and use a value called DATA_COUNT in your SCRIPTS source file.

```
ABSOLUTE DATA_COUNT = 6
```

The output file will contain something similar to the following.

```
#define A_DATA_COUNT      0x00000006L

ULONG A_DATA_COUNT_Used[ ] = {
     0x00000011L,
     0x00000018L
};
```

The array A_DATA_COUNT_Used lists the offsets into the compiled SCRIPTS code where the value is actually used. To change it in the SCRIPTS code, simply use the offsets as array indices. For example, to change the value of DATA_COUNT from 6 to 10:

```
SCRIPT[A_DATA_COUNT_Used[0]] = 10L;
SCRIPT[A_DATA_COUNT_Used[1]] = 10L;
```

This process is called *patching*. Besides changing absolute values, you can change pointers to external buffers, relative addresses, and other public-access elements.

The output file also lists entry points into your SCRIPTS code. If your code contained the entry points TEST_UNIT_READY, INQUIRY, and RESET_DEVICE, they would appear as follows.

```
#define Ent_TEST_UNIT_READY    0x00000110L
#define Ent_INQUIRY            0x00000192L
#define Ent_RESET_DEVICE       0x00000210L
```

When you tell the SCRIPTS processor where to begin execution, you can pass the address of the SCRIPTS array plus the offset to the specific routine.

Table Indirect Addressing

Patching is handy, but it can be cumbersome for making frequent changes. Most of the Symbios Logic chips also support *table indirect* operations. These chips provide an extra register that you set with the address of a table in your C program. The table entries contain information for device selection or data transfer operations.

These entries are actually structures that contain two DWORD elements.

```
typedef struct {
    DWORD count;
    DWORD address;
} table_entry;
```

For device selection, the count is an encoded value that holds SCSI control parameters, timing factors for synchronous data transfer, and the target device SCSI ID. The address is reserved and set to 0. For other operations, the address points to a buffer in physical memory and the count indicates the size of the buffer.

Table indirect operations can be tricky to work with, as they require keeping two sets of books. Your SCRIPTS code holds a table declaration and references to its entries. However, this does not actually generate any code or allocate any memory. The table is just a placeholder, and the references indicate offsets into the table.

The actual work is done in the C side of your code. You declare the table again, making sure that the entries are identical and in the same order as in the SCRIPTS code. You may also define some mnemonic values for indices into the table, corresponding to the names used in the SCRIPTS code.

This is also where you actually allocate memory for the table and align it on a DWORD boundary. Once you have the memory, you fill the table with the desired values and set the table address in the proper register. The code below shows the process from both the SCRIPTS side and the C side.

Listing 8-2. SCRIPTS Table Declaration

```
TABLE my_table \
    select_info = ??, \
    cmd_buf = ??, \
    msg_buf = ??, \
    data_buf = ??
```

Listing 8-3. C Table Declaration

```
typedef struct {            // table entry definition
    DWORD count;
    DWORD address;
} table_entry;

table_entry *my_table;      // pointer to table
BYTE command_buf[6];        // command buffer
BYTE message_buf[2];        // message buffer
BYTE data_buf[32];          // data buffer
BYTE targ_id;               // target SCSI ID

#define TABLE_SIZE 4        // number of table entries

enum table_offsets {        // table offsets
    SELECT_INFO = 0,
    CMD_BUF,
    MSG_BUF,
    DATA_BUF
}


table_entry *alloc_table(WORD nentries)
{
    BYTE *ptr;              // temporary pointer
    WORD seg, off;         // pointer parts
    table_entry *newptr = NULL;

    ptr = malloc(nentries * sizeof(table_entry) + 4);

    if (ptr) {
    // allocated table memory
    // DWORD align the buffer
        seg = FP_SEG(ptr);
        off = FP_OFF(ptr);
        off += (4 - (off & 0x03));
        newptr = (table_entry *) MK_FP(seg, off);
    }
```

(Continued)

Listing 8-3. (*Continued*)

```
    return newptr;
}


my_table = alloc_table(TABLE_SIZE);

if (my_table != NULL) {
// allocated table memory
// fill the table entries
    my_table[SELECT_INFO].count = (0x00000300L & targ_id) << 16;
    my_table[SELECT_INFO].address = 0L;

    my_table[CMD_BUF].count = 6L;
    my_table[CMD_BUF].address = getPhysAddr(command_buf);

    my_table[MSG_BUF].count = 2L;
    my_table[MSG_BUF].address = getPhysAddr(message_buf);

    my_table[DATA_BUF].count = 32L;
    my_table[DATA_BUF].address = getPhysAddr(data_buf);
}
```

To make the table available to the SCRIPTS code, set the *Data Structure Address* (DSA) register on the chip to the physical address of the table.

```
IOWrite32(io_base + DSA, getPhysAddr(my_table));
```

With the flexibility of table indirect operation, you can simply change addresses, byte counts, or target device information in your C code instead of patching the SCRIPTS array. This makes it easy to reuse your SCRIPTS code for different commands or functions.

Detecting SCRIPTS Program Completion

It's nice to know when your SCRIPTS program has completed. There are a few different ways to detect this, all of which focus on the ISTAT register on the chip. This register contains information about interrupts that occur during SCSI operations. Specifically, it tells you the source of the interrupt.

You will normally end your SCRIPTS program with an `INT` instruction, which halts execution of the SCRIPTS code. It takes a value for an argument, storing it in a register where you can retrieve it later. This lets you return a value from your SCRIPTS code to your C program.

A SCSI error may also cause your SCRIPTS code to end abnormally. An unexpected disconnect, a reset, or a phase mismatch may terminate your program if it's not prepared to handle these conditions.

The ISTAT register contains two important flags that direct you to further information. The *DMA Interrupt Pending* (DIP) flag at bit 0 tells you to check the *DMA Status* (DSTAT) register for the source of the interrupt. Bit 2 of this register is set if the interrupt came from an INT instruction in the SCRIPTS code. If this is the case, the *DMA SCRIPTS Pointer Save* (DSPS) register holds the value returned by the INT instruction.

If the *SCSI Interrupt Pending* (SIP) flag at bit 1 is set, a SCSI error caused the interrupt. Two other registers, *SCSI Interrupt Status 0* and *1* (SIST0 and SIST1) hold information about the error that occurred.

Many of these interrupt conditions may be masked through settings in other registers. You must make sure that you test for valid conditions. You also must be aware of which SCSI error conditions are fatal and which are not.

Polling for Completion

The ISTAT register is unique in that you can access it from your C program while your SCRIPTS code executes. By polling the register in a loop you can detect when the SCRIPTS code completes by testing whether bit 0 or 1 is set. This is the simplest to program, but it wastes CPU cycles to constantly poll.

You may also poll the contents of a data buffer or status byte in your C code to detect completion. This runs the risk of failing to detect when the program stops because of a SCSI error.

Hardware Interrupt on Completion

A more elegant but more complex way to detect completion is through hardware interrupts. If you enable them in the *DMA Control* (DCNTL) register, the chip will generate an IRQ when an interrupt occurs. If you are comfortable with writing hardware interrupt handlers, you may wish to use this method. In your handler, check the same registers as described above to determine the source of the interrupt.

The IRQ level used depends on how the chip is configured. If you are using a PCI SCSI adapter, you can retrieve the IRQ level through PCI BIOS calls. Let's look at how to do that as we discuss initializing and setting up the chip.

Initialization and Housekeeping

Before you can even think about running a SCRIPTS program, there are housekeeping issues that demand your attention. You'll want to interrogate the controller to find out how it's configured and what features it supports. You'll need to reset the SCSI functions and choose reasonable default values for the control registers.

PCI BIOS Functions

The SYM8251S host adapter is a PCI board based on the Symbios Logic SYM53C825 SCSI I/O controller chip. Using functions available through the INT 0x1A and the PCI BIOS function (0xB1) ID you can locate installed boards, and query and set their configurations. First, though, you need to know if the machine your program is running on has a current PCI BIOS installed.

Calling the PCI interrupt subfunction 0x01 returns the identification string " ICP" in the EDX register if a version 2 BIOS is present. Older versions return the string in the CX:DX registers. To access the extended register EDX requires 80386 instructions. Many C compilers don't support these instructions in inline assembly code, so you may need to build them in a separate assembly module. Listing 8-4 illustrates how to check for the presence of a PCI BIOS.

Listing 8-4. Detecting PCI BIOS Version

```
WORD PCI_GetPCIBIOSVersion(pci_bios *ppcibios)
{
    WORD r_ax, r_bx, r_cx, r_dx;   // register variables
    DWORD r_edx;
    DWORD pci_sig;                 // PCI signature
    WORD retval = PCI_NO_BIOS;
    pci_sig = 0x20494350L;         // " ICP" signature
    // call PCI function to check for BIOS
    r_ax = ((PCI_FUNCTION_ID << 8) | PCI_BIOS_PRESENT);
    asm {
        .386
        mov ax, [r_ax]
        int PCI_BIOS_INT
        mov DWORD PTR [r_edx], edx
        mov [r_dx], dx
        mov [r_cx], cx
        mov [r_bx], bx
        mov [r_ax], ax
    }
```

(Continued)

Listing 8-4. (*Continued*)

```
    if (r_dx == LOWORD(pci_sig)) {
    // PCI BIOS is present
        if (r_cx == HIWORD(pci_sig) &&
            (r_bx & 0xff00) == 0x0100) {
        // PCI BIOS version 1.x
            retval = PCI_BIOS_REV_1X;
        }
        else if (r_edx == pci_sig) {
        // PCI BIOS version 2.x
            retval = PCI_BIOS_REV_2X;
        }
        else {
        // unknown version
            retval = PCI_UNKNOWN_BIOS;
        }
        if (ppcibios != NULL) {
        // fill BIOS info struct
            ppcibios->access = (r_ax & 0xff);
            ppcibios->version = r_bx;
            ppcibios->lastbus = (r_cx & 0xff);
        }
    }
    return retval;
}
```

Save the PCI BIOS information in a structure for later use. Though this function provides information about the BIOS version and the number of busses, its main purpose is to assure us that there is a PCI bus present on this machine.

Subfunction 0x02 lets us search for a specific device on the PCI bus. Each device is identified by a vendor ID, a device ID, and a device index. In Listing 8-5 we use a structure to hold PCI device information. We set the device ID for the 53C825 chip, which is 0x003. The Symbios Logic vendor ID is 0x1000.

Listing 8-5. Locating a PCI Device

```
int PCI_FindDevice(pci_device *ppcidevice)
{
// struct REGPACK regs;
    WORD r_ax, r_bx, r_cx, r_dx, r_si;
    DWORD config;
    int retval = 0;
```

(Continued)

Listing 8-5. (*Continued*)

```
// make sure we have a PCI BIOS
   if (PCI_GetPCIBIOSVersion(NULL) != PCI_NO_BIOS) {
// PCI BIOS is present
   // call PCI function to find device
   r_ax = ((PCI_FUNCTION_ID << 8) |
      (PCI_FIND_DEVICE));
   r_cx = ppcidevice->dev_id;
   r_dx = PCI_SYM_VENDOR_ID;
   r_si = ppcidevice->dev_index;
   asm {
      .386
      mov ax, [r_ax]
      mov cx, [r_cx]
      mov dx, [r_dx]
      mov si, [r_si]
      int PCI_BIOS_INT
      mov ax, 0
      adc ax, 0
      mov [r_bx], bx
      mov [r_ax], ax
   }
   if (r_ax == 0) {
   // carry bit is clear—call succeeded
      // save device bus number
      ppcidevice->bus_num = ((r_bx & 0xFF00) >> 8);
      // save device number
      ppcidevice->dev_num = (r_bx & 0x00FF);
      // save device function
      ppcidevice->function = (r_bx & 0x0007);
      // get command register
      ppcidevice->command =
         (WORD) PCI_GetConfigRegister(
         ppcidevice, PCI_CONFIG_REG_CMD);
      // get revision ID
      ppcidevice->rev_id =
         (BYTE) PCI_GetConfigRegister(
         ppcidevice, PCI_CONFIG_REG_REVID);
      // get subsystem and vendor ID
      config = PCI_GetConfigRegister(
         ppcidevice, PCI_CONFIG_REG_SUBV);
      ppcidevice->sub_ven_id = (WORD) config;
      ppcidevice->sub_id = (WORD) (config >> 16);
      // get I/O base address
      config = PCI_GetConfigRegister(
         ppcidevice, C8XX_CONFIG_REG_IOB);
      ppcidevice->io_base = (config & 0xFFFFFFFEL);
```

(Continued)

Listing 8-5. (*Continued*)

```
        // get ROM base address
        ppcidevice->rom_base = PCI_GetConfigRegister(
            ppcidevice, PCI_CONFIG_REG_ROM);
        // get interrupt number
        config = PCI_GetConfigRegister(
            ppcidevice, PCI_CONFIG_REG_INTL);
        ppcidevice->intl = (BYTE) config;
        retval = 1;
    }
  }
  return retval;
}
```

If the function succeeds, it returns the location of the adapter by bus number and device number. We use this to get further information from the board. Revision and ID numbers, the I/O base address, and the interrupt level used all are available through PCI queries.

The `PCI_GetConfigRegister` function uses subfunction 0x0A to read configuration registers. Once again, we use a structure to pass and return PCI device information. The `offset` parameter points to a specific register we wish to read.

Listing 8-6. Querying PCI Device Configuration

```
DWORD PCI_GetConfigRegister(pci_device *ppcidevice,
    WORD offset)
{
    WORD r_ax, r_bx, r_di, r_dx, r_cx;
    DWORD r_ecx;
    WORD pci_version;
    DWORD retval = 0L;

    // get PCI version
    pci_version = PCI_GetPCIBIOSVersion(NULL);
    if (!(pci_version == PCI_NO_BIOS ||
        retval == PCI_UNKNOWN_BIOS)) {
    // PCI BIOS present
        // call PCI function to read register
        r_ax = ((PCI_FUNCTION_ID << 8) |
            (PCI_READ_CONFIG_DWORD));
```

(Continued)

Listing 8-6. (*Continued*)

```
    // set bus number and device number to search
    r_bx = ((ppcidevice->bus_num & 0xff) << 8) |
        (ppcidevice->dev_num & 0xff);
    // set configuration register offset
    r_di = offset;
    asm {
        .386
        mov ax, [r_ax]
        mov bx, [r_bx]
        mov di, [r_di]
        int PCI_BIOS_INT
        mov DWORD PTR [r_ecx], ecx
        mov [r_dx], dx
        mov [r_cx], cx
    }
    if (pci_version == PCI_BIOS_REV_1X) {
    // PCI version 1.x
        retval = r_dx;
        retval = (retval << 16) | r_cx;
    }
    else if (pci_version == PCI_BIOS_REV_2X) {
    // PCI version 2.x
        retval = r_ecx;
    }
}
return retval;
}
```

Depending on the PCI version, this function returns the requested information in the ECX or CX:DX registers.

Now that we have the controller's base I/O address, we can initialize the control registers.

Initializing SCSI Control Registers

The control registers are set to hardware default values when the chip is powered up. These usually are sufficient for most purposes. If your controller board or your motherboard is equipped with a SCSI BIOS, it may have changed some of the values on bootup. If you aren't happy with these settings, you are free to change them.

It is absolutely necessary to have the documentation for your controller chip before you attempt to fine-tune the register settings. Many of the settings are bit-encoded into the registers. Others pertain to features like Wide SCSI or Fast-20 SCSI that your controller may not support. Proceeding without the documentation is like taking off on a cross-country trip without a road map. You may get where you want to go, but it's more likely you'll get lost somewhere along the way.

Sample Code

To illustrate how all these pieces fit together, let's use them to build a simple utility. Starting with a SCRIPTS module to handle general SCSI functions, we'll add supporting C code to create a program that will query the SCSI bus and print information about devices it finds. If it encounters a direct access device, it will read and display the contents of the first block.

This requires only a few SCSI functions. `Test Unit Ready`, `Device Inquiry`, and `Request Sense` will apply to all devices. For direct access devices, we'll also use `Read Capacity` and `Read` (the 6-byte version).

The generic SCRIPTS module, GENSCSI.SS, handles selection, message phases, and data phases. It also handles disconnect/reselect sequences. For more advanced applications, you'll need to flesh it out by addding support for synchronous or wide transfer negotiation. The sample code in the Symbios Logic Software Developer's Kit includes some examples of this. For our purposes, we'll omit those features to make the code easy to follow.

The C modules are broken up by functions. SPCI.C contains PCI BIOS interface code. Initialization code for the 53C800 chip family is isolated in S8XX.C. Actual implementation of standard SCSI functions is contained in SSCSI.C. Utility functions reside in the SDK file GEN_TOOLS.C.

In the main module, SQUERY.C, we start by initializing the host adapter using PCI calls. We gather configuration details about the host adapter, information about the I/O port used, and support for Wide SCSI or Fast SCSI. Wide SCSI support is important because it tells us how many devices to look for.

Next we set up buffers for the SCRIPTS array and data buffers for the SCSI calls. Message buffers, Command Descriptor Blocks, and data buffers are allocated and aligned on DWORD boundaries. These are filled with the proper values as we use them.

Finally, we search for devices that respond to a `Test Unit Ready` command. Many of them may respond with a `Unit Attention` status, so we need to retrieve sense data using the `Request Sense` command. You should expect a `Unit Attention` condition the first time a device is accessed after powering up. The code contains a retry loop for this purpose.

A Device Inquiry follows for any SCSI ID that responds to the `Test Unit Ready` command. The program prints out the device type, identification strings, and other parameters.

If it finds a direct access device, the program issues a `Read Capacity` command. This reports the number and size of data blocks on the medium. If you are using a removable media drive like the Iomega Zip drive, this call will fail if there is no disk present. The first call after you insert the medium will return sense data indicating that the medium has changed. Again, we have to anticipate this condition and recover from it.

The final call for direct access devices reads the first block on the medium and prints it out in both hexadecimal and ASCII. Block 0 on a formatted Zip disk contains an Iomega signature in the first few bytes.

Generic SCRIPTS Code

The heart of our sample program is the SCRIPTS code contained in GEN-SCSI.SS. Let's examine it more closely.

We start by declaring the architecture for which we are compiling. In this case, it's the 53C825 chip.

```
;---------- set architecture for 53C825
ARCH 825
```

Next we declare some constants. These are values that the SCRIPTS code will return to its parent program.

```
;---------- set constant values
ABSOLUTE err_cmd_complete =      0x00000000
ABSOLUTE err_not_msgout =        0x00000001
ABSOLUTE err_bad_reselect =      0x00000002
ABSOLUTE err_bad_phase =         0x00000004
```

Now comes a critical part. We declare a table of buffers because we are using table indirect addressing for our data transfers. It's not really important what we call it, because a SCRIPTS module can only contain a single table.

Remember that simply declaring a table does not allocate memory for it. That part is done in your supporting C code. In the example below, the values that follow each table element are simply placeholders for debugging information.

In SCRIPTS syntax, a table declaration is a single line of code followed by a carriage return. We've used backslashes as line continuation characters to separate the table elements and make the code more readable.

```
;---------- set up table definitions
TABLE table0 \
   scsi_id = ID {0x33, 0x00, 0x00, 0x00}, \
   msgout_buf = {0x80, 0x00}, \
   cmd_buf = {0x00, 0x00, 0x00, 0x00, 0x00, 0x00}, \
   stat_buf = ??, \
   msgin_buf = 2 {??}, \
   exmsgin_buf = 4 {??} \
   datain_buf = 0x40 {??}
```

Following the table declaration, we declare an entry point for the code, and a name for the script. The script name will be used to name the SCRIPTS array in the compiled code.

```
;---------- entry point for general SCSI script
ENTRY start_scsi

PROC GEN_SCRIPT:
```

Finally, we begin the actual code with a SELECT ATN instruction. Our C code has already filled the scsi_id buffer with information about the target we are selecting. If the host adapter is itself selected or reselected during this step, execution will branch to the bad_reselect label.

```
;---------- start SCSI target selection
start_scsi:

; select device from encoded SCSI ID
; set ATN for message out after select
SELECT ATN FROM scsi_id, REL(bad_reselect)
```

Because we set the ATN flag during selection, a Message Out phase follows. We'll send the Identify message, telling the target whether it has disconnect privileges. We set up the msgout_buf buffer in our C code.

```
;---------- send identify message
; exit if not message out phase
INT err_not_msgout, WHEN NOT MSG_OUT

; send identify message
MOVE FROM msgout_buf, WHEN MSG_OUT
JUMP REL(handle_phase)
```

After sending the Identify message we jump to a phase handler routine. This routine simply examines the bus phase and jumps to a corresponding routine. Here it's a Command phase that follows Message Out.

```
;---------- send SCSI command
send_cmd:

; send command block to target
MOVE FROM cmd_buf, WHEN CMD
JUMP REL(handle_phase)
```

Once again, it's back to the phase handler after the Command phase. The command issued determines what happens next. For a command like Test Unit Ready no data transfer takes place—we move directly to the Status phase. In the example, we just read the status byte into a buffer.

```
;---------- get SCSI status
get_status:

; read status byte from data bus
MOVE FROM stat_buf, WHEN STATUS
JUMP REL(handle_phase)
```

A Message In phase follows the Status phase. We read the message byte and clear the ACK bit. If things went well, the message is Command Complete, and we jump to our exit code. If we arrived here at some other point in the command execution, we must handle other messages.

The other messages we check for are Disconnect and extended messages. If we detect a Disconnect message, we branch to a routine that waits for a disconnect to occur. For extended messages, we read another byte from the bus before jumping to the phase handler. Any other messages are ignored.

```
;---------- get SCSI message input
get_msgin:

; read message byte from data bus
MOVE FROM msgin_buf, WHEN MSG_IN
CLEAR ACK

; handle Command Complete message
JUMP REL(cmd_complete), IF 0x00

; handle Disconnect message
JUMP REL(wait_disconnect), IF 0x04

; handle extended message
JUMP REL(ext_msgin), IF 0x01
JUMP REL(handle_phase)
```

```
;---------- handle extended message
ext_msgin:

; read extended message from data bus
MOVE FROM exmsgin_buf, WHEN MSG_IN
CLEAR ACK
JUMP REL(handle_phase)
```

If we issued a command that reads or returns data, the phase handler will dispatch us to the data input routine. The number of bytes to read and the destination address are contained in `data_buf`. Once again, we set this up in our C code.

The process would be similar for commands that send or write data to a device. Data direction is determined by the command.

```
;---------- get data input
get_datain:

; read data from bus
MOVE FROM datain_buf, WHEN DATA_IN
JUMP REL(handle_phase)
```

Here is the dispatch table we use to handle the different bus phases. Unexpected phases exit with an error code.

```
;---------- handle SCSI phases
handle_phase:

; jump to appropriate handler for phase
JUMP REL(get_status), WHEN STATUS
JUMP REL(get_msgin), WHEN MSG_IN
JUMP REL(get_datain), WHEN DATA_IN
JUMP REL(send_cmd), WHEN COMMAND
; unhandled phase
INT err_bad_phase
```

This is our normal exit handler, reached by a `Command Complete` message. We expect a bus disconnect, so we clear the register bits that generate an error on disconnect. When disconnect occurs, we return with a success code.

```
;---------- SCSI command execution complete
cmd_complete:

; command complete - wait for disconnect
MOVE SCNTL2 & 0x7F to SCNTL2
```

```
CLEAR ACK
WAIT DISCONNECT
INT err_cmd_complete
```

Selection or reselection errors come to this error handler. It simply exits with an error code.

```
;---------- handle invalid select or reselect
bad_reselect:

; unhandled reselect
INT err_bad_reselect
```

If we received a `Disconnect` message, we wait here for disconnect to occur. Notice that we have cleared the bits that generate an error on disconnect. After disconnect, we clear any remaining data in the SCSI and DMA registers, and wait for reselection. Once we are reselected, we wait for an `Identify` message from the target and branch to the error handler.

This approach to the disconnect/reselect process is light on error checking. For more robust applications, you'll want to process the `Save Data Pointers` message that precedes the `Disconnect` message, and save other information to ensure that there are no gaps or overlaps in your data transfers.

```
;---------- handle disconnect before reselect
wait_disconnect:

MOVE SCNTL2 & 0x7F to SCNTL2
CLEAR ACK
WAIT DISCONNECT

; clear DMA and SCSI fifos
MOVE CTEST3 | 0x04 to CTEST3
MOVE STEST3 | 0x02 to STEST3

; wait for reselect
WAIT RESELECT REL(bad_reselect)

; expect identify message
MOVE FROM msgin_buf, WHEN MSG_IN
CLEAR ACK

; shortcut to update sync and wide options
SELECT FROM scsi_id, REL(handle_phase)
```

Examine the sample code and the SCRIPTS routines. Experiment with it, adding handlers for other commands or messages.

The Symbios Logic ftp site is a good source for other examples, and for the NASM compiler used to build the SCRIPTS code. After you work with it, you'll see how powerful SCRIPTS can be for low-level SCSI development.

Chapter 9

SCSI Target-Mode Programming

Most of this book discusses SCSI programming from the perspective of using a host adapter to control peripheral devices. In this chapter things are turned around and SCSI is looked at from a target peripheral's point of view. Target-mode SCSI programming has long been considered a specialty practiced by few outside the mass-storage industry. It conjures visions of a lone programmer working late at night deep within the bowels of an R&D lab, taking nourishment from a bottle of Mountain Dew dripping into an I.V. tube. Needless to say, this chapter isn't written to help these poor souls. Rather, we hope to give the rest of you a feel for the "other side" of SCSI, along with some practical advice on how to turn your PC into a SCSI target device.

From a programmer's perspective a typical SCSI implementation contains three distinct components: hardware, drivers (including ASPI), and applications. The hardware component handles the physical portions of a SCSI transaction, including bus arbitration, selection, and data transfer. The driver component manages the hardware, responding to phase changes, handling message bytes, and providing an interface to the application. The application component gets the work done—working with SCSI commands and orchestrating things at a higher level. I'll try to break things up into these same categories as we discuss target-mode SCSI programming.

When I first took on the task of writing a PC-based target-mode application I hoped to find a software library or driver package that would help manage the low-level details of the SCSI bus. What I really wanted was a sort of "reverse-ASPI" driver; something that would simply hand me an incoming CDB and data buffer and let me get on with the real work. I wasn't interested in SCSI bus phase changes, message bytes, and the like—I just wanted to get the job done. I knew that the *Common Access Method* (ANSI CAM) specification had provisions for target-mode SCSI programming, but I wasn't able to find a single PC-based SCSI adapter that provided functional CAM drivers. In the end, I couldn't find any libraries or packages that helped with target-mode programming, and I had to develop my own code from the hardware on up. Fortunately, I was already familiar with SCSI host-mode programming and with the command sets of the devices I was trying to emulate. The SCSI-2 specification is remarkably complete, and it did contain most of the information that I really needed. These factors at least made the task manageable, but, boy, what I'd have given for a bit of target-mode advice and a few samples. The code and techniques presented in this chapter are provided with the hope that I can save someone reading this from a similar frustration.

Hardware

Not all SCSI host adapters are suitable for target-mode programming. Some cards are designed only for the SCSI initiator role and simply cannot respond to a selection request from another initiator. Others contain embedded firmware that is optimized for host-mode transactions at the expense of target-mode support. In some cases you can download special target-mode firmware to these cards, but in most cases you're out of luck. But by far the biggest obstacle to target-mode programming on most adapters is a lack of documentation. Very few PC SCSI card manufacturers will admit that their cards are capable of supporting target-mode operation, and even fewer have any documentation that tells how to accomplish it. I've often found it necessary to select a SCSI chipset that fits my needs directly from a semiconductor manufacturer, then work backward to find a PC card that uses that particular chipset. This usually leaves me without support from the card supplier, but at least I'll have access to the SCSI chipset documentation directly from the semiconductor manufacturer's datasheets.

The SCSI chipset I'll be using for the examples below is the Symbios Logic 53C400A. The 53C400A is an older, relatively low-end SCSI chip that combines NCR's 53C80E SCSI core with an ISA bus interface. I selected it as our example because of its low-level programming interface to the SCSI bus. The 53C400A provides a minimal amount of hardware support for SCSI bus arbitration, selection, and handshaking without hiding too many of the details involved in SCSI transactions. This allows us to learn about the SCSI bus in detail while still achieving reasonable transfer rates for most applications.

Handling SCSI Phases

Before we proceed, let's take a moment to review the different phases of a SCSI transaction. This transaction begins with the bus arbitration and selection phases, providing the means for an initiator to grab the SCSI bus and establish a link to a particular target device. After selection, the target device takes over the SCSI bus and controls the sequencing of the SCSI bus phase changes. If the initiator asserts the `ATN` signal, the target will enter the Message Out phase, reading message bytes from the initiator. These messages typically specify the target LUN and disconnect privileges, but other messages may be sent as well. After the message bytes have been received and processed, the target will enter the Command phase and supervise the transfer of the SCSI *Command Descriptor Block* (CDB) from the host. Once this is finished, the target can begin processing the command.

At this point the target may decide to disconnect from the SCSI bus if it is performing a lengthy command (only if the `Identify` message gave it permission to disconnect). This involves a Message In phase, in which the target sends a `Save Data Pointers` message, a `Disconnect` message, and then releases control of the SCSI bus by entering the bus-free state. When the target is ready to reconnect it performs the bus arbitration and reselection phases, sends an `Identify` message to indicate which LUN is reconnecting, then continues with the data or status transfer. If a SCSI bus parity error is encountered during a transfer, the target might issue a `Restore Data Pointers` message to the host and restart the data transmission. Finally, the target enters the Status phase and sends the `command` status to the initiator to mark the end of the process, then releases control of the SCSI bus by entering the bus-free state.

In the sample code below we'll see how the 53C400A responds to a selection and handles the various phases of a SCSI transaction. The code below assumes the existence of a `WriteReg()` routine that writes values into a 53C400A register, and a `ReadReg()` routine that reads the value of a specified 53C400A register. The code uses register names and values that are specific to the 53C400A, but you should be able to follow the intent of the code from the comments. Of course, other SCSI chipsets will require different low-level code sequences, but the sample code below should help you by showing how to handle the various SCSI bus phases.

The first requirement is to initialize and enable the 53C400A. We do this by resetting the chip, enabling target-mode operation (at the expense of traditional host-mode operation), and clearing the interrupt state.

Listing 9-1. Chip Initialization

```
WriteReg(CR0,0x80);          // Reset the 53C400A chip
WriteReg(MR,0x40);           // Enable target-mode operation
WriteReg(SER,1 << ID);       // Specify our target SCSI id
ReadReg(RIR);                // Read/reset the SCSI interrupt
WriteReg(CR0,0x10);          // Enable the SCSI interrupt
```

Now we simply wait for an interrupt telling us that the 53C400A has been selected as the target by another host adapter. We'll do this by polling just to keep things simple for this example, but most implementations would install a real interrupt handler. Once we've detected an interrupt we'll check for exceptional conditions such as a bus reset or parity error. If we've been selected as the target of a SCSI transaction we'll also have to figure out the SCSI ID of the initiator. Note that we double-check the selection bits on the SCSI bus to make sure that we are the legitimate target of the selection. In the real world, false selections can occur because of glitches on the data bus, or from quirks in the arbitration/selection handling on some older host adapters. Once we've decided that we have been properly selected, we'll assert the BSY signal to notify the initiator that we've taken control of the SCSI bus. The initiator should acknowledge this by dropping the SEL signal. Most newer SCSI chipsets will handle all of this for us automatically, but on the 53C400A we'll see exactly what needs to be done.

Listing 9-2. Responding to Selection

```
while (!(ReadReg(ISR) & IRQ))
// Wait for an interrupt
    ;

irq_cause = ReadReg(ISR);    // save the interrupt source
ReadReg(RIR);                // Reset 53C400A interrupt
```

(Continued)

Listing 9-2. (*Continued*)

```
if (irq_cause & BUS_RESET)       // Bus reset interrupt?
    {
    ProcessBusReset();           // handle it elsewhere
    return;
    }

if (irq_cause & PARITY_ERROR)
// Parity error?
    {
    ProcessParityError();        // handle it elsewhere
    return;
    }

// This must be a selection interrupt. Get the
// selection ID bits from the SCSI data bus and
// make sure our ID bit is set (we could have
// interrupted with an invalid selection due to
// a glitch on the SCSI bus).

selection_id = ReadReg(DATA);
if (!(selection_id & (1 << ID)))
    {
    // Our SCSI ID bit isn't set, so we aren't
    // really selected!  Ignore the selection.
    return;
    }

// Now determine the SCSI ID of the initiator
// by finding which other ID bit is set.

selection_id &= ~ID;         // first clear our ID bit
for (initiator=0; initiator<8; initiator++)
    {
    if (selection_id & 1)
        break;
    selection_id >>= 1;
    }

// We have a valid selection, assert BSY and wait
// for the host to drop the SEL signal to end the
// selection phase

WriteReg(ICR,BSY);
while (ReadReg(CSC) & SEL)
    ;
```

At this point we've completed the SCSI arbitration and selection phases and, as the selected target, we have control of the SCSI bus. The SCSI-2 specification now requires a Message Out phase with at least an Identify message, but older SCSI-1 initiators may skip this stage. We'll examine the state of the ATN signal to determine whether the initiator has any message bytes to send us. As you examine the code below, note that we explicitly control the SCSI bus phase by setting and clearing the various signals. You'll also see that we strobe in each message byte individually via the REQ and ACK signals. The 53C400A is capable of automated transfers of 128-byte data blocks, but for smaller chunks we're on our own.

Listing 9-3. Message In Phase

```
while (ReadReg(ISR) & ATN)      // Host message waiting?
    {
    WriteReg(TCR,MSG|CD);       // set MSG and C/D signals
                                // to enter MSG OUT phase

    WriteReg(TCR,MSG|CD|REQ);   // Now also assert REQ to
                                // request msg byte from host

    while (!ReadReg(ISR) & ACK)
    // Wait for host to ACK, so data is available
        ;

    msg_byte = ReadReg(DATA);   // Read first message byte

    WriteReg(TCR,MSG|CD);       // release REQ, leave MSG+CD

    if (msg_byte & 0x80)        // Is it an Identify message?
        {
        // extract Identify information
        ok_to_disconnect = msg_byte & 0x40;
        luntar = msg_byte & 0x20;
        lun = msg_byte & 0x07;
        }
    else if ((msg_byte == 0x06) || (msg_byte == 0x0C))
        {
        // Abort or Bus Device Reset message
        WriteReg(TCR,0);        // release MSG and CD lines
        WriteReg(ICR,0);        // release BSY line
        return;
        }
```

(Continued)

Listing 9-3. (Continued)

```
    else if ((msg_byte == 0x08))
        {
        // NOP, so just ignore it
        }
    else
        {
        // This sample won't handle any other message bytes
        // so return a Message Reject back to the host
        WriteReg(TCR,MSG|CD|IO);      // Enter MSG IN phase
        WriteReg(DATA,0x07);          // MESSAGE REJECT
        WriteReg(ICR,BSY|DB);         // Turn on data bus
        WriteReg(TCR,MSG|CD|IO|REQ);  // Assert REQ
        while (!ReadReg(ISR) & ACK)   // Wait for host to ACK
            ;
        WriteReg(TCR,MSG|CD|IO);      // Release REQ
        WriteReg(ICR,BSY);            // Turn off data bus
        }
    }
```

That was a lot, and we only handled a few messages. Real-world implementations typically handle several others, including the Synchronous and Wide Data Transfer Request messages. I typically create message I/O subroutines to clean up the code a bit, but for this example I thought it best to show the bus phase changes up front.

After the Message Out phase (messages from the host to the target), a target will enter the Command phase to collect the *Command Descriptor Block* (CDB) from the host. This is pretty straightforward—the only complexity rises from the need to interpret the first command byte to determine the CDB length.

Listing 9-4. Command Phase

```
WriteReg(TCR,CD);              // Select the COMMAND phase
WriteReg(TCR,CD|REQ);          // Assert REQ signal
while (!ReadReg(ISR) & ACK)    // Wait for host to ACK
    ;
cdb_byte[0] = ReadReg(DATA);   // Get first byte of CDB
WriteReg(TCR,CD);              // De-assert REQ
switch (cdb_byte[0] >> 5)
// Extract the command group code
// to determine the CDB length
```

(Continued)

Listing 9-4. (*Continued*)

```
        {
    case 0:
        cdb_len = 6;
        break;
    case 1:
    case 2:
        cdb_len = 10;
        break;
    case 5:
        cdb_len = 12;
        break;
    default:
    // Reserved or vendor-specific, treat as
    // an error and force early termination
        cdb_len = 0;
    }

// Now read the remaining CDB bytes
for (i=1; i<cdb_len; i++)
    {
    WriteReg(TCR,CD|REQ);       // Assert REQ
    while (!ReadReg(ISR) & ACK) // Wait for host to ACK
        ;
    cdb_byte[i] = ReadReg(DATA); // Get next CDB byte
    WriteReg(TCR,CD);           // Clear REQ
    }
```

At this point we have a complete SCSI Command Descriptor Block ready for processing. We know which LUN should receive the CDB because of the Identify message received from the host. (If the message came from a SCSI-1 initiator, we can either assume a LUN of 0, or retrieve it from the upper three bits of cdb_byte[1]. This lack of an Identify message was one of the many problems encountered with multiple LUNs before the SCSI-2 standard.)

If the command requires additional data, we would enter a Data Out phase (out of the host, in to our target), strobing each byte with the REQ/ACK signals just as we did above. We may also send additional messages to the host by entering a Message In phase (in to the host, out of the target) and strobing out the message data, just as we did with the Message Reject message above. If the command required a significant delay before the data was available, we might disconnect at this point and reconnect when the data is ready. For our example, let's assume that we've received a standard Inquiry command.

Listing 9-5. Responding to Inquiry Command

```
if (cdb_byte[0] == INQUIRY)
    {
    // Send back inquiry data. Assume the correct inquiry
    // data is stored in the inq_byte[] array.
    nbytes = cdb_byte[4];                // Get requested length

    if (nbytes > sizeof(inq_byte))   // Truncate requested
        nbytes = sizeof(inq_byte);   // length to actual

    WriteReg(TCR,IO);                    // Select DATA IN phase

    WriteReg(ICR,BSY|DB);                // Turn on data bus

    for (i=0; i<nbytes; i++)
        {
        WriteReg(DATA,inq_byte[i]); // Write the next byte
        WriteReg(TCR,IO|REQ);           // Set the REQ line
        while (!ReadReg(ISR) & ACK) // Wait for host to ACK
            ;
        WriteReg(TCR,IO);               // Clear the REQ line
        }

    WriteReg(ICR,BSY);                   // turn off data bus
    }
```

At this point we should check for an active ATN signal from the host indicating that it has additional message bytes to send. Real-world implementations should check for such messages between every phase change, and also at the end of every data block during a data transfer. In our example we'll skip this check and proceed to the final step, sending the status byte and the command complete message back to the host, and releasing control of the SCSI bus.

Listing 9-6. Sending Status and Command Complete

```
status_byte = 0x00;           // GOOD status
WriteReg(TCR,CD|IO);          // Select STATUS phase
WriteReg(ICR,BSY|DB);         // Turn on data bus
WriteReg(DATA,status_byte); // Send the status byte
WriteReg(TCR,CD|IO|REQ);     // Set the REQ line
while (!ReadReg(ISR) & ACK) // Wait for host to ACK
    ;
```

(Continued)

Listing 9-6. (*Continued*)

```
WriteReg(TCR,CD|IO);            // Clear the REQ line
WriteReg(TCR,MSG|CD|IO);        // Enter MSG IN phase
WriteReg(DATA,COMMAND_COMPLETE); // Send command complete
WriteReg(TCR,MSG|CD|IO|REQ);    // Set the REQ line
while (!ReadReg(ISR) & ACK)     // Wait for host to ACK
    ;
WriteReg(ICR,BSY);              // Turn off data bus
WriteReg(TCR,0);                // Release all SCSI lines
WriteReg(ICR,0);                // to enter BUS FREE
```

As you've seen, managing the SCSI bus isn't a trivial task. We've examined a typical transaction, but haven't really gone into any significant detail regarding message and error handling. Also, we've been working directly with the hardware. That gets pretty boring and is better left to the chipset's data sheet, especially since you're likely to use a completely different SCSI adapter for your target-mode project. Rather than continue with a long, drawn-out presentation of the details of 53C400A programming, wouldn't it be a better idea to hide this complexity behind the sort of target-mode API that I hinted at earlier? For any of you who might be interested in these low-level details, I refer you to the target-mode source code included on the CD-ROM that accompanies this book.

Target-Mode API

Let's start by considering the functional requirements for a target-mode SCSI interface. First and foremost, it should be easy to understand and to use, just like the ASPI interface is for host-mode programming. ASPI's biggest asset is its simplicity. It foregoes little-used SCSI features like tagged queues and asynchronous event notification in favor of a simple, easy to understand interface. Our target-mode interface should do the same. Let's not worry about every feature of SCSI target-mode programming, but instead concentrate on those features we need to get the job done. Also, a target-mode SCSI interface should insulate applications from hardware-specific details. This should allow us to run the same application with different implementations of the target-mode interface, just like ASPI applications should run with any ASPI implementation.

Please note that I'm not trying to create a standard interface specification here—I'll just be describing an API that has worked well for me over the past few years. I hope you will find it useful if you decide to write any

PC-based target-mode applications. You'll find the complete source code for a 53C400A TSPI driver included on the CD-ROM that accompanies this book. Of course, you'll probably want to use another SCSI chipset for your target-mode application. If so, you'll have to modify the TSPI driver to work with your specific hardware. I've tried to keep the hardware-specific code separate from the more general-purpose target-mode routines to make this process easier.

I've arrived at this particular API by the notorious trial and error design process. They provide a fairly complete and (I hope) easy to understand routines that insulate applications from the details of the SCSI bus transactions. The functional goals for the API include:

- pass full CDBs to the application for processing
- provide Read/Write routines that the application can call to transfer data buffers
- handle SCSI message bytes transparently (as much as possible)
- provide for disconnect/reconnect sequences
- allow for multiple LUNs

Let's jump right in by examining the core data structures and routines that comprise the API, which I call the *Target-mode SCSI Programming Interface*, or TSPI. (Pretty original, huh?) I've modeled its interface along the same lines as ASPI. The interface has a single entry point, `tspi_SendCommand()`, which is passed a pointer to a structure describing the command. Since you're already familiar with ASPI from Chapter 7, you shouldn't have much trouble with this interface.

I wanted to keep the application code as simple as possible, while providing enough flexibility to work with most existing host adapters. The TSPI interface works very much like ASPI. It has a single entry point called `tspi_SendCommand(void *)`, which takes a pointer to a structure that contains all the information necessary to execute a given TSPI command. We'll see how to issue TSPI commands a bit later. Right now let's look at the command structures used to pass information across the TSPI interface.

Listing 9-7. TSPI Command Structures

```
typedef struct TSPI_EVENT_s
// Holds incoming SCSI CDBs and bus events
   {
   unsigned char  CommandCode;    // Type of command
   unsigned char  Error;          // Returns error status
```
(Continued)

Listing 9-7. (*Continued*)

```
    unsigned short Flags;          // TSPI_FLAG_xxxx
    unsigned char  AdapterIndex;   // Adapter number
    unsigned char  InitiatorId;    // Who sent it
    unsigned char  Lun;            // Our LUN
    unsigned char  Reserved1[15];  // Reserved for API use
    unsigned long  Timeout;        // In milliseconds
    unsigned char  Reserved2[3];   // Reserved (alignment)
    unsigned char  CdbLength;      // Length of CDB
    unsigned char  CdbByte[16];    // CDB data bytes
    } TSPI_EVENT;

typedef struct TSPI_CMD_
// Generic TSPI cmd
    {
    unsigned char  CommandCode;    // Type of command
    unsigned char  Error;          // Returns error status
    unsigned short Flags;          // TSPI_FLAG_xxxx
    unsigned char  AdapterIndex;   // Adapter number
    unsigned char  InitiatorId;    // Host SCSI ID
    unsigned char  Lun;            // Our LUN
    unsigned char  Reserved1[15];  // Reserved for API use
    unsigned long  Parm[6];        // Generic parameters
    } TSPI_CMD;

typedef struct TSPI_XFER_s
// Data transfer cmd
    {
    unsigned char  CommandCode;    // Type of command
    unsigned char  Error;          // Returns error status
    unsigned short Flags;          // TSPI_FLAG_xxxx
    unsigned char  AdapterIndex;   // Adapter number
    unsigned char  InitiatorId;    // Host SCSI ID
    unsigned char  Lun;            // Our LUN
    unsigned char  Reserved1[15];  // Reserved for API use
    unsigned long  TransferLength; // Bytes to read/write
    void *         TransferAddress;// Data buffer address
    unsigned long  ResidualLength; // Bytes NOT sent
    unsigned long  Reserved2[3];   // Reserved (alignment)
    } TSPI_XFER;

// Flags
#define TSPI_FLAG_BusReset         0x0001
#define TSPI_FLAG_DeviceReset      0x0002
#define TSPI_FLAG_HostMsgWaiting   0x0004
#define TSPI_FLAG_SaveDataPointers 0x0008
```

(Continued)

Listing 9-7. (*Continued*)

```
// Command Codes
#define TSPI_CMD_AdapterInfo        0
#define TSPI_CMD_AttachLUN          1
#define TSPI_CMD_DetachLUN          2
#define TSPI_CMD_GetEvent           3
#define TSPI_CMD_ReadFromHost       4
#define TSPI_CMD_WriteToHost        5
#define TSPI_CMD_CompleteCommand    6
#define TSPI_CMD_SendMessage        7
#define TSPI_CMD_GetMessage         8
#define TSPI_CMD_Disconnect         9
#define TSPI_CMD_Reconnect          10

// Error Codes
#define TSPI_ERR_None               0
#define TSPI_ERR_InvalidCommand     1
#define TSPI_ERR_Busy               2
#define TSPI_ERR_InvalidAdapter     3
#define TSPI_ERR_InvalidTarget      4
#define TSPI_ERR_InvalidLUN         5
#define TSPI_ERR_LunNotAvailable    6
#define TSPI_ERR_Timeout            7
    .
    .
    .
```

You'll note that the first few fields of each structure are identical. The TSPI manager uses the CommandCode field to interpret the remaining fields. The TSPI_EVENT structure is used to retrieve SCSI commands and events as they arrive at the target. The TSPI_XFER structure is used to manage the transfer of data buffers across the SCSI bus. Finally, the TSPI_CMD structure is used to control the remaining portions of a SCSI transaction, including disconnect/reconnect sequences and command completion. The TSPI_CMD structure is also used to control the TSPI interface itself. Let's take a closer look at the TSPI commands.

Adapter Inquiry (TSPI_CMD_AdapterInfo)

This command is used to obtain information about a specific target-mode adapter managed by the TSPI driver. To issue an adapter inquiry command you must set the CommandCode field to TSPI_CMD_AdapterInfo and set the AdapterIndex field to the 0-based index of the target-mode adapter you wish to query. If you specify an adapter that doesn't exist, the

Error field will return `TSPI_ERR_InvalidAdapter`. Otherwise, the `Parm[ ]` array will return information pertaining to that adapter.

On entry:

CommandCode	`TSPI_CMD_AdapterInfo`
AdapterIndex	0-based adapter index
Flags	Must be 0

On return:

Error	Error code
Parm[0]	Total number of target-mode adapters managed by the TSPI manager
Parm[1]	TSPI version number supported by this adapter, e.g. 0x00000104 (1.04)
Parm[2]	Target adapter SCSI ID
Parm[3-5]	Reserved for future use, currently return 0

Listing 9-8. TSPI Adapter Inquiry

```
TSPI_CMD info;
info.CommandCode = TSPI_CMD_AdapterInfo;
info.AdapterIndex = 0;
info.Flags = 0;
tspi_SendCommand(&info);
NumAdapters = info.Parm[0];
printf("%lu target-mode adapters available\n",
    NumAdapters);
while (info.AdapterIndex < NumAdapters)
    {
    if (info.Error)
        printf("Adapter %lu, error %u\n",
            info.AdapterIndex
            info.Error);
    else
        printf("Adapter %lu, ID=%lu version %lu.%02lu\n",
            info.AdapterIndex,
            info.Parm[2],
            info.Parm[1] >> 8,
            info.Parm[1] & 0xFF);

    info.AdapterIndex++;
    }
```

This example also illustrates another TSPI behavior. All nonreserved parameters are left alone, unless they are specifically documented as returning a value. This can simplify the application code since it won't have to constantly reinitialize structures.

Attach LUN (TSPI_CMD_AttachLUN)

This command is used to notify the TSPI manager that your application will handle SCSI commands for the specified LUN. You must do this before issuing any other TSPI commands that use this LUN. If this command completes without an error your application should start issuing `TSPI_CMD_GetEvent` commands to retrieve incoming SCSI commands and bus events.

On entry:

CommandCode	`TSPI_CMD_AttachLUN`
AdapterIndex	Adapter to attach (0-n)
Lun	LUN to attach (0-7)
Flags	Must be 0

On return::

Error	Error code

Listing 9-9. TSPI Attach LUN

```
TSPI_CMD attach;
attach.CommandCode = TSPI_CMD_AttachLUN;
attach.AdapterIndex = 0;
attach.Lun = 0;
attach.Flags = 0;
tspi_SendCommand(&attach);
if (!attach.Error)
    printf("LUN %u is now enabled\n",attach.lun);
```

We'll describe the callback routine in more detail later.

Detach LUN (TSPI_CMD_DetachLUN)

This command is used to notify the TSPI manager that your application will no longer be responding to SCSI commands for the specified LUN.

You must issue this command to detach any previously attached LUNs before your application terminates.

On entry:

CommandCode	`TSPI_CMD_DetachLUN`
AdapterIndex	Adapter to detach from, same as for `TSPI_CMD_AttachLUN`
LUN	LUN to attach from, same as for `TSPI_CMD_AttachLUN`
Flags	Must be 0

On return:

Error	Error code

Listing 9-10. TSPI Detach LUN

```
TSPI_CMD attach;      // used in original call to
                      // TSPI_CMD_AttachLUN
TSPI_CMD detach;
detach.CommandCode = TSPI_CMD_DetachLUN;
detach.AdapterIndex = attach.AdapterIndex;
detach.Lun = attach.Lun;
detach.Flags = 0;
tspi_SendCommand(&detach);
if (!detach.Error)
    printf("LUN %u is now disabled\n",detach.Lun);
```

Get Event (TSPI_CMD_GetEvent)

This command is used to retrieve SCSI commands for execution. The TSPI manager will buffer a single incoming command for each attached LUN, and the application uses the `TSPI_CMD_GetEvent` command to retrieve it. Most applications will sit in a loop waiting for events and then processing them as they arrive. Note that you must use a TSPI_EVENT structure with this command.

On entry:

CommandCode	`TSPI_CMD_GetEvent`
AdapterIndex	Adapter number, same as for `TSPI_CMD_ AttachLUN`
Lun	LUN, same as for `TSPI_CMD_AttachLUN`
Flags	Must be 0
Timeout	Number of milliseconds to wait for an incoming SCSI command or bus reset event. A value of 0 indicates that the command should return immediately if no command or event is pending.

On return:

Error	Error code
Flags	The flag bits will be updated to indicate the current status of the SCSI bus at the end of this command. `TSPI_FLAG_BusReset` will be set if the SCSI bus has been reset. `TSPI_FLAG_DeviceReset` will be set if the TSPI manager has received a `Device Reset` message for the target. `TSPI_FLAG_HostMsgWaiting` will be set if the initiator is asserting the ATN signal, indicating that it has a message to send to us. If so, use the `TSPI_CMD_GetMessage` command to get the message.
CdbLength	Number of valid CDB bytes in the `CdbByte[]` array. A value of 0 indicates that there is no CDB associated with this event. This can happen if the `TSPI_FLAG_ BusReset` or `TSPI_FLAG_DeviceReset` flag bits are set.
CdbByte[]	This array contains the SCSI Command Descriptor Block received from the initiator. Its length is determined by the `CdbLength` field.

Listing 9-11. TSPI Get Event

```
TSPI_CMD attach;      // used in original call to
                      // TSPI_CMD_AttachLUN
TSPI_EVENT event;
while (!quit)
    {
    event.CommandCode = TSPI_CMD_GetEvent;
```

(Continued)

Listing 9-11. (*Continued*)

```
event.AdapterIndex = attach.AdapterIndex;
event.Lun = attach.Lun;
event.Timeout = 100;      // 100 milliseconds
event.Flags = 0;
tspi_SendCommand(&event);
if (event.Error == TSPI_ERR_None)
    {
    if (event.Flags & TSPI_FLAG_BusReset)
        printf("Bus reset detected\n");
    if (event.Flags & TSPI_FLAG_DeviceReset)
        printf("Device reset detected\n");
    if (event.CdbLength > 0)
        ProcessCdb(&event);
    }
else if (event.Error != TSPI_ERR_Timeout)
    {
    printf("Error %u, quitting...\n",event.Error);
    quit = 1;
    }
}
```

Read Data From Host (TSPI_CMD_ ReadFromHost)

This command causes the TSPI manager to read a data buffer from the initiator. This is required for commands that write data or parameters to the target device (e.g., `Write`). The specified adapter will enter a Data Out phase, and the specified number of bytes will be read from the initiator and placed in the application's data buffer. Note that you don't have to read the entire data buffer from the host at one time. You can break it into as many transfers as you wish, issuing this command once for each chunk of data you wish to read. Of course, larger chunks will generally lead to better performance, so don't make your buffers too small. Note also that the structure passed to the `tspi_SendCommand()` routine is a TSPI_XFER structure rather than a TSPI_CMD structure.

On entry:

CommandCode	TSPI_CMD_ReadFromHost
AdapterIndex	Adapter number from the original TSPI_EVENT structure
InitiatorId	Initiator SCSI ID from the original TSPI_EVENT structure

LUN	LUN from the original TSPI_EVENT structure
Flags	Must be 0
TransferLength	Number of bytes to transfer
TransferAddress	Pointer to the buffer that will receive the data bytes from the host. This buffer must be large enough to hold the number of bytes requested.

On return:

Error	Error code
Flags	The flag bits will be updated to indicate the current status of the SCSI bus at the end of this command. TSPI_FLAG_BusReset will be set if the SCSI bus has been reset. TSPI_FLAG_HostMsgWaiting will be set if the initiator is asserting the ATN signal, indicating that it has a message to send to us. If so, use the TSPI_CMD_GetMessage command to get the message.
ResidualCount	Number of requested data bytes NOT transferred. This value is the requested transfer length minus the number of bytes actually received. If the entire requested transfer length was received, this field will be 0.

Listing 9-12. TSPI Read Data From Host

```
TSPI_EVENT *event;  // original incoming event structure
TSPI_XFER   xfer;   // our transfer structure
char block_buf[512];
xfer.CommandCode = TSPI_CMD_ReadFromHost;
xfer.AdapterIndex = event->AdapterIndex;
xfer.InitiatorId = event->InitiatorId;
xfer.Lun = event->Lun;
xfer.Flags = 0;
xfer.TransferLength = sizeof(block_buf);
xfer.TransferAddress = &block_buf[0];
tspi_SendCommand(&xfer);
if (!xfer.Error)
    printf("%lu bytes received\n",
    xfer.TransferLength - xfer.ResidualCount);
```

Write Data To Host (TSPI_CMD_ WriteToHost)

This command causes the TSPI manager to send a data buffer to the initiator. This is required for commands that read data or parameters from the target device (e.g., `Read`). The specified adapter will enter a Data In phase, and the specified number of bytes will be sent to the host from the application's data buffer. Note that you don't have to send the entire data buffer to the host at one time. You can break it into as many transfers as you wish, issuing this command once for each chunk of data you wish to send. Of course, larger chunks will generally lead to better performance, so don't make your buffers too small. Note that the structure passed to the `tspi_SendCommand()` routine is a TSPI_XFER structure rather than a TSPI_CMD structure.

On entry:

CommandCode	`TSPI_CMD_WriteToHost`
AdapterIndex	Adapter number from the original TSPI_EVENT structure
InitiatorId	Initiator SCSI ID from the original TSPI_EVENT structure
LUN	LUN from the original TSPI_EVENT structure
Flags	Must be 0
TransferLength	Number of bytes to transfer
TransferAddress	Pointer to the buffer that contains the data bytes that will be sent to the host.

On return:

Error	Error code
Flags	The flag bits will be updated to indicate the current status of the SCSI bus at the end of this command. `TSPI_FLAG_BusReset` will be set if the SCSI bus has been reset. `TSPI_FLAG_HostMsgWaiting` will be set if the initiator is asserting the ATN signal, indicating that it has a message to send to us. If so, use the `TSPI_CMD_GetMessage` command to get the message.
ResidualCount	Number of requested data bytes NOT transferred. This value is the requested transfer length minus the number of bytes actually sent. If the entire requested transfer length was sent, this field will be 0.

Listing 9-13. TSPI Write Data To Host

```
TSPI_EVENT *event;    // original incoming event structure
TSPI_XFER   xfer;     // our transfer structure
char block_buf[512];
xfer.CommandCode = TSPI_CMD_WriteToHost;
xfer.AdapterIndex = event->AdapterIndex;
xfer.InitiatorId = event->InitiatorId;
xfer.Lun = event->Lun;
xfer.Flags = 0;
xfer.TransferLength = sizeof(block_buf);
xfer.TransferAddress = &block_buf[0];
tspi_SendCommand(&xfer);
if (!xfer.Error)
    printf("%lu bytes sent\n",
        xfer.TransferLength - xfer.ResidualCount);
```

Complete Command (TSPI_CMD_CompleteCommand)

This command is used to signal the end of a SCSI command received via the callback routine. It causes the TSPI manager to send the final STATUS byte back to the initiator and disconnect from the SCSI bus. All SCSI commands received via the callback routine must have a corresponding `TSPI_CMD_CompleteCommand` command to terminate them. Once this command is sent for a given TSPI_EVENT received via the callback routine you should not access any fields within that TSPI_EVENT structure, since the TSPI manager may immediately reuse it for another command. This shouldn't be a practical restriction, since `TSPI_CMD_Complete-Command` will be the last command issued for a given event.

On entry:

CommandCode	`TSPI_CMD_CompleteCommand`
AdapterIndex	Adapter number from the original TSPI_EVENT structure
InitiatorId	Initiator SCSI ID from the original TSPI_EVENT structure
LUN	LUN from the original TSPI_EVENT structure
Flags	Must be 0
Parm[0]	Status byte to send back to the initiator. This is typically one of the following: 0x00 – Good

> 0x02 – Check condition
>
> 0x08 – Busy
>
> 0x18 – Reservation Conflict
>
> 0x22 – Command Terminated
>
> Refer to the SCSI specification for a complete list of possible status bytes.

On return:

Error   Error code

Listing 9-14. TSPI Complete Command

```
TSPI_EVENT *event;  // original incoming event structure
TSPI_CMD   cmd;
cmd.CommandCode = TSPI_CMD_CompleteCommand;
cmd.AdapterIndex = event->AdapterIndex;
cmd.InitiatorId = event->InitiatorId;
cmd.Lun = event->Lun;
cmd.Flags = 0;
cmd.Parm[0] = 0x02; // Check condition
tspi_SendCommand(&cmd);
if (!cmd.Error)
    printf(" Error %u\n",cmd.Error);
```

Send Message To Host (TSPI_CMD_SendMessage)

This command is used to send a message to the initiator. This command is provided to allow the application to send an arbitrary SCSI message to the host. It follows the same format as the `TSPI_CMD_WriteToHost` command, except that the data will be send during a Message In phase. Note that the structure passed to the `tspi_SendCommand()` routine is a TSPI_XFER structure rather than a TSPI_CMD structure.

On entry:

CommandCode	`TSPI_CMD_WriteToHost`
AdapterIndex	Adapter number from the original TSPI_EVENT structure
InitiatorId	Initiator SCSI ID from the original TSPI_EVENT structure

LUN	LUN from the original TSPI_EVENT structure
Flags	Must be 0
TransferLength	Number of message bytes to transfer
TransferAddress	Pointer to the buffer that contains the message bytes that will be sent to the host. The application is responsible for the formatting of the message bytes.

On return:

Error	Error code
Flags	The flag bits will be updated to indicate the current status of the SCSI bus at the end of this command. `TSPI_FLAG_BusReset` will be set if the SCSI bus has been reset. `TSPI_FLAG_HostMsgWaiting` will be set if the initiator is asserting the ATN signal, indicating that it has a message to send to us (possibly a `Message Reject` message). If so, use the `TSPI_CMD_GetMessage` command to get the message.
ResidualCount	Number of requested message bytes NOT transferred. This value is the requested transfer length minus the number of bytes actually sent. If the entire requested transfer length was sent, this field will be 0. Note that if the initiator requests a MESSAGE OUT phase, this routine will terminate early to allow for timely processing of the host's message. This field will indicate where in the message buffer the host asserted ATN.

Listing 9-15. TSPI Send Message To Host

```
TSPI_EVENT *event;  // originally passed to callback routine
TSPI_XFER   xfer;   // our transfer structure
char msg_buf[4];
msg_buf[0] = RESTORE_POINTERS;    // restore saved pointers
xfer.CommandCode = TSPI_CMD_SendMessage;
xfer.AdapterIndex = event.AdapterIndex;
xfer.InitiatorId = event.InitiatorId;
xfer.Lun = event.Lun;
xfer.Flags = 0;
```

(Continued)

Listing 9-15. (*Continued*)

```
xfer.TransferLength = 1;
xfer.TransferAddress = &msg_buf[0];
tspi_SendCommand(&xfer);
if (!xfer.Error)
    printf("%lu bytes sent\n",
        xfer.TransferLength - xfer.ResidualCount);
```

Get Message From Host (TSPI_CMD_GetMessage)

This command is used to get a message from the initiator. You might do this if the `TSPI_FLAG_HostMsgWaiting` bit is set upon return from another command. This indicates that the initiator has the ATN signal asserted to request a Message Out phase. This command allows an application to read that message. Note that messages arriving before the command phase of a transaction will be automatically handled by the TSPI manager. This includes nearly all of the message handling required for most applications, including `Identify` messages, `Synchronous` and `Wide Negotiation`, and the `Bus Device Reset` message. However, the TSPI manager does not automatically handle messages that arrive during or after the data transfer phases. These may include the `Abort`, `Disconnect` (from host), and `Initiator Detected Error` messages. Also, an initiator may send a parity error message after a Data In transfer to indicate an error in the data. The `TSPI_FLAG_HostMsgWaiting` bit indicates the presence of such a message. If this bit is set you should issue a `TSPI_CMD_GetMessage` command to read the message from the host. If it was a `Parity Error` message, you might want to send a `Restore Pointers` message and retry the transfer.

This command follows the same general format as the `TSPI_CMD_ReadFromHost` command, except that the data will be send during a Message In phase. Note that the structure passed to the `tspi_SendCommand()` routine is a TSPI_XFER structure rather than a TSPI_CMD structure. Also note that more than one message may be read into your buffer if the host sends multiple messages during a single Message Out phase.

On entry:

CommandCode	`TSPI_CMD_GetMessage`
AdapterIndex	Adapter number from the original TSPI_EVENT structure

InitiatorId	Initiator SCSI ID from the original TSPI_EVENT structure
LUN	LUN from the original TSPI_EVENT structure
Flags	Must be 0
TransferLength	Number of bytes to transfer
TransferAddress	Pointer to the buffer that will receive the message bytes from the host. This buffer must be large enough to hold the number of bytes requested.

On return:

Error	Error code
Flags	The flag bits will be updated to indicate the current status of the SCSI bus at the end of this command. TSPI_FLAG_BusReset will be set if the SCSI bus has been reset. TSPI_FLAG_HostMsgWaiting will be set if the initiator is still asserting the ATN signal, indicating that it has another message to send to us.
ResidualCount	Number of requested data bytes NOT transferred. This value is the requested transfer length minus the number of bytes actually received. If the entire requested transfer length was received, this field will be 0. You should use this field to calculate how many message bytes were actually received.

Listing 9-16. TSPI Get Message From Host

```
TSPI_EVENT *event;   // originally passed to callback routine
TSPI_XFER   xfer;    // our transfer structure
char msg_buf[16];
xfer.CommandCode = TSPI_CMD_GetMessage;
xfer.AdapterIndex = event.AdapterIndex;
xfer.InitiatorId = event.InitiatorId;
xfer.Lun = event.Lun;
xfer.Flags = 0;
xfer.TransferLength = sizeof(msg_buf);
xfer.TransferAddress = &msg_buf[0];
tspi_SendCommand(&xfer);
if (!xfer.Error)
    ProcessMessageBytes( msg_buf,
          xfer.TransferLength -
          xfer.ResidualCount)
```

Disconnect (TSPI_CMD_Disconnect)

This command causes the TSPI manager to send a disconnect message to the initiator and then disconnect from the SCSI bus. This allows an application to free the SCSI bus for other transactions while the application is carrying out a lengthy operation. The application must issue a `TSPI_CMD_Reconnect` command before sending any other commands to the TSPI manager for that LUN.

On entry:

CommandCode	`TSPI_CMD_Disconnect`
AdapterIndex	Adapter number from the original TSPI_EVENT structure
InitiatorId	Initiator SCSI ID from the original TSPI_EVENT structure
LUN	LUN from the original TSPI_EVENT structure
Flags	If the `TSPI_CMD_SaveDataPointer` bit is set, the TSPI manager will send a `Save Data Pointer` message to the initiator before disconnecting. This flag is almost always set when you are breaking a transfer up into smaller chunks.

On return:

Error	Error code

Listing 9-17. TSPI Disconnect

```
TSPI_EVENT *event;  // original incoming event structure
TSPI_CMD    cmd;
cmd.CommandCode = TSPI_CMD_Disconnect;
cmd.AdapterIndex = event->AdapterIndex;
cmd.InitiatorId = event->InitiatorId;
cmd.Lun = event->Lun;
cmd.Flags = TSPI_FLAG_SaveDataPointer;
tspi_SendCommand(&cmd);
if (!cmd.Error)
    printf(" Error %u\n",cmd.Error);
```

Reconnect (TSPI_CMD_Reconnect)

This command causes the TSPI manager to reselect an initiator to continue a SCSI transaction. See the `TSPI_CMD_Disconnect` command for additional information.

On entry:

CommandCode	`TSPI_CMD_Reconnect`
AdapterIndex	Adapter number from the original TSPI_EVENT structure
InitiatorId	Initiator SCSI ID from the original TSPI_EVENT structure
LUN	LUN from the original TSPI_EVENT structure
Flags	Must be 0

On return:

Error	Error code
Flags	The `TSPI_FLAG_HostMsgWaiting` will be set if the initiator is asserting the ATN signal, indicating that it has a message to send to us. If so, use the `TSPI_CMD_GetMessage` command to get the message from the host.

Listing 9-18. TSPI Reconnect

```
TSPI_EVENT *event;  // original incoming event structure
TSPI_CMD    cmd;
cmd.CommandCode = TSPI_CMD_Reconnect;
cmd.AdapterIndex = event->AdapterIndex;
cmd.InitiatorId = event->InitiatorId;
cmd.Lun = event->Lun;
cmd.Flags = 0;
tspi_SendCommand(&cmd);
if (!cmd.Error)
    printf("Unable to reconnect, error %u\n",cmd.Error);
```

Connecting to the TSPI Manager

The TSPI interface was designed to exist in a separate executable from the applications that use it. This typically would be a device driver or

Windows DLL (just like ASPI). For our MS-DOS example, we'll connect to it in very much the same way we connected to the ASPI manager. We'll open the TSPI manager's device driver and get the address of the TSPI manager's entry point. This is done by the following code sample:

Listing 9-19. Getting the TSPI Entry Point

```
        .DATA
TspiEntryPoint      DD 0            ; address of entry point
TspiHandle          DW 0            ; file handle
AspiDriverName      DB "TSPIMGR$",0   ; TSPI device name

        .CODE
GetTspiEntryPoint PROC
     push   ds                      ; save current data segment
     mov    ax,@DATA                ; load local data segment
     mov    ds,ax
     lea    dx,TspiDriverName       ; load offset of driver name
     mov    ax,3D00h                ; MS-DOS open file
     int    21h
     jc     failed
     mov    [TspiHandle],ax         ; save file handle

     mov    bx,[TspiHandle]         ; load file handle
     lea    dx,TspiEntryPoint       ; address of buffer
     mov    cx,4                    ; length = 4 bytes
     mov    ax,4402h                ; MS-DOS IOCTL read
     int    21h
     jc     failed

     mov    bx,[TspiHandle]         ; load file handle
     mov    ax,3E00h                ; MS-DOS close file
     int    21h

   ; return the address of the TSPI entry point
     mov    ax,word ptr [TspiEntryPoint]
     mov    dx,word ptr [TspiEntryPoint+2]
     pop    ds
     ret

failed:
     mov    ax,0                    ; return NULL on error
     mov    dx,0
     pop    ds
     ret
GetTspiEntryPoint ENDP
```

An application can then use the following sequence to connect to the TSPI manager:

Listing 9-20. Connecting to the TSPI Manager

```
BYTE NumAdapters;

VOID (FAR *tspi_SendCommand)(void FAR *p);

tspi_SendCommand = GetTspiEntryPoint();
if (tspi_SendCommand)
    {
    TSPI_CMD tspi_info;
    memset( &tspi_info, 0, sizeof(tspi_info) );
        tspi_info.CommandCode = TSPI_CMD_AdapterInquiry;
        tspi_info.AdapterIndex = 0;
    tspi_SendCommand( &tspi_info );
    if (tspi_info.Error)
        {
        // Something is wrong
        NumAdapters = 0;
        }
    else
        {
        // TSPI manager is installed and running
        NumAdapters = tspi_info.Parm[0];
        }
    }
else
    {
    // TSPI manager is not installed
    NumAdapters = 0;
    }
```

Using the TSPI Interface

Now that we've defined a target-mode SCSI interface for PCs, let's look at how you might use it from within a target-mode application. First you should define the SCSI command set that your application will support. If your application will be emulating a device type already defined by the SCSI specification, this is easy—just grab the SCSI spec and implement the command set defined for that device type. Maybe this won't seem easy when you look at the myriad of mode sense/select pages, buffering and logging options, and other features. Try implementing a bare-bones emulation at first, and then add features as required. If you're writing code for the initiator (host) side as well, you can often get away with a minimal implementation of the command set.

If your application doesn't match any of the defined SCSI device types, you'll have to define your own command set. This shouldn't be too difficult, as the command set probably will be dictated by the functionality you require. You may want to place all of your operations in vendor-specific commands, or you may be able to use variations of existing commands (i.e., `read` and `write`) to meet your specific needs. Whichever route you choose, be sure to implement all of the mandatory SCSI commands so that your application will be compatible with existing host adapters and software. Also, be sure to set the most significant bit of the `Peripheral Qualifier` field in your inquiry data. This marks your device type as vendor-specific, and should keep other applications from trying to use it.

If you define your own vendor-unique commands, you should keep them as "SCSI-like" as possible. For example, the opcode, LUN, and control byte fields are common to all current SCSI commands, so don't redefine them in your vendor-unique commands.

Also, keep your CDBs either 6, 10, or 12 bytes long, and use the existing command group codes if possible. Some host adapter drivers and software won't handle other lengths.

Your application should use standard sense keys and ASC/ASCQ codes wherever possible. This will help eliminate confusion on the host side, and some host applications can make retry and error recovery decisions based on these values.

Be prepared to respond to an `Inquiry` or `Test Unit Ready` command at any time. This is important if your device supports commands that can complete before the operation is actually finished. As an example, check out the `Rewind` command for sequential access (tape) devices. It contains an `Immediate` bit that, when set, instructs the device not to wait for the rewind operation to finish before completing the SCSI `Rewind` command. Then, the host might later issue a `Test Unit Ready` command to determine if the rewind has actually finished. Since rewind operations can take a great deal of time, this feature is often used by tape applications. Note that with the TSPI manager you don't have to worry about additional SCSI commands arriving until the current SCSI command has completed. The warning above applies only to SCSI commands that can complete early, but which may leave the device unable to accept additional media access-type commands until some later time.

Let's take a look at a simple target-mode application that implements a few frequently used SCSI commands. As with the earlier examples, this code leaves out a few details, but you should be able to follow along. Check out the companion CD-ROM for a more complete example.

Listing 9-21. TSPI Sample Application

```
#define SENSE_LEN    18
unsigned char SenseData[SENSE_LEN];

#define INQUIRY_LEN  36
unsigned char InquiryData[INQUIRY_LEN] =
    { your inquiry data here };

void (FAR *tspi_SendCommand)(void FAR *p);

int main(int argc, char *argv[])
    {
    TSPI_CMD      cmd;
    TSPI_EVENT    event;

    tspi_SendCommand = GetTspiEntryPoint();
    if (!tspi_SendCommand)
        {
        printf("TSPI manager not installed\n");
        return 3;
        }

    // Attach to LUN 0 on the Adapter 0
    cmd.CommandCode = TSPI_CMD_AttachLUN;
    cmd.Adapter = 0;
    cmd.Lun = 0;
    tspi_SendCommand(&cmd);
    if (cmd.Error)
        {
        printf("Error %u trying to attach LUN\n",
            cmd.Error);
        return 4;
        }

    SetSenseData(SKEY_NoSense, 0, 0);

    while (!kbhit())    // Run until a key is pressed
        {
        event.CommandCode = TSPI_CMD_GetEvent;
        event.AdapterIndex = cmd.AdapterIndex;
        event.Lun = cmd.Lun;
        event.Timeout = 100;    // 100 milliseconds
        tspi_SendCommand(&event);
        if (event.Error == TSPI_ERR_None)
```

(Continued)

Listing 9-21. (*Continued*)

```
            {
            if (event.Flags & TSPI_FLAG_BusReset)
                printf("Bus reset detected\n");
            if (event.Flags & TSPI_FLAG_DeviceReset)
                printf("Device reset detected\n");
            if (event.CdbLength > 0)
                ProcessCdb(&event);
            }
        else if (event.Error != TSPI_ERR_Timeout)
            {
            printf("Error %u, quitting...\n",event.Error);
            break;
            }
        }

    // Detach from LUN before we exit
    cmd.CommandCode = TSPI_CMD_DetachLUN;
    cmd.Adapter = 0;
    cmd.Lun = 0;
    tspi_SendCommand(&cmd);
    return 0;
    }


void ProcessCdb(TSPI_EVENT *event)
    {
    int status;
    TSPI_CMD cmd;

    switch (event->CdbByte[0])
        {
        case TEST_UNIT_READY:
            status = TestUnitReady(event);
            break;
        case INQUIRY:
            status = Inquiry(event);
            break;
        case REQUEST_SENSE:
            status = RequestSense(event);
            break;
        default:
            // Unsupported command
            SetSenseData( SKEY_IllegalRequest,
                    ASC_InvalidCommandCode, 0 );
            status = CHECK_CONDITION;
        }
```

(Continued)

Listing 9-21. (*Continued*)

```c
    // Now we tell the TSPI manager that we're done,
    // and send the status byte back to the initiator

    cmd.CommandCode = TSPI_CMD_CompleteCommand;
    cmd.AdapterIndex = event->AdapterIndex;
    cmd.TargetId = event->TargetId;
    cmd.Parm[0] = status;
    tspi_SendCommand(&cmd);
    }

void SetSenseData( int skey, int asc, int asq )
    {
    int i;
    for (i=0; i<SENSE_LEN; i++)
        SenseData[i] = 0;
    SenseData[0] = 0x70;    // Current error
    SenseData[2] = skey & 0x0F; // Sense Key
    SenseData[12] = asc;    // Additional sense code
    SenseData[13] = asq;    // Additional qualifier
    }

int TestUnitReady(TSPI_EVENT *event)
    {
    // Assume a global 'Ready' variable
    // indicates our ready status
    if (Ready)
        return GOOD;
    else
        return CHECK_CONDITION;
    }
int RequestSense(TSPI_EVENT *event)
    {
    // Send sense data back to host
    TSPI_XFER xfer;
    xfer.CommandCode = TSPI_CMD_WriteToHost;
    xfer.AdapterIndex = event->AdapterIndex;
    xfer.InitiatorId = event->InitiatorId;
    xfer.TargetId = event->TargetId;
    xfer.Lun = event->Lun;
    if (event->CdbByte[4] > SENSE_LEN)
        xfer.TransferLength = SENSE_LEN;
    else
        xfer.TransferLength = event->CdbByte[4];
    xfer.TransferAddress = &SenseData[0];
```

(Continued)

Listing 9-21. (*Continued*)

```
    tspi_SendCommand(&xfer);
    if (xfer.Error)
        {
        }
    return GOOD;
    }

int Inquiry(TSPI_EVENT *event)
    {
    if (event->CdbByte[1] & EVPD_BIT)
        {
        // We don't support vital page data in this
        // example, so return a CHECK CONDITION
        SetSenseData( SKEY_IllegalRequest,
                ASC_InvalidFieldInCdb, 0)
        return CHECK_CONDITION;
        }
    else
        {
        // Send standard inquiry data back to host
        TSPI_XFER xfer;
        xfer.CommandCode = TSPI_CMD_WriteToHost;
        xfer.AdapterIndex = event->AdapterIndex;
        xfer.InitiatorId = event->InitiatorId;
        xfer.TargetId = event->TargetId;
        xfer.Lun = event->Lun;
        if (event->CdbByte[4] > INQUIRY_LEN)
            xfer.TransferLength = INQUIRY_LEN;
        else
            xfer.TransferLength = event->CdbByte[4];
        xfer.TransferAddress = &InquiryData[0];
        tspi_SendCommand(&xfer);
        return GOOD;
        }
    }
```

Chapter 10

SCSI Support under Windows

With the enormous installed base of computers running Microsoft Windows, we'd be remiss if we didn't spend some time discussing native SCSI support under Windows. I'll start by reminding you that ASPI managers are available for each current version of Windows (3.x, 95, and NT). In an ideal world, that would be enough said—you could write ASPI-compliant code, and aside from a few initialization details, you wouldn't have to worry which operating system it ran on. Unfortunately, this is the real world, and there are some additional requirements and restrictions you should note when using ASPI under Windows. In this chapter we'll take a look at these requirements, and then move on to a look at how SCSI is supported on the Windows 95 and NT operating systems.

ASPI for Windows 3.x

Windows 3.x is really a graphical operating environment that sits on top of DOS. (I'll bet you haven't heard that before!) For our purposes, the important difference between Windows 3.x and the others is that Windows 3.x still uses DOS for many of its services, and that DOS device drivers (such as ASPI managers) can still be loaded and used. This is important because although there is a true ASPI for Windows 3.x specification (more about this later), not all SCSI adapter vendors provided the Windows 3.x WinASPI drivers required to use it. Windows 3.x applications that had to run with all SCSI adapters were forced to bypass WinASPI support, and instead use DOS Protected Mode Interface (DPMI) calls to access the real-mode ASPI drivers directly. Unfortunately, this technique still has some limitations. For example, any SRB and data buffers that you pass to a real-mode ASPI manager must lie in real-mode addressable memory below one megabyte. This often means that an application must copy data buffers to and from the DOS addressable space. For a detailed description of how to use DPMI services to access real-mode ASPI managers, read Brian Sawert's article "The Advanced SCSI Programming Interface" in the March 1994 issue of *Dr. Dobb's Journal*.

Adaptec eventually released an ASPI specification and drivers that support Windows 3.x applications. Their implementation still uses DOS ASPI drivers, but it also has a Windows 3.x Virtual Device Driver (VxD) and a DLL that applications can call directly from Windows 3.x applications. The VxD handles most of the enhanced-mode memory management issues automatically, so applications don't have to copy data buffers back and forth from the DOS addressable memory space. Also, applications that use WinASPI aren't restricted to using that precious little bit of DOS addressable memory available under Windows 3.x for SRBs and data buffers. They can use the regular Windows `GlobalAlloc()` routine to allocate memory above the one megabyte limit, and pass them directly to the WinASPI manager. The only restriction is that an application must page-lock the memory to prevent enhanced-mode Windows 3.x from swapping it out to disk while the ASPI operation was in progress. This is done by allocating memory with the GMEM_FIXED attribute, and then calling `GlobalPageLock()` to lock it in place. If your application uses ASPI posting (callbacks) you should also page-lock your code segment and any data segments used by the post routine to keep them from being moved or swapped out to disk.

ASPI for Win32 (Windows 95 and NT)

Windows 95 and NT both have SCSI support built right into the operating system. This allows for a much more robust implementation of ASPI for these systems. In particular, you no longer need to worry about page-locking your code segments and data buffers. When necessary, these functions are carried out by the SCSI drivers themselves. However, the ASPI for Win32 specification does make some changes that you need to note. First, the layout of the SRB structure has changed a bit. Fields have been moved around for better 32-bit alignment, and the `SRB_CDBByte[]` array is now always 16 bytes long, and is followed by a new field that receives any returned sense data bytes. This means that you no longer have to take the length of the CDB into account when looking at the sense data.

ASPI for Win32 (95 and NT) also provides a new method for notifying your application that an SRB has completed, called *Event Notification*. With this method, you provide the handle to a regular Win32 event object that will be signaled when the SRB completes. After starting the SRB, your application can call `WaitForSingleObject()` to block until the SRB completes. This frees up processor time that would otherwise be wasted while your application polls for the SRB's completion. Event Notification is the preferred method for waiting for an SRB to complete under Windows 95 and NT. It is even faster and more efficient than posting, which requires the ASPI for Win32 manager to launch a separate thread to monitor SRBs for completion. This is done because the post routine cannot be run at interrupt time under Windows 95 and NT (like it can under DOS). The extra thread provides a way for the ASPI for Win32 manager to simulate the callback to the post routine, but at the expense of some additional system overhead.

The Windows 95 and NT SCSI Model

Both Windows 95 and NT contain a series of layered device drivers that provide different levels of SCSI support. At the lowest level are hardware-specific drivers that manage SCSI bus transaction. In the middle lies a driver that provides a single, consistent interface to all of the SCSI adapters on the system. And at the top are class drivers that implement the different personalities of the various SCSU device types. Although the implementation details differ between the two operating systems, conceptually they provide very similar SCSI model.

At the lowest software level are SCSI *miniport* drivers that are responsible for the direct control of a SCSI interface adapter. Miniport drivers initialize SCSI adapters, transmit I/O requests to the hardware, handle interrupts, and perform adapter-level error recovery and logging. In short, miniport drivers are small, stripped-down SCSI I/O modules that hide the hardware-specific details of a particular SCSI adapter. They provide higher-level SCSI modules with a consistent low-level interface to different SCSI adapters, regardless of the actual hardware interface.

As you can see from Figure 10-1, a SCSI miniport driver doesn't have to control a traditional SCSI adapter as long as it implements the defined SCSI miniport interface. This allows peripheral vendors to use a different bus interface to their hardware with a minimal amount of device driver support. As long as they can make their interface look like SCSI at some

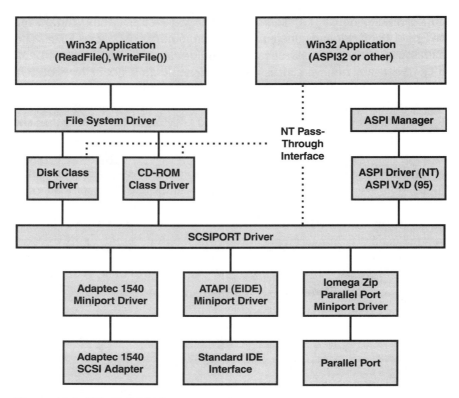

Figure 10-1. Win32 SCSI Support Model

level, they can rely on the higher-level Windows drivers to do most of the work required to control their device. For example, ATAPI devices have a command set nearly identical to SCSI, but they communicate over an IDE bus. The Windows ATAPI miniport driver accepts the low-level SCSI commands and sends them out over the IDE bus. It hides the IDE-specific features of the interface behind a SCSI shell. Similarly, Iomega supplies a miniport driver that mimics the SCSI interface over a parallel port to communicate with their Zip drives.

Sitting atop these miniport drivers is a mid-level driver called the SCSIPORT driver. The SCSIPORT driver provides a single entry point for all SCSI requests in the system. It initializes the various miniport drivers in the system, converts system-specific SCSI I/O requests into standard SCSI *Command Descriptor Blocks* (CDBs), and passes these requests through to the appropriate miniport driver. Since hardware-specific details are hidden by the miniport drivers, higher-level drivers can call the SCSI-PORT driver to carry out any SCSI I/O operation without regard to the actual hardware interface employed. Under Windows NT, applications can also send SCSI I/O requests directly to the SCSIPORT driver via the `DeviceIoControl()` routine—more about this a bit later. Unfortunately, Windows 95 doesn't provide the same support for applications—only VxDs and other system components can call the SCSIPORT driver.

The highest level of SCSI-specific support in the Windows layered device driver model rests in the SCSI *class drivers*. Each class driver is responsible for handling I/O requests for a particular type of SCSI device. There are several standard SCSI class drivers shipped with Windows, including those that handle disk drives, tape drives, and CD-ROM drives. Each of these device types requires a significantly different high-level interface, but can use the SCSIPORT driver to carry out the lower-level SCSI I/O requests. For example, file system drivers will call upon the disk class driver to carry out high-level, block-oriented I/O requests. The disk class driver will convert the file system requests into a series of SCSI I/O requests, which it will then pass along to the SCSIPORT driver. Tape class drivers have a completely different high-level interface, one suited to sequential access rather than block access, and they know about tape-specific concepts such as filemarks and end-of-tape warnings. The tape class driver converts these high-level tape requests into one or more SCSI I/O requests, which are again passed along to the SCSIPORT driver. The CD-ROM and scanner class drivers are similarly unique, each implementing a different high-level interface, but calling on the SCSIPORT driver to carry out SCSI I/O requests.

You might be asking where ASPI fits into this picture. The Windows NT ASPI manager uses a custom device driver (ASPI32.SYS) to call directly into the SCSIPORT driver. The Windows 95 implementation makes calls into the APIX VxD, which then connects to the SCSIPORT driver. In either case, the ASPI manager must be careful not to allow applications direct access to certain devices used by the system. You certainly shouldn't be able to issue commands to a SCSI hard drive while Windows is trying to update the file system. The ASPI managers for Windows 95 and NT deal with this by simply hiding these system-reserved devices from your application. If you want access to these devices from your application, you should use the standard file system services. If you really want to muck about with a hard drive while it's being used by Windows, you'll have to write your own device driver to manage it.

Windows NT SCSI Pass-Through Interface

Earlier I mentioned that applications could issue SCSI commands directly to the SCSIPORT driver under Windows NT. This is accomplished via a slightly documented mechanism called the SCSI *Pass-Through Interface,* or SPTI. Applications can issue various SCSI-specific IOCTL calls directly to any SCSI class or port driver. That driver will then route the SCSI command through the chain of drivers, and eventually out to the device. If a particular device has been claimed by a class driver, you must issue the SCSI pass-through commands to that class driver rather than the SCSI port driver. This restriction prevents applications from issuing commands without the knowledge of the class drivers, and allows the class driver to maintain control of the device state.

To use the SCSI pass-through interface you must first open the class or port driver in charge of the device. Direct-access devices are usually claimed by the file-system drivers, and you can open them via their drive letter. Other devices are accessed by their class driver name. You can access unclaimed devices directly through their SCSI adapter driver. Examples of each of these device names appear below:

Device Name Examples

\\.\C:	Hard drive C
\\.\D:	CD-ROM drive D
\\.\Tape0:	Tape drive 0
\\.\Scsi0:	SCSI adapter 0
\\.\Scsi2:	SCSI adapter 2

Opening the driver is as simple as opening a file:

Listing 10-1. Opening a Device Driver

```
handle = CreateFile( "\\\\Scsi2:",
    GENERIC_WRITE | GENERIC_READ,
    FILE_SHARE_READ | FILE_SHARE_WRITE,
    NULL, OPEN_EXISTING, 0, NULL );
```

Once you've opened the device you can issue IOCTL calls to get the inquiry data for any devices controlled by the driver, get the host adapter capabilities, execute SCSI commands, or re-scan the SCSI bus to look for new devices. The IOCTL codes and the structures that they use are defined in various header files distributed with the Windows NT Device Driver Kit (DDK). The required header files are:

- DEVIOCTL.H
- NTDDDISK.H
- NTDDSCSI.H

The calls available via the SCSI pass-through interface are:

- IOCTL_SCSI_GET_INQUIRY_DATA
- IOCTL_SCSI_GET_CAPABILITIES
- IOCTL_SCSI_GET_ADDRESS
- IOCTL_SCSI_RESCAN_BUS
- IOCTL_SCSI_PASS_THROUGH
- IOCTL_SCSI_PASS_THROUGH_DIRECT

Let's examine each of these in turn.

IOCTL_SCSI_GET_INQUIRY_DATA

This IOCTL command is used to retrieve information describing each SCSI bus and device controlled by the driver. Let's look at the structures used to describe this information, and then at some sample code that walks through the list of busses and devices.

Listing 10-2. SCSI Get Inquiry Data

```
typedef struct _SCSI_ADAPTER_BUS_INFO
    {
    UCHAR NumberOfBuses;          // How many SCSI busses
    SCSI_BUS_DATA BusData[1];     // Array of data structures
    } SCSI_ADAPTER_BUS_INFO, *PSCSI_ADAPTER_BUS_INFO;

typedef struct _SCSI_BUS_DATA
    {
    UCHAR NumberOfLogicalUnits;  // Logical devices
    UCHAR InitiatorBusId;        // SCSI adapter's ID
    ULONG InquiryDataOffset;     // Inquiry data buffer
    }SCSI_BUS_DATA, *PSCSI_BUS_DATA;

typedef struct _SCSI_INQUIRY_DATA
    {
    UCHAR PathId;                // Which SCSI bus
    UCHAR TargetId;              // Which SCSI target
    UCHAR Lun;                   // Which SCSI LUN
    BOOLEAN DeviceClaimed;       // Claimed by driver?
    ULONG InquiryDataLength;     // Inquiry data length
    ULONG NextInquiryDataOffset;// Next LUN's data
    UCHAR InquiryData[1];        // This LUN's data
    }SCSI_INQUIRY_DATA, *PSCSI_INQUIRY_DATA;
```

(Continued)

Listing 10-2. (*Continued*)

```
ULONG bus,n;
SCSI_ADAPTER_BUS_INFO *adapter;
char inq_buf[4096];
DeviceIoControl( device_handle, // from CreateFile()
    IOCTL_SCSI_GET_INQUIRY_DATA,
    NULL, 0,
    &inq_buf, sizeof(inq_buf),
    &n, NULL );

// Scan through the adapter inquiry data, printing out
// information for each BUS/TID/LUN encountered
adapter = (SCSI_ADAPTER_BUS_INFO *) inq_buf;
printf("Bus TID LUN Claimed Inquiry Data\n");
printf("--- --- --- ------- ----------------------\n");
for (bus=0; bus<adapter->NumberOfBuses; bus++)
    {
    // Get offset to first logical unit's inquiry data
    ULONG inq_offset =
        adapter->BusData[bus].InquiryDataOffset;

    while ( inq_offset != 0)    // end of list?
        {
        // Get pointer to the inquiry data
        // within the returned buffer
        SCSI_INQUIRY_DATA *inq;
        inq = (SCSI_INQUIRY_DATA *) (inq_buf + inq_offset);

        // Print BUS/TID/LUN, and whether or not
        // the device is claimed by a class driver.
        printf("%3lu %3u %3u %s ",
            bus, inq->TargetId, inq->Lun,
            inq->DeviceClaimed ? "  Yes " : "  No   " );

        // Now print out the device's SCSI inquiry data
        for (int i=0; i<8; i++)
            printf("%02X ",inq->InquiryData[i]);
        printf("%.28s\n",&inq->InquiryData[8]);

        // Get offset to next logical unit's inquiry data
        inq_offset = inq->NextInquiryDataOffset;
        }
```

IOCTL_SCSI_GET_CAPABILITIES

This command is used to determine the capabilities and limitations of the underlying SCSI adapter and miniport driver. This includes the maximum transfer length allowed, how many pages that transfer may span, and the alignment requirement for any data buffers passed to it.

Listing 10-3. SCSI Get Capabilities

```
typedef struct _IO_SCSI_CAPABILITIES
    {
    ULONG Length;                       // Length of this structure
    ULONG MaximumTransferLength;// Maximum transfer length
    ULONG MaximumPhysicalPages;  // How many physical pages
                                 // the transfer can span
    ULONG SupportedAsynchronousEvents; // Async event allowed
    ULONG AlignmentMask;         // Alignment requirement
    BOOLEAN TaggedQueuing;       // Tagged queueing allowed
    BOOLEAN AdapterScansDown;    // Adapter scans BIOS
    BOOLEAN AdapterUsesPio;      // Adapter uses programmed I/O
                                 // (as opposed to bus-master
                                 // or DMA transfers)
    } IO_SCSI_CAPABILITIES, *PIO_SCSI_CAPABILITIES;

IO_SCSI_CAPABILITIES caps;

DeviceIoControl( device_handle, // from CreateFile()
    IOCTL_SCSI_GET_INQUIRY_DATA,
    NULL, 0,
    &caps, sizeof(caps),
    &n, NULL );
```

You always should respect the transfer limits returned by this command. Larger transfers will fail, and may cause some versions of Windows NT to crash. Since applications don't have access to the physical page layout of their data buffers, you should limit your transfers to the smaller of the MaximumTransferLength and the worst-case page layout of your buffer, which is (MaximumPhysicalPages-1) * PAGE_SIZE.

IOCTL_SCSI_GET_ADDRESS

This command is used to return addressing information for a particular device. Note that this command is valid only for class drivers. You can use this information to determine the SCSI adapter, bus, and target ID to which a device is attached.

Listing 10-4. SCSI Get Address

```
typedef struct _SCSI_ADDRESS
    {
    ULONG Length;               // Length of this structure
    UCHAR PortNumber;           // Which SCSI device controls
    UCHAR PathId;               // Which bus it's on
    UCHAR TargetId;             // Its target ID
    UCHAR Lun;                  // Its logical unit number
    }SCSI_ADDRESS, *PSCSI_ADDRESS;

SCSI_ADDRESS addr;

DeviceIoControl( device_handle, // from CreateFile()
    IOCTL_SCSI_GET_ADDRESS,
    NULL, 0,
    &addr, sizeof(addr),
    &n, NULL );
```

Note that the `PathId`, `TargetId`, and `LUN` fields are also returned by the `IOCTL_SCSI__GET_INQUIRY_DATA` command. The `PortNumber` field can be used to create the device name for the port driver. For example, a `PortNumber` of 2 would indicate that the device is controlled via the "\\\Scsi2" port driver.

IOCTL_SCSI_RESCAN_BUS

This command causes the driver to rescan its SCSI bus, looking for new devices. It collects SCSI inquiry data for newly attached devices, while preserving any class driver claims on existing devices.

Listing 10-5. SCSI Rescan Bus

```
DeviceIoControl( device_handle, // from CreateFile()
    IOCTL_SCSI_RESCAN_SCSI_BUS,
    NULL, 0,
    NULL, 0,
    &n, NULL );
```

An application can then reissue the `IOCTL_SCSI_INQUIRY_DATA` command to check for any new devices.

IOCTL_SCSI_PASS_THROUGH and IOCTL_SCSI_PASS_THROUGH_DIRECT

These commands are used to send SCSI commands to a target device. The `IOCTL_SCSI_PASS_THROUGH` command uses a single structure for the SRB and data buffer, while `IOCTL_SCSI_PASS_THROUGH_DIRECT` allows you to specify the address of a separate data buffer for I/O transfers. The structures used by these commands are as follows:

Listing 10-6. SCSI Pass-Through

```
typedef struct _SCSI_PASS_THROUGH
    {
    USHORT Length;              // Length of this structure
    UCHAR ScsiStatus;           // Returned target status
    UCHAR PathId;               // Path ID
                                // (from SCSI_INQUIRY_DATA)
    UCHAR TargetId;             // Target ID
                                // (from SCSI_INQUIRY_DATA)
    UCHAR Lun;                  // LUN
                                // (from SCSI_INQUIRY_DATA)
    UCHAR CdbLength;            // Length of SCSI CDB
    UCHAR SenseInfoLength;      // Sense buffer length
    UCHAR DataIn;               // Direction flag (see below)
    ULONG DataTransferLength;   // Data bytes to transfer
    ULONG TimeOutValue;         // timeout, in seconds
    ULONG DataBufferOffset;     // offset of data buffer
    ULONG SenseInfoOffset;      // offset of sense buffer
    UCHAR Cdb[16];              // CDB bytes
    } SCSI_PASS_THROUGH, *PSCSI_PASS_THROUGH;

typedef struct _SCSI_PASS_THROUGH_DIRECT
    {
    USHORT Length;              // Length of this structure
    UCHAR ScsiStatus;           // Returned target status
    UCHAR PathId;               // Path ID
                                // (from SCSI_INQUIRY_DATA)
    UCHAR TargetId;             // Target ID
                                // (from SCSI_INQUIRY_DATA)
    UCHAR Lun;                  // LUN
                                // (from SCSI_INQUIRY_DATA)
    UCHAR CdbLength;            // Length of SCSI CDB
```

(Continued)

Listing 10-6. (*Continued*)

```
    UCHAR SenseInfoLength;        // Sense buffer length
    UCHAR DataIn;                 // Direction flag (see below)
    ULONG DataTransferLength;     // Data bytes to transfer
    ULONG TimeOutValue;           // timeout, in seconds
    PVOID DataBuffer;             // address of data buffer
    ULONG SenseInfoOffset;        // offset of sense buffer
    UCHAR Cdb[16];                // CDB bytes
} SCSI_PASS_THROUGH_DIRECT, *PSCSI_PASS_THROUGH_DIRECT;
```

Note that these structures are almost identical, with the exception of the `DataBufferOffset` and `DataBuffer` fields. The IOCTL_SCSI_ PASS_THROUGH command expects the data buffer to be addressed as an offset from the start of the SCSI_PASS_THROUGH structure, while the IOCTL_SCSI_PASS_THROUGH_DIRECT command allows you to specify a pointer that directly addresses the buffer. Also note that the `Sense-InfoOffset` in each structure indicates an offset from the start of the structure. Applications typically embed these structures within their own data structures, like the following:

Listing 10-7. SCSI Pass-Through Request

```
typedef struct _NT_SCSI_REQUEST
    {
    SCSI_PASS_THROUGH  spt;
    unsigned char sense[16];
    unsigned char data[1];
    } NT_SCSI_REQUEST;

typedef struct _NT_SCSI_REQUEST_DIRECT
    {
    SCSI_PASS_THROUGH_DIRECT  spt;
    unsigned char sense[16];
    } NT_SCSI_REQUEST_DIRECT;
```

This allows you to use the `offsetof()` macro to specify the offset of the sense buffer (and the data buffer offset for the IOCTL_SCSI_PASS_ THROUGH command).

Listing 10-8. SCSI Pass-Through Data Buffers

```
NT_SCSI_REQUEST sr;
sr.spt.SenseInfoOffset = offsetof(NT_SCSI_REQUEST,sense);
sr.spt.DataBufferOffset = offsetof(NT_SCSI_REQUEST,data);

NT_SCSI_REQUEST_DIRECT srd;
char data_buffer[1024];
srd.spt.SenseInfoOffset = offsetof(NT_SCSI_REQUEST,sense);
srd.spt.DataBuffer = &data_buffer[0];
```

The following example shows how you can use the `IOCTL_SCSI_PASS_THROUGH_DIRECT` command to implement a SCSI I/O routine. Your application can use a similar routine to handle all of the I/O commands for SCSI devices.

Listing 10-9. Using SCSI Pass-Through

```
int ScsiCommand( HANDLE device_handle,
    SCSI_INQUIRY_DATA *inq,
    void *cdb_buf, unsigned cdblen,
    void *data_buf, unsigned long dlen,
    int direction,
    void *sense_buf, unsigned slen,
    long timeout )
    {
    NT_SCSI_REQUEST_DIRECT a;
    ULONG returned;

    memset(&a,0,sizeof(a));
    a.spt.Length = sizeof(a.spt);
    a.spt.PathId = inq->PathId;
    a.spt.TargetId = inq->TargetId;
    a.spt.Lun = inq->Lun;
    a.spt.CdbLength = cdblen;
    a.spt.SenseInfoLength = sizeof(a.sense);
    a.spt.DataIn = direction;
    a.spt.DataTransferLength = dlen;
    a.spt.TimeOutValue = timeout;
    a.spt.DataBuffer = data_buf;
    a.spt.SenseInfoOffset =
        offsetof(NT_SCSI_REQUEST_DIRECT,sense);
    memcpy( a.spt.Cdb, cdb_buf, cdblen );
```

(Continued)

Listing 10-9. (*Continued*)

```
if (!DeviceIoControl( h,
    IOCTL_SCSI_PASS_THROUGH_DIRECT,
    &a, sizeof(a), &a, sizeof(a),
    &returned, NULL) )
    {
    int x = GetLastError(); // See why it failed
    if (sense_buf && slen)
        memset(sense_buf,0,slen);
                            // clear sense area
    return 0xFF;            // return error status
    }

if (sense_buf && slen)
    memcpy( sense_buf, a.sense,
        (slen < sizeof(a.sense)) ? slen :
         sizeof(a.sense) );

return a.spt.ScsiStatus;
}
```

Chapter 11

Unix SCSI Implementations

The rest of this book covers how to write SCSI device drivers and applications in the ever-popular MS-DOS/Windows/Windows95/NT environment. That seems to be the general trend these days, yet SCSI doesn't really get to shine in most platforms of that type. A personal desktop system with one user clicking away at the keyboard, even a programmer doing software development, only begins to tap the capabilities of a high-performance SCSI I/O subsystem.

In server systems running UNIX, the multitasking abilities of SCSI are put to real advantage. Since any number of users are requesting data from multiple disks, CD-ROMs, etc., the single-minded nature of IDE would not be well tolerated. Because of this, virtually all current servers have SCSI I/O.

In the paragraph above, I mentioned systems running UNIX. UNIX is not really one operating system anymore. Ever since U.C. Berkeley started independent development from the AT&T version 7 code base, UNIX has branched many times. A number of attempts at standardizing UNIX systems has resulted in operating systems that are basically source code compatible at the application programming interface level. However, every UNIX kernel is completely unique inside! Unfortunately, this is the domain of the UNIX device driver developer.

The various UNIX vendors never felt the need to be compatible below the application level. Even when the PC vendors agreed on a standard SCSI API, the UNIX vendors paid it no mind. That thinking is readily apparent when one begins to write SCSI device drivers for more than one UNIX platform. Each platform has its own entirely different SCSI API, not to mention a whole different kernel architecture and set of kernel I/O support functions.

This situation has provided employment for a large number of driver writers since 1985 or so. After a while ANSI decided to create a standard SCSI API specification called *Common Access Method* (CAM), but it wasn't really in a usable state until about 1991 or so. By then the UNIX vendors were pretty much locked in to their proprietary APIs. Only Digital Equipment Corporation adopted CAM as their native UNIX SCSI API.

UNIX systems provide an application environment that is quite different from the MS-DOS/Windows environment. User applications are not allowed to directly access system hardware. In order to perform I/O an application must make a system call, like "read," for example. The O/S will then decide which device driver is in control of the device from which the data is to be read from and build a request asking that the desired data be transferred into the user's memory buffer.

Another method that is used by some special applications is for the O/S to provide what is called a SCSI pass-through driver. In this case the application builds its own SCSI commands and hands them to the pass-through driver to be delivered to the device. Once the command completes the status is returned to the calling application. An example of this type of application is a music CD playing utility.

Some UNIX systems have all the device drivers linked into one large monolithic kernel file. When the system boots, the entire O/S image is loaded into memory and executed. Other systems go through a dynamic process during boot that loads only the drivers that are needed currently. Other drivers can be loaded and unloaded as needed. This dynamic approach is being used more and more since it conserves system resources. It does, however, make the drivers themselves more complicated to write.

This chapter will not attempt to explain in detail how to write SCSI drivers and applications for all UNIX platforms. To do that would take an entire book for each O/S. I simply want to give the reader a glimpse of the SCSI environment in the various UNIX variants. Then I'll single out one popular UNIX variant and give more detail on it.

A Brief Description of UNIX Device Drivers

In UNIX systems applications are protected from each other's transgressions by the kernel's intervention. All I/O is done via system calls into the

UNIX kernel. A device driver is a program that runs at the kernel's privilege level that performs I/O to a particular type of I/O device. All UNIX I/O is made to look to the application like file I/O, even when the I/O is to a hardware device like a terminal screen. There is a "special file" (also called a *device node*) for each device that appears in the filesystem (usually in the /dev directory). These have names like /dev/tty0 for a terminal or /dev/hd0 for a hard disk. The names are made up by the driver writer, but can be changed or have links made to them by the system administrator. All these special files really do is store the "major and minor numbers" for that device. The major number is used as an index into a table of all the device drivers in the kernel and the minor number can be used in any manner desired by the driver writer. It usually is used to specify which unit the I/O is to go to.

There are two main types of UNIX drivers, called *block* and *character*. Block devices are used to access devices that are clearly block oriented (like disks). Character devices are used for everything else.

Block drivers have three major entry points: Open, Close, and Strategy. Character drivers have a few more: Open, Close, Read Write, and Ioctl.

Take a look at Figure 11-1 to understand how all the pieces fit together.

Drivers operate in two processor contexts: User and Kernel. When the driver is opened by the user application and a data request is made, the driver is acting as a privileged extension of the user application (User context). Once the user's request has been submitted to the device, the application is put to sleep (blocked from further execution), until the device interrupts the currently running process by causing the driver's interrupt handler to execute. The interrupt handler runs in kernel context. It issues a wakeup call that will cause the application to resume execution where it left off with the requested data in its buffer, where it was placed either by the interrupt handler using polled I/O or by the device itself using DMA. Modern UNIX drivers also need to be aware that their interrupt handler may run on a different processor than the one running the application program. This means that some form of locking must be done on any structures or variables that are accessed by an instance of the driver.

A driver's strategy routine is actually called by the kernel's file system code when a user process asks for data using standard file I/O calls. The data read this way is stored in the kernel's "buffer cache" so that other processes that need the same data can get it without another disk read operation being done.

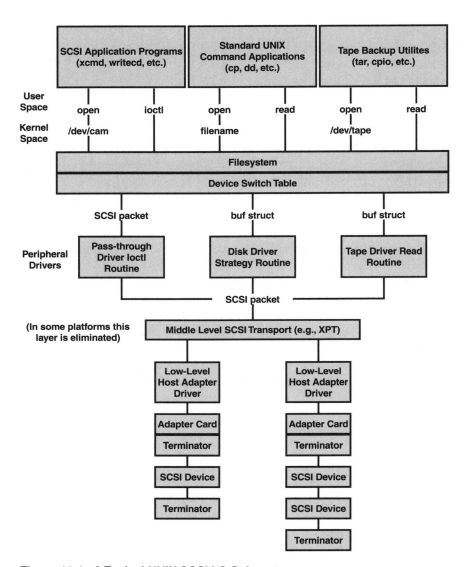

Figure 11-1. A Typical UNIX SCSI I/O Subsystem

The specific kernel function names that perform all the housekeeping operations involved in accomplishing the above mentioned data transfer are different for each flavor of UNIX.

Comparison of UNIX Implementations

Here are some key points of the most popular UNIX variants in outline form, which I hope will make it easy to compare them. The following tables could also act as a guide in getting a driver writer started in developing drivers for the various platforms.

Table 11-1. AIX Version 4.1 Features

Feature	Description
Platform	Power RISC and Power PC architectures
Kernel type	Fully dynamic
Kernel—memory handling (allocate/free)	xmattach(), xmalloc(), xmfree()
Kernel—data space conversion	copyin(), copyout(), uiomove()
Kernel—process blocking (sleeping)	e_sleep(), wakeup()
Kernel—data access locking	lockl(), unlockl(), lock_alloc(), simple_lock_init(), unlock_ enable(), lock_free(), disable_lock(), i_enable(), i_disable()
Kernel—other functions	fp_opendev(), fp_close(), fp_ioctl(), pincode(), unpincode(), pinu(), unpinu(), errsave(), bzero(), uphysio(), devswadd(), devswdel()
Kernel—other structures	buf, sc_buf, sc_iocmd
SCSI-related header files	/usr/include/sys/scsi.h, trcmacros.h, err_rec.h, errids.h, trchkid.h, lock_alloc.h, cdrom.h, scdisk.h
SCSI adapter driver interface	devstrat(sc_buf)
Required driver entry points	drivernameconfig, drivernameopen, drivernameclose, driver- nameread, drivernamewrite, drivernameioctl, drivernamestrategy
SCSI pass-through interface	fd = openx("/dev/rcd0", O_RDONLY, NULL, SC_DIAGNOSTIC)
	ioctl(fd, CDIOCMD or DKIOCMD, &sc_iocmd)
Driver support commands	smit, lsdev, odme, odmadd, odmdelete, odmget, odmchange, odmshow, trace, errpt, errclear, cfgmgr, installp

(Continued)

Table 11-1. AIX Version 4.1 Features *(Continued)*

Feature	Description
Driver support files	/etc/drivers/*, /etc/methods/*, /lib/kernex.exp
Error logging	errsave(), errrpt
Example driver source	Under Ver 3.x, a few partial examples were included with the O/S (in /usr/lpp/bos/samples/). Better examples are included on a diskette in the IBM Device Driver manual mentioned below. Another source of sample driver code is on IBM's ftp site at ftp://ftp.austin.ibm.com/pub/developer/aix/ddriver/writedd.tar.Z
Debugging	A very primitive kernel debugger is included with the O/S. It requires that a dumb terminal be attached to a serial port.
	Kernel printf is active only with switch in the "service" position.
Available driver documentation	"Writing a Device Driver for AIX Version 3.2" (IBM P/N GG24-3629-01)
	"Writing a Device Driver for AIX Version 4.1" (IBM P/N SC23-2593-03)
	"Kernel Extensions and Device Support Programming Concepts" (IBM P/N SC23-2611-03)
Comments	AIX drivers are more complicated than some because of the required interaction with the ODM (Object Data Manager) database for device information. All device topology and identification information is stored in the ODM.
	AIX SCSI adapter drivers need to realize that the sc_buf passed to it may contain a list of transfers to be done, or only one. There is more than one if the buf structure pointer in the sc_buf is not NULL. An editor called odme, which could be used to edit the ODM database directly, used to be supplied in version 3.x, but it is no longer available in 4.x.
	The "export" files in /lib show which functions are exported by each module. It is useful to look in kernex.exp to determine the exact names of kernel functions. If your driver will have any entry points other than the standard ones, you must create one of these export files for your driver too. This includes any of your symbols you may want to find in the kernel debugger.

Table 11-2. HP-UX 10.x Features

Feature	Description
Platform	HP9000/8xx series PA-RISC architecture
Kernel type	Monolithic
	Note: As of HP-UX 10.xx, HP-UX supports two different driver subsystems: Workstation I/O (WSIO) and Server I/O (SIO). Generally, WSIO drivers control devices on EISA, HSC, and some built-in busses, while SIO drivers control HP-IO bus devices.
Kernel—memory handling (allocate/free)	kmalloc(), kfree(), io_get_mem(), io_rel_mem()
Kernel—data space conversion	copyin(), copyout(), bvtospace(), pvtospace(), minphys()
Kernel—process blocking (sleeping)	biowait(), get_sleep_lock(), sleep(), wakeup()
Kernel—data access locking	alloc_spinlock(), spinlock(), spinunlock()
Kernel—other functions	physio(), timeout(), biodone(), bzero(), bcopy(), bcmp()
Kernel—other structures	buf, sctl_io, iovec, uio
SIO—other functions	io_send(), io_get_trn(), io_get_frame(), io_port_info(), sio_get_pda()
SIO—SCSI-related header files	/usr/include/sio/llio.h, sys/sio_drv.h
SIO—SCSI adapter driver interface	io_send(io_req) A driver must "bind" to a Device Adapter Manager (DAM) for each SCSI target it wants to control. No other driver can then be bound to those devices.
WSIO—data access locking	scsi_lun_lock(), scsi_lun_unlock()
WSIO—other functions	scsi_lun_open(), scsi_lun_close(), scsi_ioctl(), scsi_init_inquiry_data(), scsi_read(), scsi_write(), scsi_enqueue(), scsi_dequeue(), scsi_dequeue_bp(), scsi_cmd(), scsi_ddsw_init(), scsi_strategy(), scsi_enqueue_cnt(), scsi_mode_sense(), scsi_mode_fix(), scsi_mode_select(), scsi_wr_prot(), scsi_action(), scsi_sense_action(), scsi_snooze(), scsi_sleep(), scsi_log_io()
WSIO—SCSI-related header files	/usr/include/sys/wsio.h, sys/scsi_ctl.h

(Continued)

Table 11-2. HP-UX 10.x Features *(Continued)*

Feature	Description
WSIO—SCSI adapter driver interface	scsi_start()
SCSI-related header files	/usr/include/sys/scsi.h, scsi_meta.h
Required driver entry points	drivername (I/O message port server)
SCSI pass-through interface	fd = open("/dev/rdsk/c0t5d0", ...)
	ioctl(fd, SIOC_IO or SIOC_SET_CMD, &sctl)
	Other IOCTL commands:
	SIOC_INQUIRY, SIOC_EXCLUSIVE, SIOC_XSENSE, SIOC_IO, SIOC_PRIORITY_MODE, SIOC_CMD_MODE, SIOC_SET_ CMD, SIOC_RETURN_STATUS, SIOC_GET_TGT_PARMS, SIOC_GET_BUS_PARMS, SIOC_GET_LUN_LIMITS, SIOC_ SET_LUN_LIMITS, SIOC_GET_TGT_LIMITS, SIOC_SET_ TGT_LIMITS, SIOC_GET_BUS_LIMITS, SIOC_SET_BUS_ LIMITS, SIOC_RESET_DEV, SIOC_RESET_BUS
Driver support commands	swinstall, swremove, swpackage, ioscan, uxgen
Driver support files	/sbin/rc2.d/Sxxx and Kxxx scripts, /stand/system, /usr/conf/master.d/drivername, /usr/conf/lib/driverlib.a
Error logging	/var/adm/messages, dmesg
Debugging	Source-level kernel debugger called ddb, which is based on dbx. Requires a second machine on the same IP subnet.
Comments	Server type SCSI adapters use the 'scsi1' (narrow) or 'scsi3' (wide) adapter drivers. Workstation type SCSI adapters use either the 'c700' (narrow) or 'c720' (fast/wide) adapter drivers.
	The driver being used by a SCSI adapter can be seen using the command "ioscan -kf".
	Warning! Some HP PA RISC documentation shows bit 0 as the MSB. There were major changes between HP-UX ver 9.x and 10.x. All kernel intersubsystem communication is done via messages.

Table 11-3. SCO ODT 3 Features

Feature	Description
Platform	Intel architecture based PCs
Kernel type	Monolithic
Kernel—data space conversion	ktop(), ptok(), paddr(), vtop(), copyin(), copyout()
Kernel—process blocking (sleeping)	iowait(), sleep(), wakeup(), iodone()
Kernel—data access locking	spl6(), splx()
Kernel—other functions	bcopy(), printf(), delay(), major(), minor(), panic(), physio(), suser(), signal(), timeout()
Kernel—other structures	buf, scsi_io_req, scsi_dev_cfg, u
SCSI-related header files	/usr/include/sys/scsi.h
SCSI adapter driver interface	scsi_ha_cfg[0](&scsi_io_req)
Required driver entry points	drxinit, drxopen, drxclose, drxread, drxwrite, drxioctl, drxstrategy, drxstart, drxintr
SCSI pass-through interface	fd = open("/dev/rcd0", ...) ioctl(fd, SCSIUSERCMD, &sc)
Driver support commands	link_unix, custom
Driver support files	/etc/conf/cf.d/mscsi, mdevice, sdevice, /etc/conf/pack.d/drxx/driver.o
Error logging	cmn_err, /var/adm/messages
Example driver source	Comes with SCO Driver Book mentioned below.
Debugging	An assembler-level kernel debugger is available from SCO for developers.
Available driver documentation	Kettle, Peter and Steve Statler. *Writing Device Drivers for SCO UNIX: A Practical Approach.* Reading, Massachusetts: Addison-Wesley, 1993.
Comments	AT&T System V based. Evolved into Microsoft Xenix and around 1990 into SCO UNIX and Open Desktop.

Table 11-4. Solaris 2.5 Features

Feature	Description
Platform	Sun SPARC architecture
Kernel type	Fully dynamic
Kernel—memory handling (allocate/free)	scsi_alloc_consistent_buf(), scsi_free_consistent_buf(), kmem_alloc(), kmem_zalloc(), kmem_free()
Kernel—data space conversion	copyin(), copyout()
Kernel—process blocking (sleeping)	sleep(), wakeup(), biowait(), biodone(), bioerror(), cv_init, cv_wait(), cv_wait_sig(), cv_signal(), cv_broadcast(), cv_destroy()
Kernel—data access locking	mutex_init(), mutex_enter, mutex_exit()
Kernel—other functions	ddi_get_soft_state, ddi_soft_state_fini(), ddi_soft_state_zalloc(), ddi_soft_state_free(), mod_remove(), mod_info(), ddi_getprop(), ddi_get_parent(), ddi_get_instance(), ddi_get_driver_private(), scsi_init_pkt(), ddi_create_minor_node(), ddi_remove_minor_ node(), ddi_get_name(), ddi_name_to_major(), ddi_report_dev(), scsi_reset(), scsi_destroy_pkt(), scsi_probe(), scsi_unprobe(), scsi_errmsg(), makecom_g0(), bzero(), bcopy(), physio(), getrbuf(), freerbuf()
Kernel—other structures	buf, uscsi_cmd, iovec, uio
SCSI-related header files	/usr/include/sys/scsi/scsi.h
SCSI adapter driver interface	scsi_transport(scsi_pkt)
Required driver entry points	drivername_open, drivername_close, drivername_read, drivername_write, drivername_ioctl, drivername_strategy, drivername_info, drivername_identify, drivername_probe, drivername_attach, drivername_detach, _init, _fini, _info
SCSI pass-through interface	fd=open("/dev/rdsk/c0t2l0s0", ...) ioctl(fd, USCSICMD, &uscsi_cmd)
Driver support commands	add_drv, rem_drv, drvconfig, pkgmk, pkginfo, pkgtrans, pkgchk, pkgadd, pkgrm, prtconf, sysdef
Driver support files	/usr/kernel/drv/driver.conf, /etc/devlink.tab, proto.drivername, /etc/system, /etc/rc2/
Error logging	/var/adm/messages

(Continued)

Table 11-4. Solaris 2.5 Features *(Continued)*

Feature	Description
Example driver source	ftp://opcom.sun.ca/pub/drivers/svr4_sample_drivers.tar.Z
Debugging	Assembler-level kernel debugger is built into the system boot PROM and can be activated by booting with a command line option. It can then be entered by typing "L1-A" or ("Stop-A"). Another primitive debugger called "adb" is also provided.
Available driver documentation	http://www.sun.com/smcc/solaris-migration/docs/ Solaris 2.x DDK (Driver Development Kit) "Writing Device Drivers" (Sun P/N 800-6502-06)
Comments	On SPARC systems, DMA goes through the memory management hardware so scatter/gather isn't necessary for transfers up to 16 MB. Development is rather convenient since drivers can be loaded and unloaded without rebooting.

Table 11-5. Digital UNIX (Formerly OSF/1) Ver. 4.x Features

Feature	Description
Platform	Digital Alpha architecture
Kernel type	Monolithic (but driver loading/unloading is possible)
Kernel—memory handling (allocate/free)	contig_malloc(), contig_free(), MALLOC()
Kernel—data space conversion	copyin(), copyout()
Kernel—process blocking (sleeping)	biodone(), iodone(), mpsleep(), sleep(), spldevhigh(), splx(), wakeup()
Kernel—data access locking	lock_init(), lock_done(), lock_read(), lock_write(), lock_terminate()
Kernel—other functions	physio(), devsw_add(), devsw_del(), devsw_get(), getnewbuf(), brelse(), bzero(), major(), minor()
Kernel—other structures	buf, uagt_struct, CCB_SCSIIO, CCB_GETDEV, CCB_PATHINQ, etc.

(Continued)

Table 11-5. Digital UNIX (Formerly OSF/1) Ver. 4.x Features *(Continued)*

Feature	Description
SCSI-related header files	/usr/include/io/cam/cam.h, scsi_all.h, scsi_cdbs.h, scsi_direct.h, scsi_opcodes.h, uagt.h, dec_cam.h, xpt.h, scsi_status.h, buf.h, ioctl.h
SCSI adapter driver interface	xpt_action(&ccb), xpt_ccb_alloc(), xpt_ccb_free()
Required driver entry points	drivername_open, drivername_close, drivername_read, drivername_write, drivername_ioctl, drivername_strategy
SCSI pass-through interface	fd=open("/dev/cam", ...) ioctl(fd, UAGT_CAM_IO, &uagt_struct)
Driver support commands	uerf, /sbin/doconfig, /sbin/ddr_config, /usr/sbin/sysconfig
Driver support files	/etc/ddr.dbase, sysconfigtab, /sys/conf/hostname
Error logging	cam_logger, /var/adm/messages, binary.errlog
Debugging	dbx –k, dbx –remote, Ladebug (All are full source level debuggers.)
Available driver documentation	Digital UNIX Device Driver Writing Manual Set (DEC P/N QA-MT5AH-GZ)
Comments	A large set of common routines for simplifying the sending and receiving of CAM CCBs is available for use by SCSI peripheral drivers. See the ccmn_xxxx routines in the CAM driver writer's manual (part of the document set above).

Table 11-6. Linux (Kernel Ver. 2.0.x) Features

Feature	Description
Platform	Intel x86 architecture-based PCs, Digital Alpha architecture, Sun SPARC architecture
Kernel type	Partially dynamic
Kernel—memory handling (allocate/free)	kmalloc(), kfree(), free_pages(), scsi_init_malloc(), scsi_init_free(), brelse()
Kernel—data space conversion	put_user(), get_user(), verify_area(), memcpy_tofs(), memcpy_fromfs()

(Continued)

Table 11-6. Linux (Kernel Ver. 2.0.x) Features *(Continued)*

Feature	Description
Kernel—process blocking (sleeping)	sleep_on(), wake_up()
Kernel—data access locking	save_flags(), cli(), sti(), restore_flags()
Kernel—other functions	printk(), panic(), memset(), suser(), init_module(), register_blkdev(), unregister_blkdev(), register_chrdev(), unregister_chrdev(), scsi_register_device(), scsi_register_host(), scsi_unregister_device(), scsi_unregister_host(), scsi_register_module(), scsi_unregister_module(), scsi_init(), scsi_done(), check_sense(), scsi_abort(), scsi_reset(), scsi_build_commandblocks(), scsi_dev_init()
Kernel—other structures	buf, Scsi_Cmnd, Scsi_Device_Template, drx_fops
SCSI-related header files	/usr/src/linux/drivers/scsi/scsi.h, scsi_ioctl.h
SCSI adapter driver interface	scsi_do_cmd(SCpnt, cmd, buffer, bufflen, done_rtn, timeout, retries)
Required driver entry points (character drivers)	drx_init, drx_open, drx_release, drx_finish, drx_attach, drx_detach, drx_detect, drx_ioctl, drx_read, drx_write, do_drx_request
Required driver entry points (block drivers)	check_media_change, drx_revalidate
SCSI pass-through interface (character drivers)	fd=open("/dev/sg0", ...) write(fd, scsi_command, nbytes) read(fd, scsi_results, nbytes)
SCSI pass-through interface (block drivers)	fd = open("/dev/scd0", ...) ioctl(fd, SCSI_IOCTL_SEND_COMMAND, buff)
Driver support commands	make depend, make zlilo
Driver support files	/lib/modules/version/*, /usr/src/linux/kernel/drivers/*
Error logging	logger(), syslog(), printk(), /etc/syslog.conf, /usr/sbin/syslogd, /var/log/messages
Example driver source	/usr/src/linux/kernel/drivers/scsi/sd.*, st.*, sg.c

(Continued)

Table 11-6. Linux (Kernel Ver. 2.0.x) Features *(Continued)*

Feature	Description
Debugging	printk(), gdb, /proc/*
	A handy feature of the /proc filesystem: "cat /proc/scsi/scsi" will show all attached SCSI devices. There is also another "directory" /proc/scsi/adaptername/. There are "files" in there (0, 1 ...) for each SCSI bus's parameters.
Available driver documentation	Beck, Michael. *Linux Kernel Internals.* Reading, Massachusetts: Addison-Wesley, 1996. See also documentation files that accompany the Linux distribution: *Linux Kernel Hacker's Guide* (Michael K. Johnson); *Writing Linux Device Drivers* (Michael K. Johnson); *Linux SCSI HOWTO* (Drew Eckhardt); *Linux SCSI Programming HOWTO* (Heiko Ei Felt).
Comments	The Linux disk driver only has one interface, unlike most other UNIX disk drivers that provide both a block and character interface. It also has no strategy routine.
	Linux is not derived from AT&T or BSD sources.

After comparing the kernel environments in the above UNIX platforms, it should be apparent that to write UNIX drivers one needs to concentrate on one platform at a time. Writing one that's portable between multiple platforms is almost unthinkable, given the current state of affairs. This may change at some point. There are efforts afoot to standardize and modularize UNIX drivers at two different levels. The *Universal Device Interface* (UDI) is one such idea, and Intel's I2O standard is another.

If the purpose of writing your first UNIX SCSI driver is to learn how to do it, I can't think of a better platform to start with than Linux. It provides a powerful yet inexpensive environment to learn the basics of UNIX driver writing. Linux runs on just about any hardware. To get started, I'd recommend buying one of the several CD-ROM install-based releases, such as Slackware or Red Hat, for the Intel X86-based PC. For the more adventurous, Linux can also be downloaded from the Internet from many sites via ftp or http protocol. The Linux web site at http://www.linux.org contains links to download sites for several different distributions.

Once you have a running Linux system, install the kernel sources (if they weren't installed with the rest of the O/S). In the /usr/src/linux/drivers directory you'll find the source code for all the drivers that have been written for Linux. One of the best ways to learn how to write a driver is to look at examples of working drivers. To get you started, I'm going to walk you through the SCSI disk driver (sd.c), and the SCSI passthrough driver (also referred to as the "SCSI Generic" driver) (sg.c).

Don your hip boots, and let's get started.

The Linux SCSI Disk Driver

I'm just going to show each driver entry point routine in isolation from the surrounding glue code that allows it to compile and links the driver into the kernel.

The excerpts below are from the source files: /usr/src/linux/kernel/drivers/scsi/sd.c, sd_ioctl.c, scsi.c, sd.h

Listing 11-1. Linux sd_open Routine

```
static int sd_open(struct inode * inode, struct file * filp)
{
    int target;
    target =  DEVICE_NR(inode->i_rdev);

    if(target >= sd_template.dev_max || !rscsi_disks[target].device)
        return -ENXIO;   /* No such device */

/*
 * Make sure that only one process can do a check_change_disk at
 * one time. This is also used to lock out further access when the
 * partition table is being reread.
 */

    while (rscsi_disks[target].device->busy)
        barrier();
    if(rscsi_disks[target].device->removable) {
        check_disk_change(inode->i_rdev);

        /*
         * If the drive is empty, just let the open fail.
         */
        if ( !rscsi_disks[target].ready )
           return -ENXIO;

        /*
         * Similarly, if the device has the write protect tab set,
         * have the open fail if the user expects to be able to write
         * to the thing.
         */
        if ( (rscsi_disks[target].write_prot) && (filp->f_mode & 2))
           return -EROFS;
    }
```

(Continued)

Listing 11-1. (*Continued*)

```
/*
 * See if we are requesting a nonexistent partition.  Do this
 * after checking for disk change.
 */
if(sd_sizes[MINOR(inode->i_rdev)] == 0)
    return -ENXIO;

if(rscsi_disks[target].device->removable)
    if(!rscsi_disks[target].device->access_count)
        sd_ioctl(inode, NULL, SCSI_IOCTL_DOORLOCK, 0);

rscsi_disks[target].device->access_count++;
if (rscsi_disks[target].device->host->hostt->usage_count)
    (*rscsi_disks[target].device->host->hostt->usage_count)++;
if(sd_template.usage_count) (*sd_template.usage_count)++;
return 0;
}
```

The `sd_open` routine gets two arguments as input: a pointer to an inode structure and a pointer to a file structure. The first thing the routine does is check that the device actually exists and has media in the drive.

The `rscsi_disks[]` array is used to keep track of all information about each disk in the system. If all goes well the routine returns 0 meaning success.

Listing 11-2. Linux sd_release Routine

```
static void sd_release(struct inode * inode, struct file * file)
{
    int target;
    fsync_dev(inode->i_rdev);

    target =  DEVICE_NR(inode->i_rdev);

    rscsi_disks[target].device->access_count--;
    if (rscsi_disks[target].device->host->hostt->usage_count)
        (*rscsi_disks[target].device->host->hostt->usage_count)--;
    if(sd_template.usage_count) (*sd_template.usage_count)--;
```
(Continued)

Listing 11-2. (*Continued*)

```
    if(rscsi_disks[target].device->removable) {
        if(!rscsi_disks[target].device->access_count)
            sd_ioctl(inode, NULL, SCSI_IOCTL_DOORUNLOCK, 0);
    }
}
```

The `sd_release` routine gets two arguments as input: a pointer to an inode structure and a pointer to a file structure. The routine doesn't do much except decrement some count variables and unlock the media in removable media drives.

Listing 11-3. Linux sd_init Routine

```
/*
 * The sd_init() function looks at all SCSI drives present,
 * determines their size, and reads partition table entries
 * for them.
 */

static int sd_registered = 0;

static int sd_init()
{
    int i;

    if (sd_template.dev_noticed == 0) return 0;

    if(!sd_registered) {
        if (register_blkdev(MAJOR_NR,"sd",&sd_fops)) {
            printk("Unable to get major %d for SCSI disk\n",
                MAJOR_NR);
            return 1;
        }
        sd_registered++;
    }

    /* We do not support attaching loadable devices yet. */
    if(rscsi_disks) return 0;

    sd_template.dev_max = sd_template.dev_noticed +
        SD_EXTRA_DEVS;
```

(Continued)

Listing 11-3. (*Continued*)

```
rscsi_disks = (Scsi_Disk *)
    scsi_init_malloc(sd_template.dev_max *
    sizeof(Scsi_Disk), GFP_ATOMIC);
memset(rscsi_disks, 0, sd_template.dev_max *
    sizeof(Scsi_Disk));

sd_sizes = (int *)
    scsi_init_malloc((sd_template.dev_max << 4) *
    sizeof(int), GFP_ATOMIC);
memset(sd_sizes, 0, (sd_template.dev_max << 4) * sizeof(int));

sd_blocksizes = (int *)
    scsi_init_malloc((sd_template.dev_max << 4) *
    sizeof(int), GFP_ATOMIC);

sd_hardsizes = (int *)
    scsi_init_malloc((sd_template.dev_max << 4) *
    sizeof(int), GFP_ATOMIC);

for(i=0;i<(sd_template.dev_max << 4);i++){
    sd_blocksizes[i] = 1024;
    sd_hardsizes[i] = 512;
}
blksize_size[MAJOR_NR] = sd_blocksizes;
hardsect_size[MAJOR_NR] = sd_hardsizes;
sd=(struct hd_struct *)
    scsi_init_malloc((sd_template.dev_max<<4) *
    sizeof(struct hd_struct), GFP_ATOMIC);

sd_gendisk.max_nr = sd_template.dev_max;
sd_gendisk.part = sd;
sd_gendisk.sizes = sd_sizes;
sd_gendisk.real_devices = (void *) rscsi_disks;
return 0;
}
```

The `init` routine gets no input arguments. It simply registers the driver with the kernel, which gives it a place in the devswitch table. Then it allocates space for the `rscsi_disks[]` array and a couple of other arrays and initializes a few values in them.

Listing 11-4. Linux sd_finish Routine

```
static void sd_finish()
{
    int i;

    blk_dev[MAJOR_NR].request_fn = DEVICE_REQUEST;

    sd_gendisk.next = gendisk_head;
    gendisk_head = &sd_gendisk;

    for (i = 0; i < sd_template.dev_max; ++i)
        if (!rscsi_disks[i].capacity &&
            rscsi_disks[i].device)
        {
            if (MODULE_FLAG &&
                !rscsi_disks[i].has_part_table) {
                sd_sizes[i << 4] = rscsi_disks[i].capacity;
            /* revalidate does sd_init_onedisk via MAYBE_REINIT*/
                revalidate_scsidisk(MKDEV(MAJOR_NR, i << 4), 0);
            }
            else
                i=sd_init_onedisk(i);
            rscsi_disks[i].has_part_table = 1;
        }

    /* If our host adapter is capable of scatter-gather,
     * then we increase the read-ahead to 16 blocks (32 sectors).
     * If not, we use a two block (4 sector) read ahead.
     */
    if(rscsi_disks[0].device &&
        rscsi_disks[0].device->host->sg_tablesize)
        read_ahead[MAJOR_NR] = 120;   /* 120 sector read-ahead */
    else
        read_ahead[MAJOR_NR] = 4;     /* 4 sector read-ahead */

    return;
}
```

The finish routine hooks the driver's "request function" into the blk_ dev[] array, reads in the partition table and then initializes the host adapter that the disks are attached to.

Listing 11-5. Linux sd_detect Routine

```
static int sd_detect(Scsi_Device * SDp){
    if(SDp->type != TYPE_DISK && SDp->type != TYPE_MOD)
        return 0;

    printk("Detected scsi %sdisk sd%c at ",
        SDp->removable ? "removable " : "",
        'a'+ (sd_template.dev_noticed++));
    printk("scsi%d, channel %d, id %d, lun %d\n",
        SDp->host->host_no, SDp->channel,
        SDp->id, SDp->lun);

    return 1;
}
```

The detect routine simply checks to see if we have a hard disk or Magneto Optical disk to use and prints a message during boot time.

Listing 11-6. Linux sd_attach Routine

```
static int sd_attach(Scsi_Device * SDp){
    Scsi_Disk * dpnt;
    int i;

    if(SDp->type != TYPE_DISK && SDp->type != TYPE_MOD)
        return 0;

    if(sd_template.nr_dev >= sd_template.dev_max) {
        SDp->attached--;
        return 1;
    }

    for(dpnt = rscsi_disks, i=0; i<sd_template.dev_max;
        i++, dpnt++)
        if(!dpnt->device) break;

    if(i >= sd_template.dev_max)
        panic ("scsi_devices corrupt (sd)");

    SDp->scsi_request_fn = do_sd_request;
    rscsi_disks[i].device = SDp;
```

(Continued)

Listing 11-6. (*Continued*)

```
    rscsi_disks[i].has_part_table = 0;
    sd_template.nr_dev++;
    sd_gendisk.nr_real++;
    return 0;
}
```

The `attach` routine checks again for the presence of a hard disk or Magneto Optical disk and that we have not reached the maximum number of drives that can be supported by this driver. It then checks through the `rscsi_disks[]` array to make sure all disks have an entry in it. If there are serious inconsistencies, the system panics. A few values in the `rscsi_disks[]` array are initialized and the number of attached devices is incremented.

Listing 11-7. Linux sd_detach Routine

```
static void sd_detach(Scsi_Device * SDp)
{
    Scsi_Disk * dpnt;
    int i;
    int max_p;
    int start;

    for(dpnt = rscsi_disks, i=0; i<sd_template.dev_max;
        i++, dpnt++)
        if(dpnt->device == SDp) {

        /* If we are disconnecting a disk driver,
         * sync and invalidate everything */
            max_p = sd_gendisk.max_p;
            start = i << sd_gendisk.minor_shift;

            for (i=max_p - 1; i >=0 ; i--) {
                int minor = start+i;
                kdev_t devi = MKDEV(MAJOR_NR, minor);
                sync_dev(devi);
                invalidate_inodes(devi);
                invalidate_buffers(devi);
                sd_gendisk.part[minor].start_sect = 0;
                sd_gendisk.part[minor].nr_sects = 0;
                sd_sizes[minor] = 0;
            }
```

(Continued)

Listing 11-7. (*Continued*)

```
            dpnt->has_part_table = 0;
            dpnt->device = NULL;
            dpnt->capacity = 0;
            SDp->attached--;
            sd_template.dev_noticed--;
            sd_template.nr_dev--;
            sd_gendisk.nr_real--;
            return;
        }
    return;
}
```

The `sd_detach` routine's main task is to flush all unwritten data out to the physical disk (specified by SDp), and then clear some variables to indicate that the device is no longer available.

Listing 11-8. Linux revalidate_scsidisk Routine

```
#define DEVICE_BUSY rscsi_disks[target].device->busy
#define USAGE rscsi_disks[target].device->access_count
#define CAPACITY rscsi_disks[target].capacity
#define MAYBE_REINIT  sd_init_onedisk(target)
#define GENDISK_STRUCT sd_gendisk

/* This routine is called to flush all partitions and
 * partition tables for a changed scsi disk, and then
 * reread the new partition table. If we are revalidating
 * a disk because of a media change, then we enter with
 * usage == 0. If we are using an ioctl, we automatically
 * have usage == 1 (we need an open channel to use an ioctl :-),
 * so this is our limit.
 */
int revalidate_scsidisk(kdev_t dev, int maxusage){
    int target;
    struct gendisk * gdev;
    unsigned long flags;
    int max_p;
    int start;
    int i;

    target =  DEVICE_NR(dev);
    gdev = &GENDISK_STRUCT;
```

(Continued)

Listing 11-8. (*Continued*)

```
    save_flags(flags);
    cli();
    if (DEVICE_BUSY || USAGE > maxusage) {
        restore_flags(flags);
        printk("Device busy for revalidation (usage=%d)\n",
            USAGE);
        return -EBUSY;
    }
    DEVICE_BUSY = 1;
    restore_flags(flags);

    max_p = gdev->max_p;
    start = target << gdev->minor_shift;

    for (i=max_p - 1; i >=0 ; i--) {
        int minor = start+i;
        kdev_t devi = MKDEV(MAJOR_NR, minor);
        sync_dev(devi);
        invalidate_inodes(devi);
        invalidate_buffers(devi);
        gdev->part[minor].start_sect = 0;
        gdev->part[minor].nr_sects = 0;
        /*
         * Reset the blocksize for everything so that we
         * can read the partition table.
         */
        blksize_size[MAJOR_NR][minor] = 1024;
    }

#ifdef MAYBE_REINIT
    MAYBE_REINIT;
#endif

    gdev->part[start].nr_sects = CAPACITY;
    resetup_one_dev(gdev, target);

    DEVICE_BUSY = 0;
    return 0;
}
```

If media has changed, invalidate all stored data for it and reread the partition table, and so on. Note that where data structures are being modified, a `cli()` is done previous and a `restore_flags()` is done afterwards. This is Linux's data locking method that prevents another instance of the driver from being able to corrupt the data.

Listing 11-9. Linux do_sd_request Routine

```
/*
 * do_sd_request() is the request handler function for
 * the sd driver. Its function in life is to take block
 * device requests, and translate them into SCSI commands.
 */

static void do_sd_request (void)
{
    Scsi_Cmnd * SCpnt = NULL;
    Scsi_Device * SDev;
    struct request * req = NULL;
    unsigned long flags;
    int flag = 0;

    save_flags(flags);
    while (1==1){
        cli();
        if (CURRENT != NULL &&
            CURRENT->rq_status == RQ_INACTIVE) {
            restore_flags(flags);
            return;
        }

        INIT_SCSI_REQUEST;
        SDev = rscsi_disks[DEVICE_NR(CURRENT->rq_dev)].device;

        /*
         * I am not sure where the best place to do this is.
         * We need to hook in a place where we are likely to
         * come if in user space.
         */
        if( SDev->was_reset )
        {
        /*
         * We need to relock the door, but we might
         * be in an interrupt handler.  Only do this
         * from user space, since we do not want to
         * sleep from an interrupt.
         */
            if( SDev->removable && !intr_count )
            {
                scsi_ioctl(SDev, SCSI_IOCTL_DOORLOCK, 0);
                /* scsi_ioctl may allow CURRENT to change,
```

(Continued)

Listing 11-9. (*Continued*)

```
                    * so start over. */
                   SDev->was_reset = 0;
                   continue;
              }
              SDev->was_reset = 0;
         }

/* We have to be careful here. allocate_device will get a
free pointer, but there is no guarantee that it is queueable.
In normal usage, we want to call this, because other types
of devices may have the host all tied up, and we want to make
sure that we have at least one request pending for this type
of device. We can also come through here while servicing an
interrupt, because of the need to start another command. If
we call allocate_device more than once, then the system can
wedge if the command is not queueable. The request_queueable
function is safe because it checks to make sure that the host
is able to take another command before it returns a pointer.
*/

         if (flag++ == 0)
             SCpnt = allocate_device(&CURRENT,
             rscsi_disks[DEVICE_NR(CURRENT->q_dev)].device, 0);
         else SCpnt = NULL;

         /*
          * The following restore_flags leads to latency problems.
          * FIXME.
          * Using a "sti()" gets rid of the latency problems but causes
          * race conditions and crashes.
          */
         restore_flags(flags);

/* This is a performance enhancement. We dig down into the
request list and try to find a queueable request (i.e., device
not busy, and host able to accept another command. If we find
one, then we queue it. This can make a big difference on systems
with more than one disk drive.  We want to have the interrupts
off when monkeying with the request list, because otherwise the
kernel might try to slip a request in between somewhere.
*/
```

                                                          (*Continued*)

Listing 11-9. (*Continued*)

```
        if (!SCpnt && sd_template.nr_dev > 1){
            struct request *req1;
            req1 = NULL;
            cli();
            req = CURRENT;
            while(req){
                SCpnt = request_queueable(req,
                    rscsi_disks[DEVICE_NR(req->rq_dev)].device);
                if(SCpnt) break;
                req1 = req;
                req = req->next;
            }
            if (SCpnt && req->rq_status == RQ_INACTIVE) {
                if (req == CURRENT)
                    CURRENT = CURRENT->next;
                else
                    req1->next = req->next;
            }
            restore_flags(flags);
        }

        if (!SCpnt) return; /* Could not find anything to do */

        /* Queue command */
        requeue_sd_request(SCpnt);
    }  /* While */
}
```

This routine is essentially the scheduler portion of the SCSI disk driver. It decides whether the host adapter is ready for another command and decides which command to do next. It then calls `requeue_sd_request()` to build the actual command request.

Listing 11-10. Linux requeue_sd_request Routine

```
static void requeue_sd_request (Scsi_Cmnd * SCpnt)
{
    int dev, devm, block, this_count;
    unsigned char cmd[10];
    int bounce_size, contiguous;
    int max_sg;
    struct buffer_head * bh, *bhp;
    char * buff, *bounce_buffer;
```

(Continued)

Listing 11-10. (*Continued*)

```
repeat:

    if(!SCpnt || SCpnt->request.rq_status == RQ_INACTIVE) {
        do_sd_request();
        return;
    }

    devm =  MINOR(SCpnt->request.rq_dev);
    dev = DEVICE_NR(SCpnt->request.rq_dev);

    block = SCpnt->request.sector;
    this_count = 0;
#ifdef DEBUG
    printk("Doing sd request, dev = %d, block = %d\n",
        devm, block);
#endif

    if (devm >= (sd_template.dev_max << 4) ||
        !rscsi_disks[dev].device ||
        block + SCpnt->request.nr_sectors >
        sd[devm].nr_sects)
    {
        SCpnt = end_scsi_request(SCpnt, 0,
            SCpnt->request.nr_sectors);
        goto repeat;
    }

    block += sd[devm].start_sect;

    if (rscsi_disks[dev].device->changed)
    {
        /*
         * quietly refuse to do anything to a changed
         * disc until the changed bit has been reset
         */
        SCpnt = end_scsi_request(SCpnt, 0,
            SCpnt->request.nr_sectors);
        goto repeat;
    }
ifdef DEBUG
    printk("sd%c : real dev = /dev/sd%c, block = %d\n",
        'a' + devm, dev, block);
#endif
```

(Continued)

Listing 11-10. (*Continued*)

```
/*
 * If we have a 1K hardware sector size, prevent access
 * to single 512 byte sectors.  In theory we could handle
 * this—in fact the scsi cd-rom driver must be able to
 * handle this because we typically use 1K blocksizes,
 * and cd-roms typically have 2K hardware sectorsizes.
 * Of course, things are simpler with the cd-rom, since it
 * is read-only. For performance reasons, the filesystems
 * should be able to handle this and not force the scsi
 * disk driver to use bounce buffers for this.
 */
if (rscsi_disks[dev].sector_size == 1024)
    if((block & 1) || (SCpnt->request.nr_sectors & 1)) {
        printk("sd.c:Bad block number requested");
        SCpnt = end_scsi_request(SCpnt, 0,
            SCpnt->request.nr_sectors);
        goto repeat;
    }

switch (SCpnt->request.cmd)
{
case WRITE :
    if (!rscsi_disks[dev].device->writeable)
    {
        SCpnt = end_scsi_request(SCpnt, 0,
            SCpnt->request.nr_sectors);
        goto repeat;
    }
    cmd[0] = WRITE_6;
    break;
case READ :
    cmd[0] = READ_6;
    break;
default :
    panic ("Unknown sd command %d\n", SCpnt->request.cmd);
}

SCpnt->this_count = 0;

/* If the host adapter can deal with very large
 * scatter-gather requests, it is a waste of time
 * to cluster
 */
contiguous = (!CLUSTERABLE_DEVICE(SCpnt) ? 0 :1);
bounce_buffer = NULL;
bounce_size = (SCpnt->request.nr_sectors << 9);
```

(Continued)

Listing 11-10. (*Continued*)

```
/* First see if we need a bounce buffer for this request.
 * If we do, make sure that we can allocate a buffer.
 * Do not waste space by allocating a bounce buffer if
 * we are straddling the 16MB line
 */
if (contiguous && SCpnt->request.bh &&
    ((long) SCpnt->request.bh->b_data)
    + (SCpnt->request.nr_sectors << 9) - 1 >
       ISA_DMA_THRESHOLD
    && SCpnt->host->unchecked_isa_dma) {
    if(((long) SCpnt->request.bh->b_data) >
       ISA_DMA_THRESHOLD)
        bounce_buffer = (char *) scsi_malloc(bounce_size);
    if(!bounce_buffer) contiguous = 0;
}

if(contiguous && SCpnt->request.bh &&
    SCpnt->request.bh->b_reqnext)
    for(bh = SCpnt->request.bh, bhp = bh->b_reqnext;
        bhp; bh = bhp, bhp = bhp->b_reqnext) {
        if(!CONTIGUOUS_BUFFERS(bh,bhp)) {
            if(bounce_buffer)
                scsi_free(bounce_buffer, bounce_size);
            contiguous = 0;
            break;
        }
    }
if (!SCpnt->request.bh || contiguous) {

    /* case of page request (i.e., raw device),
     * or unlinked buffer */
    this_count = SCpnt->request.nr_sectors;
    buff = SCpnt->request.buffer;
    SCpnt->use_sg = 0;

} else if (SCpnt->host->sg_tablesize == 0 ||
    (need_isa_buffer && dma_free_sectors <= 10)) {

    /* Case of host adapter that cannot scatter-gather.
     * We also come here if we are running low on DMA
     * buffer memory. We set a threshold higher than that
     * we would need for this request so we leave room
     * for other requests.  Even though we would not need
     * it all, we need to be conservative, because if we
     * run low enough we have no choice but to panic.
     */
```

(*Continued*)

Listing 11-10. (*Continued*)

```
        if (SCpnt->host->sg_tablesize != 0 &&
            need_isa_buffer &&
            dma_free_sectors <= 10)
            printk("Warning: SCSI DMA buffer space running low.");
            printk(" Using non scatter-gather I/O.\n");

        this_count = SCpnt->request.current_nr_sectors;
        buff = SCpnt->request.buffer;
        SCpnt->use_sg = 0;

    } else {

        /* Scatter-gather capable host adapter */
        struct scatterlist * sgpnt;
        int count, this_count_max;
        int counted;

        bh = SCpnt->request.bh;
        this_count = 0;
        this_count_max =
            (rscsi_disks[dev].ten ? 0xffff : 0xff);
        count = 0;
        bhp = NULL;
        while(bh) {
            if ((this_count + (bh->b_size >> 9)) >
                this_count_max) break;
            if(!bhp || !CONTIGUOUS_BUFFERS(bhp,bh) ||
                !CLUSTERABLE_DEVICE(SCpnt) ||
                (SCpnt->host->unchecked_isa_dma &&
                ((unsigned long) bh->b_data-1) ==
                ISA_DMA_THRESHOLD)) {
                    if (count < SCpnt->host->sg_tablesize)
                        count++;
                    else break;
            }
            this_count += (bh->b_size >> 9);
            bhp = bh;
            bh = bh->b_reqnext;
        }
#if 0
        if(SCpnt->host->unchecked_isa_dma &&
            ((unsigned int) SCpnt->request.bh->b_data-1) ==
            ISA_DMA_THRESHOLD) count--;
```

(Continued)

Listing 11-10. (*Continued*)

```
#endif
        SCpnt->use_sg = count;   /* Number of chains */
        /* scsi_malloc can only allocate in chunks of
         * 512 bytes */
        count  = (SCpnt->use_sg *
            sizeof(struct scatterlist) + 511) & ~511;

        SCpnt->sglist_len = count;
        max_sg = count / sizeof(struct scatterlist);
        if(SCpnt->host->sg_tablesize < max_sg)
            max_sg = SCpnt->host->sg_tablesize;
        sgpnt = (struct scatterlist * ) scsi_malloc(count);
        if (!sgpnt) {
            printk("Warning - running *really* short on DMA buffers\n");
            SCpnt->use_sg = 0;     /* No memory left - bail out */
            this_count = SCpnt->request.current_nr_sectors;
            buff = SCpnt->request.buffer;
        } else {
            memset(sgpnt, 0, count);
            /* Zero so it is easy to fill, but only
             * if memory is available */

            buff = (char *) sgpnt;
            counted = 0;
            for(count = 0, bh = SCpnt->request.bh, bhp =
                bh->b_reqnext; count < SCpnt->use_sg && bh;
                count++, bh = bhp) {

                bhp = bh->b_reqnext;

                if(!sgpnt[count].address) sgpnt[count].address =
                    bh->b_data;
                sgpnt[count].length += bh->b_size;
                counted += bh->b_size >> 9;

                if (((long) sgpnt[count].address) +
                    sgpnt[count].length - 1 >
                    ISA_DMA_THRESHOLD &&
                    (SCpnt->host->unchecked_isa_dma) &&
                    !sgpnt[count].alt_address) {
                    sgpnt[count].alt_address =
                        sgpnt[count].address;
                    /* We try to avoid exhausting the DMA
                     * pool, since it is easier to control
                     * usage here. In other places we might
                     * have a more pressing need, and we
                     * would be in trouble if we ran out */
```

(Continued)

Listing 11-10. *(Continued)*

```
                    if(dma_free_sectors <
                       (sgpnt[count].length >> 9) + 10) {
                        sgpnt[count].address = NULL;
                    } else {
                        sgpnt[count].address = (char *)
                            scsi_malloc(sgpnt[count].length);
                    }

                    /* If we start running low on DMA buffers,
                     * we abort the scatter-gather operation,
                     * and free all of the memory we have
                     * allocated. We want to ensure that all
                     * scsi operations are able to do at least
                     * a nonscatter/gather operation */
                    if(sgpnt[count].address == NULL) {
                    /* Out of dma memory */
#if 0
                        printk("Warning: Running low on \
                            SCSI DMA buffers");
                        /* Try switching back to a non
                         * s-g operation. */
                        while(--count >= 0){
                            if(sgpnt[count].alt_address)
                                scsi_free(sgpnt[count].address,
                                    sgpnt[count].length);
                        }
                        this_count =
                            SCpnt->request.current_nr_sectors;
                        buff = SCpnt->request.buffer;
                        SCpnt->use_sg = 0;
                        scsi_free(sgpnt, SCpnt->sglist_len);
#endif
                        SCpnt->use_sg = count;
                        this_count = counted -=
                            bh->b_size >> 9;
                        break;
                    }
                }

                /* Only cluster buffers if we know that we
                 * can supply DMA buffers large enough to
                 * satisfy the request. Do not cluster a
                 * new request if this would mean that we
                 * suddenly need to start using DMA bounce
                 * buffers */
```

(Continued)

Listing 11-10. (*Continued*)

```
if(bhp && CONTIGUOUS_BUFFERS(bh,bhp)
    && CLUSTERABLE_DEVICE(SCpnt)) {
  char * tmp;

  if ((((long) sgpnt[count].address) +
       sgpnt[count].length +
       bhp->b_size - 1 > ISA_DMA_THRESHOLD &&
       (SCpnt->host->unchecked_isa_dma) &&
       !sgpnt[count].alt_address) continue;

  if(!sgpnt[count].alt_address)
      {count--; continue;}
  if(dma_free_sectors > 10)
      tmp = (char *)
          scsi_malloc(sgpnt[count].length +
              bhp->b_size);
  else {
      tmp = NULL;
      max_sg = SCpnt->use_sg;
  }
  if(tmp){
      scsi_free(sgpnt[count].address,
          sgpnt[count].length);
      sgpnt[count].address = tmp;
      count--;
      continue;
  }

  /* If we are allowed another sg chain,
   * then increment counter so we can insert
   * it. Otherwise we will end up truncating */

  if (SCpnt->use_sg < max_sg) SCpnt->use_sg++;
    }   /* contiguous buffers */
  } /* for loop */

  /* This is actually how many we are going to transfer */
  this_count = counted;

  if(count < SCpnt->use_sg || SCpnt->use_sg >
      SCpnt->host->sg_tablesize){
      bh = SCpnt->request.bh;
      printk("Use sg, count %d %x %d\n",
          SCpnt->use_sg, count, dma_free_sectors);
      printk("maxsg = %x, counted = %d this_count = %d\n",
          max_sg, counted, this_count);
```

(*Continued*)

Listing 11-10. (*Continued*)

```
            while(bh){
                printk("[%p %lx] ", bh->b_data, bh->b_size);
                bh = bh->b_reqnext;
            }
            if(SCpnt->use_sg < 16)
                for(count=0; count<SCpnt->use_sg; count++)
                    printk("{%d:%p %p %d}   ", count,
                            sgpnt[count].address,
                            sgpnt[count].alt_address,
                            sgpnt[count].length);
            panic("Ooops");
        }

        if (SCpnt->request.cmd == WRITE)
            for(count=0; count<SCpnt->use_sg; count++)
                if(sgpnt[count].alt_address)
                    memcpy(sgpnt[count].address,
                            sgpnt[count].alt_address,
                            sgpnt[count].length);
    }   /* Able to malloc sgpnt */
}   /* Host adapter capable of scatter-gather */

/* Now handle the possibility of DMA to addresses > 16Mb */

if(SCpnt->use_sg == 0){
    if (((long) buff) + (this_count << 9) - 1 >
        ISA_DMA_THRESHOLD &&
        (SCpnt->host->unchecked_isa_dma)) {
        if(bounce_buffer)
            buff = bounce_buffer;
        else
            buff = (char *) scsi_malloc(this_count << 9);
        if(buff == NULL) {
        /* Try backing off a bit if we are low on mem*/
            this_count = SCpnt->request.current_nr_sectors;
            buff = (char *) scsi_malloc(this_count << 9);
            if(!buff) panic("Ran out of DMA buffers.");
        }
        if (SCpnt->request.cmd == WRITE)
            memcpy(buff, (char *)SCpnt->request.buffer,
                this_count << 9);
    }
}
```

(Continued)

Listing 11-10. *(Continued)*

```
#ifdef DEBUG
    printk("sd%c : %s %d/%d 512 byte blocks.\n",
            'a' + devm,
            (SCpnt->request.cmd == WRITE) ?
            "writing" : "reading",
            this_count, SCpnt->request.nr_sectors);
#endif

    cmd[1] = (SCpnt->lun << 5) & 0xe0;

    if (rscsi_disks[dev].sector_size == 1024){
        if(block & 1)
            panic("sd.c:Bad block number requested");
        if(this_count & 1)
            panic("sd.c:Bad block number requested");
        block = block >> 1;
        this_count = this_count >> 1;
    }

    if (rscsi_disks[dev].sector_size == 256){
        block = block << 1;
        this_count = this_count << 1;
    }

    if (((this_count > 0xff) || (block > 0x1fffff)) &&
        rscsi_disks[dev].ten)
    {
        if (this_count > 0xffff)
            this_count = 0xffff;

        cmd[0] += READ_10 - READ_6 ;
        cmd[2] = (unsigned char) (block >> 24) & 0xff;
        cmd[3] = (unsigned char) (block >> 16) & 0xff;
        cmd[4] = (unsigned char) (block >> 8) & 0xff;
        cmd[5] = (unsigned char) block & 0xff;
        cmd[6] = cmd[9] = 0;
        cmd[7] = (unsigned char) (this_count >> 8) & 0xff;
        cmd[8] = (unsigned char) this_count & 0xff;
    }
    else
    {
        if (this_count > 0xff)
            this_count = 0xff;
```

(Continued)

Listing 11-10. (*Continued*)

```
        cmd[1] |= (unsigned char) ((block >> 16) & 0x1f);
        cmd[2] = (unsigned char) ((block >> 8) & 0xff);
        cmd[3] = (unsigned char) block & 0xff;
        cmd[4] = (unsigned char) this_count;
        cmd[5] = 0;
    }

    /*
     * We shouldn't disconnect in the middle of a sector,
     * so with a dumb host adapter, it's safe to assume
     * that we can at least transfer this many bytes between
     * each connect/disconnect.
     */

    SCpnt->transfersize = rscsi_disks[dev].sector_size;
    SCpnt->underflow = this_count << 9;
    scsi_do_cmd (SCpnt, (void *) cmd, buff,
                this_count * rscsi_disks[dev].sector_size,
                rw_intr,
                (SCpnt->device->type == TYPE_DISK ?
                 SD_TIMEOUT : SD_MOD_TIMEOUT),
                MAX_RETRIES);
}
```

The `requeue_sd_request()` routine creates all the SCSI CDBs, which then get sent to the appropriate low-level SCSI adapter driver. Notice that the driver needs to worry about such things as the ISA bus's 16MB address space and break up transfers that will cross it using bounce buffers below that limit. The driver also is concerned with whether an operation needs to be done using "scatter-gather." This means that since DMA transfers deal with physical memory addresses that don't go through the CPU's memory management unit, areas of memory that are logically contiguous may be physically separated in memory. This means that the SCSI host adapter needs to be able to follow a linked list of memory segments while transferring the data. During `read` operations it scatters the data physically into memory and during `write` operations it gathers the data together into a single stream for the disk.

Listing 11-11. Linux check_scsidisk_media_change Routine

```
static int check_scsidisk_media_change(kdev_t full_dev){
    int retval;
    int target;
    struct inode inode;
    int flag = 0;

    target =  DEVICE_NR(full_dev);

    if (target >= sd_template.dev_max ||
        !rscsi_disks[target].device) {
        printk("SCSI disk request error: invalid device.\n");
        return 0;
    }

    if(!rscsi_disks[target].device->removable) return 0;

    inode.i_rdev = full_dev;
    /* This is all we really need here */
    retval = sd_ioctl(&inode, NULL,
        SCSI_IOCTL_TEST_UNIT_READY, 0);

    if(retval){ /* Unable to test, unit probably not ready.
                 * This usually means there is no disc in
                 * the drive. Mark as changed, and we will
                 * figure it out later once the drive is
                 * available again. */

        rscsi_disks[target].ready = 0;
        rscsi_disks[target].device->changed = 1;
        return 1;
        /* This will force a flush, if called from
         * check_disk_change */
    }

    /*
     * for removable scsi disk ( FLOPTICAL ) we have to
     * recognise the presence of disk in the drive. This
     * is kept in the Scsi_Disk struct and tested at open
     */

    rscsi_disks[target].ready = 1;/* FLOPTICAL */

    retval = rscsi_disks[target].device->changed;
    if(!flag) rscsi_disks[target].device->changed = 0;
    return retval;
}
```

This routine performs a `Test Unit Ready` command to see if the media has been changed and marks a structure variable showing whether it did.

The Linux SCSI Pass-Through Driver

A SCSI pass-through driver simply provides a way for an application program to bypass some of the kernel's protection mechanisms and send a SCSI command to an attached device. Typically the pass-through driver is used to work with less common devices that don't have kernel resident drivers. Examples of these would be scanners, CD recorders, media changers (jukeboxes), etc.

Linux provides such a driver. It is called the SCSI generic driver (sg). Let's take a look at how it works. Each SCSI device that is actually attached to the system's host adapters is represented by a device special file (also called a device node). These special files are named /dev/sga, /dev/sgb, etc., to correspond with each of the SCSI devices that were present when the system booted. For example, if you booted the system with SCSI devices on host adapter 0 at IDs 1 and 3, the /dev/sga special file would correspond with the device at ID 1 and the /dev/sgb device would correspond with the device at ID 3.

Commands are sent to the devices by opening the proper device special file and doing a `write()` system call. The results are obtained by doing a `read()` system call. An error is indicated if the return value of the system call is negative. "Sounds simple enough," you say. Let's see what the pass-through driver does to create this interface for us.

Listing 11-12. Linux sg_ioctl Routine

```
/*********   sg.c  ********/

static int sg_init(void);
static int sg_attach(Scsi_Device *);
static int sg_detect(Scsi_Device *);
static void sg_detach(Scsi_Device *);

struct Scsi_Device_Template sg_template =
    {NULL, NULL, "sg", NULL, 0xff,
    SCSI_GENERIC_MAJOR, 0, 0, 0, 0,
    sg_detect, sg_init,
    NULL, sg_attach, sg_detach};
```

(Continued)

Listing 11-12. (*Continued*)

```
#ifdef SG_BIG_BUFF
static char *big_buff = NULL;
/* wait for buffer available */
sstatic struct wait_queue *big_wait;
static int big_inuse=0;
#endif

struct scsi_generic
{
    Scsi_Device *device;
    int users;    /* how many people have it open? */
    /* wait for device to be available */
    struct wait_queue *generic_wait;
    /* wait for response */
    struct wait_queue *read_wait;
    /* wait for free buffer */
    struct wait_queue *write_wait;
    /* current default value for device */
    int timeout;
    int buff_len; /* length of current buffer */
    char *buff;    /* the buffer */
    /* header of pending command */
    struct sg_header header;
    char exclude; /* opened for exclusive access */
    char pending;  /* don't accept writes now */
    char complete; /* command complete allow a read */
};

static struct scsi_generic *scsi_generics=NULL;
static void sg_free(char *buff,int size);

static int sg_ioctl(struct inode * inode,
    struct file * file, unsigned int cmd_in,
    unsigned long arg)
{
    int result;
    int dev = MINOR(inode->i_rdev);
    if ((dev<0) || (dev>=sg_template.dev_max))
        return -ENXIO;
    switch(cmd_in)
    {
    case SG_SET_TIMEOUT:
        result = verify_area(VERIFY_READ,
            (const void *)arg, sizeof(long));
        if (result) return result;
```

(Continued)

Listing 11-12. (*Continued*)

```
          scsi_generics[dev].timeout=get_user((int *) arg);
          return 0;
     case SG_GET_TIMEOUT:
          return scsi_generics[dev].timeout;
     default:
          return scsi_ioctl(scsi_generics[dev].device,
              cmd_in, (void *) arg);
     }
}
```

The ioctl routine simply allows the application to set and get the timeout values.

Listing 11-13. Linux sg_open Routine

```
static int sg_open(struct inode * inode, struct file * filp)
{
    int dev=MINOR(inode->i_rdev);
    int flags=filp->f_flags;

    if (dev>=sg_template.dev_max ||
        !scsi_generics[dev].device)
        return -ENXIO;
    if (O_RDWR!=(flags & O_ACCMODE))
        return -EACCES;

  /*
   * If we want exclusive access, then wait until the
   * device is not busy, and then set the flag to prevent
   * anyone else from using it.
   */
   if (flags & O_EXCL)
   {
       while(scsi_generics[dev].users)
       {
           if (flags & O_NONBLOCK)
               return -EBUSY;
           interruptible_sleep_on(
               &scsi_generics[dev].generic_wait);
           if (current->signal & ~current->blocked)
               return -ERESTARTSYS;
       }
```

(Continued)

Listing 11-13. (*Continued*)

```
        scsi_generics[dev].exclude=1;
}
else
    /*
     * Wait until nobody has an exclusive open on
     * this device.
     */
    while(scsi_generics[dev].exclude)
    {
        if (flags & O_NONBLOCK)
            return -EBUSY;
        interruptible_sleep_on(
            &scsi_generics[dev].generic_wait);
        if (current->signal & ~current->blocked)
            return -ERESTARTSYS;
    }

/*
 * OK, we should have grabbed the device.  Mark the
 * thing so that other processes know that we have it,
 * and initialize the state variables to known values.
 */
if (!scsi_generics[dev].users
    && scsi_generics[dev].pending
    && scsi_generics[dev].complete)
{
    if (scsi_generics[dev].buff != NULL)
        sg_free(scsi_generics[dev].buff,
        scsi_generics[dev].buff_len);
    scsi_generics[dev].buff=NULL;
    scsi_generics[dev].pending=0;
}
if (!scsi_generics[dev].users)
    scsi_generics[dev].timeout=SG_DEFAULT_TIMEOUT;
if (scsi_generics[dev].device->host->hostt->usage_count)
    (*scsi_generics[dev].
        device->host->hostt->usage_count)++;
if(sg_template.usage_count)
    (*sg_template.usage_count)++;
scsi_generics[dev].users++;
return 0;
}
```

Reserve the desired device for use by this application.

Listing 11-14. Linux sg_close Routine

```
static void sg_close(struct inode * inode, struct file * filp)
{
    int dev=MINOR(inode->i_rdev);
    scsi_generics[dev].users--;
    if (scsi_generics[dev].device->host->hostt->usage_count)
        (*scsi_generics[dev].
        device->host->hostt->usage_count)--;
    if(sg_template.usage_count) (*sg_template.usage_count)--;
    scsi_generics[dev].exclude=0;
    wake_up(&scsi_generics[dev].generic_wait);
}
```

The close routine just releases the device that was reserved by open.

Listing 11-15. Linux sg_malloc Routine

```
static char *sg_malloc(int size)
{
    if (size<=4096)
        return (char *) scsi_malloc(size);
#ifdef SG_BIG_BUFF
    if (size<=SG_BIG_BUFF)
    {
        while(big_inuse)
        {
            interruptible_sleep_on(&big_wait);
            if (current->signal & ~current->blocked)
                return NULL;
        }
        big_inuse=1;
        return big_buff;
    }
#endif
    return NULL;
}
```

The malloc routine either allocates a fresh buffer if the request is
small, or the one large buffer if the request is larger than 4K.

Listing 11-16. Linux sg_free Routine

```
static void sg_free(char *buff,int size)
{
#ifdef SG_BIG_BUFF
    if (buff==big_buff)
    {
        big_inuse=0;
        wake_up(&big_wait);
        return;
    }
#endif
    scsi_free(buff,size);
}
```

The `free` routine releases whatever buffer was allocated by the `malloc` routine.

Listing 11-17. Linux sg_read Routine

```
/*
 * Read back the results of a previous command.
 * We use the pending and complete semaphores to
 * tell us whether the buffer is available for us
 * and whether the command is actually done.
 */
static int sg_read(struct inode *inode,struct file *filp,
    char *buf,int count)
{
    int dev=MINOR(inode->i_rdev);
    int i;
    unsigned long flags;
    struct scsi_generic *device=&scsi_generics[dev];
    if ((i=verify_area(VERIFY_WRITE,buf,count)))
        return i;

    /*
     * Wait until the command is actually done.
     */
    save_flags(flags);
    cli();
    while(!device->pending || !device->complete)
```

(Continued)

Listing 11-17. (*Continued*)

```
{
    if (filp->f_flags & O_NONBLOCK)
    {
        restore_flags(flags);
        return -EAGAIN;
    }
    interruptible_sleep_on(&device->read_wait);
    if (current->signal & ~current->blocked)
    {
        restore_flags(flags);
        return -ERESTARTSYS;
    }
}
restore_flags(flags);

/*
 * Now copy the result back to the user buffer.
 */
device->header.pack_len=device->header.reply_len;

if (count>=sizeof(struct sg_header))
{
    memcpy_tofs(buf,&device->header,
        sizeof(struct sg_header));
    buf+=sizeof(struct sg_header);
    if (count>device->header.pack_len)
        count=device->header.pack_len;
    if (count > sizeof(struct sg_header)) {
        memcpy_tofs(buf,device->buff,
            count-sizeof(struct sg_header));
    }
}
else
    count= device->header.result==0 ? 0 : -EIO;

/*
 * Clean up, and release the device so that
 * we can send another
 * command.
 */
sg_free(device->buff,device->buff_len);
device->buff = NULL;
device->pending=0;
wake_up(&device->write_wait);
return count;
}
```

The read routine first checks that the buffer the caller passed in is writable by it. It then waits for the command to complete by checking bits that get set by the command_done routine below. When the data is ready it copies it out to user space using memcpy_tofs(), frees up the buffer, and wakes up anyone who's waiting for a buffer.

Listing 11-18. Linux sg_command_done Routine

```
/*
 * This function is called by the interrupt handler
 * when we actually have a command that is complete.
 * Change the flags to indicate that we have a result.
 */
static void sg_command_done(Scsi_Cmnd * SCpnt)
{
    int dev = MINOR(SCpnt->request.rq_dev);
    struct scsi_generic *device = &scsi_generics[dev];
    if (!device->pending)
    {
        printk("unexpected done for sg %d\n",dev);
        SCpnt->request.rq_status = RQ_INACTIVE;
        return;
    }

    /*
     * See if the command completed normally, or whether
     * something went
     * wrong.
     */
    memcpy(device->header.sense_buffer, SCpnt->sense_buffer,
            sizeof(SCpnt->sense_buffer));
    switch (host_byte(SCpnt->result)) {
    case DID_OK:
      device->header.result = 0;
      break;
    case DID_NO_CONNECT:
    case DID_BUS_BUSY:
    case DID_TIME_OUT:
      device->header.result = EBUSY;
      break;
    case DID_BAD_TARGET:
    case DID_ABORT:
    case DID_PARITY:
    case DID_RESET:
    case DID_BAD_INTR:
      device->header.result = EIO;
      break;
```

(Continued)

Listing 11-18. (*Continued*)

```
        case DID_ERROR:
          /*
           * There really should be DID_UNDERRUN and DID_OVERRUN
           * error values, and a means for callers of scsi_do_cmd
           * to indicate whether an underrun or overrun should
           * signal an error.  Until that can be implemented, this
           * kludge allows for returning useful error values
           * except in cases that return DID_ERROR that might be
           * due to an underrun.
           */
          if (SCpnt->sense_buffer[0] == 0 &&
              status_byte(SCpnt->result) == GOOD)
            device->header.result = 0;
          else device->header.result = EIO;
          break;
        }

        /*
         * Now wake up the process that is waiting for the
         * result.
         */
        device->complete=1;
        SCpnt->request.rq_status = RQ_INACTIVE;
        wake_up(&scsi_generics[dev].read_wait);
}
```

The command_done routine gets control when an interrupt comes in from the SCSI adapter signifying that it has finished a command (for better or for worse). The routine saves away the sense data from the result and checks for errors. It then wakes up the caller that sent this command in the first place.

Listing 11-19. Linux sg_write Routine

```
static int sg_write(struct inode *inode,
    struct file *filp,const char *buf,int count)
{
    int bsize,size,amt,i;
    unsigned char cmnd[MAX_COMMAND_SIZE];
    kdev_t devt = inode->i_rdev;
    int dev = MINOR(devt);
    struct scsi_generic * device=&scsi_generics[dev];
```

(Continued)

Listing 11-19. (*Continued*)

```
    int input_size;
    unsigned char opcode;
    Scsi_Cmnd * SCpnt;

    if ((i=verify_area(VERIFY_READ,buf,count)))
        return i;
    /*
     * The minimum scsi command length is 6 bytes.
     * If we get anything less than this, it is
     * clearly bogus.
     */
    if (count<(sizeof(struct sg_header) + 6))
        return -EIO;

    /*
     * If we still have a result pending from a previous
     * command, wait until the result has been read by the
     * user before sending another command.
     */
    while(device->pending)
    {
        if (filp->f_flags & O_NONBLOCK)
            return -EAGAIN;
#ifdef DEBUG
        printk("sg_write: sleeping on pending request\n");
#endif
        interruptible_sleep_on(&device->write_wait);
        if (current->signal & ~current->blocked)
            return -ERESTARTSYS;
    }

    /*
     * Mark the device flags for the new state.
     */
    device->pending=1;
    device->complete=0;
    memcpy_fromfs(&device->header,buf,
        sizeof(struct sg_header));

    device->header.pack_len=count;
    buf+=sizeof(struct sg_header);


    /*
     * Now we need to grab the command itself from
     * the user's buffer.
     */
```

Listing 11-19. (*Continued*)

```
opcode = get_user(buf);
size=COMMAND_SIZE(opcode);
if (opcode >= 0xc0 &&
    device->header.twelve_byte) size = 12;

/*
 * Determine buffer size.
 */
input_size = device->header.pack_len - size;
if( input_size > device->header.reply_len)
{
    bsize = input_size;
} else {
    bsize = device->header.reply_len;
}

/*
 * Don't include the command header itself
 * in the size.
 */
bsize-=sizeof(struct sg_header);
input_size-=sizeof(struct sg_header);

/*
 * Verify that the user has actually passed
 * enough bytes for this command.
 */
if( input_size < 0 )
{
    device->pending=0;
    wake_up( &device->write_wait );
    return -EIO;
}

/*
 * Allocate a buffer that is large enough to hold the
 * data that has been requested.  Round up to an even
 * number of sectors, since scsi_malloc allocates in
 * chunks of 512 bytes.
 */
amt=bsize;
if (!bsize)
    bsize++;
bsize=(bsize+511) & ~511;
```

(*Continued*)

Listing 11-19. (*Continued*)

```
    /*
     * If we cannot allocate the buffer, report
     * an error.
     */
    if ((bsize<0) || !(device->buff=
        sg_malloc(device->buff_len=bsize)))
    {
        device->pending=0;
        wake_up(&device->write_wait);
        return -ENOMEM;
    }

#ifdef DEBUG
    printk("allocating device\n");
#endif

    /*
     * Grab a device pointer for the device we want to
     * talk to.  If we don't want to block, just return
     * with the appropriate message.
     */
    if (!(SCpnt=allocate_device(NULL,device->device,
        !(filp->f_flags & O_NONBLOCK))))
    {
        device->pending=0;
        wake_up(&device->write_wait);
        sg_free(device->buff,device->buff_len);
        device->buff = NULL;
        return -EAGAIN;
    }
#ifdef DEBUG
    printk("device allocated\n");
#endif

    SCpnt->request.rq_dev = devt;
    SCpnt->request.rq_status = RQ_ACTIVE;
    SCpnt->sense_buffer[0]=0;
    SCpnt->cmd_len = size;

    /*
     * Now copy the SCSI command from the user's
     * address space.
     */
    memcpy_fromfs(cmnd,buf,size);
    buf+=size;
```

(Continued)

Listing 11-19. (*Continued*)

```
    /*
     * If we are writing data, copy the data we are
     * writing. The pack_len field also includes the
     * length of the header and the command, so we need
     * to subtract these off.
     */
    if (input_size > 0) memcpy_fromfs(device->buff,
        buf, input_size);

    /*
     * Set the LUN field in the command structure.
     */
    cmnd[1]= (cmnd[1] & 0x1f) | (device->device->lun<<5);

#ifdef DEBUG
    printk("do cmd\n");
#endif

    /*
     * Now pass the actual command down to the low-level
     * driver. We do not do any more here—when the
     * interrupt arrives, we will then do the post
     * processing.
     */
    scsi_do_cmd (SCpnt,(void *) cmnd,
        (void *) device->buff,amt,
        sg_command_done,device->timeout,SG_DEFAULT_RETRIES);

#ifdef DEBUG
    printk("done cmd\n");
#endif

    return count;
}
```

The write routine is used to send commands to the SCSI device. It waits for any in-progress commands to complete. Potential error conditions are checked for. Allocate a buffer that's big enough for the data being transfered. The user's command (and data if necessary) are copied (memcpy_fromfs) from user space into the kernel and is executed by the scsi_do_cmd routine.

Listing 11-20. Linux sg_select Routine

```
static int sg_select(struct inode *inode, struct file *file,
    int sel_type, select_table * wait)
{
    int dev=MINOR(inode->i_rdev);
    int r = 0;
    struct scsi_generic *device=&scsi_generics[dev];

    if (sel_type == SEL_IN) {
        if(device->pending && device->complete)
        {
            r = 1;
            } else {
            select_wait(&scsi_generics[dev].read_wait, wait);
            }
    }
    if (sel_type == SEL_OUT) {
        if(!device->pending){
            r = 1;
        }
        else
        {
            select_wait(&scsi_generics[dev].write_wait, wait);
        }
    }

    return(r);
}

static struct file_operations sg_fops = {
    NULL,               /* lseek */
    sg_read,            /* read */
    sg_write,           /* write */
    NULL,               /* readdir */
    sg_select,          /* select */
    sg_ioctl,           /* ioctl */
    NULL,               /* mmap */
    sg_open,            /* open */
    sg_close,           /* release */
    NULL                /* fsync */
};
```

Check to see whether a `write` to the device would block.

Listing 11-21. Linux sg_detect Routine

```
static int sg_detect(Scsi_Device * SDp){

    switch (SDp->type) {
        case TYPE_DISK:
        case TYPE_MOD:
        case TYPE_ROM:
        case TYPE_WORM:
        case TYPE_TAPE: break;
        default:
        printk("Detected scsi generic sg%c at ");
        printk("scsi%d, channel %d, id %d, lun %d\n",
            'a'+sg_template.dev_noticed,
            SDp->host->host_no, SDp->channel,
            SDp->id, SDp->lun);
    }
    sg_template.dev_noticed++;
    return 1;
}
```

Check the type of the device that was found and display a message for
the ones we don't recognize.

Listing 11-22. Linux sg_init Routine

```
/* Driver initialization */
static int sg_init()
{
    static int sg_registered = 0;

    if (sg_template.dev_noticed == 0) return 0;

    if(!sg_registered) {
        if (register_chrdev(SCSI_GENERIC_MAJOR,"sg",&sg_fops))
        {
            printk("Unable to get major %d ",
                SCSI_GENERIC_MAJOR);
            printk("for generic SCSI device\n");
            return 1;
        }
        sg_registered++;
    }

    /* If we already have been through here, return */
    if(scsi_generics) return 0;
```

(Continued)

Listing 11-22. (*Continued*)

```
#ifdef DEBUG
    printk("sg: Init generic device.\n");
#endif

#ifdef SG_BIG_BUFF
    big_buff= (char *) scsi_init_malloc(SG_BIG_BUFF,
        GFP_ATOMIC | GFP_DMA);
#endif

    scsi_generics = (struct scsi_generic *)
        scsi_init_malloc((sg_template.dev_noticed +
            SG_EXTRA_DEVS) * sizeof(struct scsi_generic),
            GFP_ATOMIC);
    memset(scsi_generics, 0, (sg_template.dev_noticed +
        SG_EXTRA_DEVS) * sizeof(struct scsi_generic));

    sg_template.dev_max = sg_template.dev_noticed +
        SG_EXTRA_DEVS;
    return 0;
}
```

Create special files for all the available devices. Allocate a transfer buffer if necessary. Allocate enough space for the table of devices and a couple of extras.

Listing 11-23. Linux sg_attach Routine

```
static int sg_attach(Scsi_Device * SDp)
{
    struct scsi_generic * gpnt;
    int i;

    if(sg_template.nr_dev >= sg_template.dev_max)
    {
        SDp->attached--;
        return 1;
    }

    for(gpnt = scsi_generics, i=0; i<sg_template.dev_max;
        i++, gpnt++)
        if(!gpnt->device) break;
```

(Continued)

Listing 11-23. (*Continued*)

```
    if(i >= sg_template.dev_max)
        panic ("scsi_devices corrupt (sg)");

    scsi_generics[i].device=SDp;
    scsi_generics[i].users=0;
    scsi_generics[i].generic_wait=NULL;
    scsi_generics[i].read_wait=NULL;
    scsi_generics[i].write_wait=NULL;
    scsi_generics[i].buff=NULL;
    scsi_generics[i].exclude=0;
    scsi_generics[i].pending=0;
    scsi_generics[i].timeout=SG_DEFAULT_TIMEOUT;
    sg_template.nr_dev++;
    return 0;
};
```

Initialize the array of available SCSI devices.

Listing 11-24. Linux sg_detach Routine

```
static void sg_detach(Scsi_Device * SDp)
{
    struct scsi_generic * gpnt;
    int i;

    for(gpnt = scsi_generics, i=0; i<sg_template.dev_max;
        i++, gpnt++)
        if(gpnt->device == SDp) {
            gpnt->device = NULL;
            SDp->attached--;
            sg_template.nr_dev--;
            /*
             * avoid associated device /dev/sg? being
             * incremented each time module is
             * inserted/removed , <dan@lectra.fr>
             */
            sg_template.dev_noticed--;
            return;
        }
    return;
}
```

Release all the devices.

Example SCSI Pass-Through Application Program

The companion CD-ROM contains an example of a SCSI pass-through application in the Linux "SCSI Programming HOWTO" document.

Summary

I know that what I've told you in this chapter isn't enough to allow you to go right out and write UNIX SCSI drivers. I do hope, though, that I've sketched things out well enough to enable you to find and absorb the necessary information. After having written drivers for each of the above mentioned systems myself, I've found that jumping right in and writing a simple driver initially is the best way to learn it. Reading only prepares you to understand what you will encounter during the development process.

Acknowledgments

I'd like to thank Linus Torwalds and his merry band of Linux developers for producing such an impressive operating system platform for everyone to enjoy. And, most especially, for making it and its source code freely distributable.

Chapter 12

Troubleshooting and Common Mistakes

By now you've probably concluded that SCSI represents a powerful technology, but you may be intimidated by its complexity. If you're starting to think that more can go wrong with SCSI than can go right, this chapter may help put your mind at ease.

The mistakes programmers make when working with SCSI fall into a few basic categories. Certain problems crop up frequently enough that it's easy to recognize them and head them off. Some simple troubleshooting and debugging skills can save you hours of frustration.

Start with a Clean Hardware Layer

The most important thing you can do to minimize problems with SCSI is to make sure your hardware is set up correctly. Some people think that setting up a trouble-free SCSI system is a matter of trial and error. That's not the case. The rules for cable lengths, termination, and other components of the physical layer are precise, if somewhat hard to interpret.

For a handy reference to troubleshooting your physical layer, you may wish to refer to the "SCSI Game Rules," posted once a month on the *comp.periphs.scsi* newsgroup. This document is maintained by Gary Field, who also maintains the SCSI FAQ on the same forum. It's full of tips to help you understand how the SCSI game is played and what happens when you break the rules.

SCSI Bus Termination

More mythology and misinformation surrounds the subject of bus termination than any other aspect of SCSI. The simple fact is that a properly configured bus has exactly two terminators—no more, no less. The terminators must be at the ends of the bus. Often this means the host adapter is terminated, but that is not always the case. If you use both internal and external devices, the host adapter may be in the middle of the chain and should not be terminated.

Often, people will advise terminating all attached devices, just to be sure. This is bad advice—run fast and far from anyone who suggests that you do this.

Passive termination is common, but active termination is the most trouble-free. For higher transfer rates, termination becomes critical. That is why Fast SCSI protocols require active termination to work properly.

SCSI Termination Power

Termination power problems can be difficult to track down. The host adapter is required to provide a TERMPWR signal. However, this rule often is violated. Many parallel port SCSI adapters do not supply TERMPWR, relying instead on the attached peripheral to supply it. Some peripheral devices will, but often they do not. For example, the Iomega Zip drive does not supply TERMPWR, and does not work with many parallel port adapters.

If nothing provides terminator power you have serious trouble. If you're not sure if it's within range, check with a voltmeter. It should be between 4.25 and 5.25 volts on a properly terminated single-ended bus.

Be Cautious with Cables

The SCSI bus has much stricter electrical requirements than other interfaces. That's why it pays to be fussy about the cables you use. Good SCSI cables are properly shielded, have the correct impedance, and probably cost more than you think they should. This is not the place to cut corners, as a marginal cable can cost you more in the long run, causing intermittent problems that are nearly impossible to isolate.

Be aware of cable lengths. The total length of a single-ended SCSI bus should be no more than six meters. For cabling between devices, shorter is better.

And at the risk of stating the obvious, make sure both ends of your cables are connected. A cable connected at only one end is a spawning ground for electrical gremlins.

Don't Take Documentation at Face Value

As you work with SCSI devices, you'll find that often the manufacturer's documentation is only slightly more trustworthy than a supermarket tabloid. Often the documentation is written to design specifications that changed several times before the final product reached the market.

Trust nothing you read. If the programmer's specification claims that a device returns a certain error code, test it by inducing the error condition and checking how the device responds.

Be cautious with documentation that appears vague. Programmers tend to be optimistic, interpreting ambiguous information in whatever way makes the code easier to write. When in doubt seek out a second opinion, preferably from a pessimist.

Watch Out for Platform Dependencies

SCSI Byte Order

Novice SCSI programmers often are careless about byte order in SCSI commands. The rule is simple: values in SCSI Command Blocks are always in big-endian order. The most significant byte leads, the least significant byte follows.

Programmers working on Intel platforms generally are more used to little-endian values where the least significant byte leads. Be aware that you'll have to do some bit-shifting or other operations to convert values back and forth.

ASPI Byte Order

On the other hand, ASPI uses Intel order in its SCSI Request Blocks. This makes sense, since ASPI was created for Intel platforms. It can make things confusing, however, when you build a SCSI CDB with big-endian numbers, then embed it in an ASPI SRB filled with little-endian values.

A little extra attention to bookkeeping can make things go more smoothly. You may find it helpful to define macros for frequently used conversions.

Structure Alignment

It's a minor mistake, but often hard to catch. You've defined a structure in your C code to hold a SCSI Command Descriptor Block. You fill it with the proper values and send it to a device for execution, only to have sense data come back informing you that you have an invalid parameter in the CDB. What went wrong?

It's possible your structure isn't aligned properly. A SCSI CDB must be aligned on byte boundaries. Many compilers align structures on word or doubleword boundaries by default.

Check your compile options to make sure your byte-aligned structures are preserved. Inspect the structures using a debugger to make sure they look the way you expect them to.

Buffer Alignment

Buffer alignment is another potential problem. When working with ASPI, always check the host adapter capabilities. The `SC_HA_INQUIRY` function returns a buffer alignment mask. This mask tells you how to align any buffer pointers that you pass to the ASPI manager for this particular host. Violate the requirements at your own peril.

SCRIPTS code also has strict rules for buffer alignment. Registers that point to memory addresses hold DWORD values, so all buffers must fall on a DWORD boundary.

The easiest way to comply with buffer alignment rules is to align all buffers on DWORD boundaries. This will also satisfy more lenient requirements for word or byte aligned buffers. The SCSI Snooper sample application takes this approach by defining a utility class called Aligned-Buffer. The AlignedBuffer class allocates memory and returns a pointer aligned to the next doubleword boundary.

Debugging Tools

Debugging SCSI code can be a maddening experience. Too often it involves sending a CDB to a device that is, in effect, a black box. The device may perform as you expect, or it may surprise you with errors that you never anticipated.

Interactive Command Utilities

If you can invest the time, it's often worthwhile to build a utility that will let you edit a CDB, pass it to a device, and examine the output. This lets you work with a device and become familiar with it before you build any production code.

There are many commercial and public domain tools that perform this function. A tool called ASPIMenu is available from Western Digital, a manufacturer of SCSI drives and controllers. It works through your installed ASPI driver to let you interact with a SCSI device. You can download ASPIMenu without charge from the Western Digital Web site at www.wdc.com.

Virtual Devices

If you plan to work extensively with a particular device, it is sometimes helpful to simulate it in software. Set up a second host adapter in your test machine with a different SCSI ID, and connect it to the first host adapter. With the proper software, this second adapter can mimic a SCSI peripheral.

For developers writing target-mode software, this is often the only way to test code before committing it to firmware. A poorly behaved application is less likely to inflict damage on a simulated device than a real one.

Software that works with SCSI disk drives can be difficult to test safely. Many of the examples in this book use an Iomega Zip drive, which has removable media that is easily replaced. An even better solution would be to use a virtual disk drive. In the SCRIPTS sample code on the companion CD-ROM, there is an application that demonstrates target mode programming by building such a device. If you have a compatible Symbios Logic host adapter, you may want to look at this code.

SCSI Bus Analyzers

The granddaddy of all SCSI debugging tools is the SCSI bus analyzer. A bus analyzer can make errors painfully obvious. Illegal phase transitions or dead signal lines show up readily.

Bus analyzers come in many forms, but the basic purpose is to display a snapshot of the SCSI bus at any given time. A bus analyzer can show you what phase the bus is in by examining the signal lines. It can display raw data, or formatted Command Descriptor Blocks, depending on the capabilities of a particular model. Many models measure signal voltages and bus timing. Some have extensive capture and analysis capabilities that will let you walk through a sequence of commands and data transfers.

If bus analyzers have a drawback, it's that they are expensive. Most units start at several thousand dollars, which can be difficult to justify for small projects. However, if you plan to work extensively with SCSI, it's worth the investment.

Keep a Record

As you work with SCSI, you'll probably have more suggestions of your own to add to this list. As the SCSI specification evolves, so does the potential for mistakes by programmers. To keep from repeating your mistakes, try keeping a notebook or journal. You'd be surprised how much you can forget between projects if you don't have something to refer back to.

Chapter 13

Sample Application: SCSI Snooper

Up until now, we've only shown snippets of sample code to illustrate SCSI concepts. It's time to put some of this information to use in building a practical application.

Most programmers learning to use SCSI start by writing an inventory program that locates and identifies attached to the bus. We'll take this approach further.

We'll develop a C++ class library around ASPI calls that will include definitions for a SCSI interface class and SCSI device classes. We'll derive classes for specific device types through inheritance from a generic base class.

Then we'll use this class library to build a SCSI inspector utility to examine host adapters and peripherals attached to them. This is a 32-bit Windows application that runs under Windows 95 and NT.

A word of preparation is in order for the Windows NT platform. The ASPI32 service we use in this application is not part of the default NT installation. Unless you have an application that installs it for you, you will have to install it manually. For instructions on how to do this, refer to Appendix C.

Because the application is written in Microsoft Visual C++, you'll also need the files MSVCRT40.DLL and MFC40.DLL. Chances are, they're on your system already. If not, copy them from the accompanying CD-ROM into your system directory.

An Overview of the SCSI Snooper

Let's look at our sample application in action, then we'll examine how it's constructed.

The application displays a window with icons representing SCSI host adapters and attached peripherals. Clicking on the icons brings up information provided by the ASPI manager and SCSI Inquiry commands.

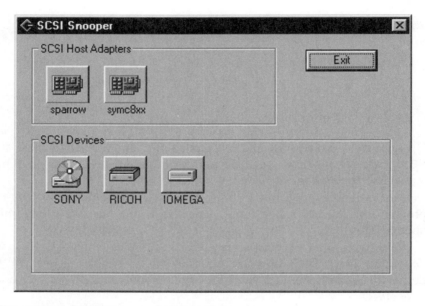

Figure 13-1. SCSI Snooper Opening Screen

The host adapter information screen displays information gleaned from the ASPI driver. It shows the host adapter number, the name of the ASPI manager, and a driver identification string.

You may see some surprises if you run this application on different machines. Many manufacturers have adopted the ASPI model for device drivers. Iomega, for example, uses an ASPI-compatible device driver for the parallel port version of their Zip drive. Modern IDE devices may use an ATAPI interface based on SCSI protocol, with ASPI-compatible drivers. When we tested the software on an IBM ThinkPad equipped with an ATAPI CD-ROM drive, the internal interface appeared on the list of ASPI hosts adapters, identifying itself as "ESDI_506."

Our example is from a Windows 95 machine equipped with Symbios Logic SYM53C825 and Adaptec 1522 host adapters. The Symbios adapter information screen shows that this is a Wide SCSI controller capable of supporting 16 devices, with an assigned SCSI ID of 7.

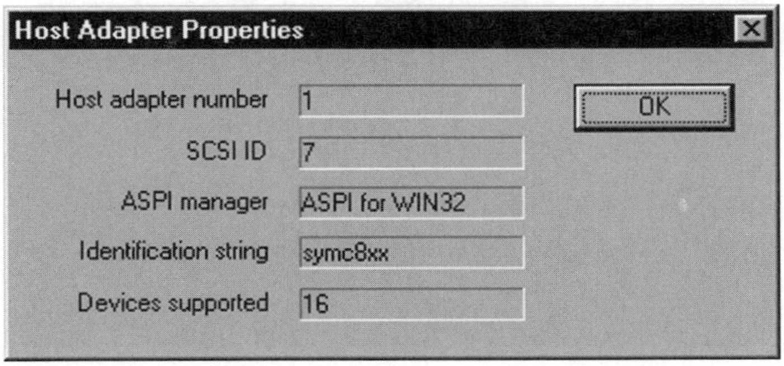

Figure 13-2. Host Adapter Information Screen

Attached peripherals are treated as a pool of devices, regardless of which host adapter they are connected to. A click on a device icon brings up a basic information screen that displays the device address, type, and identification. For the Iomega Zip drive, it looks like Figure 13-3.

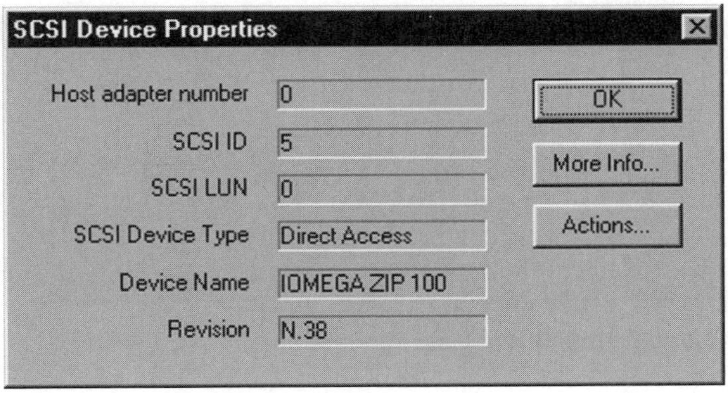

Figure 13-3. Iomega Zip Drive Basic Information

A click on the "More Info..." button brings up an advanced information screen. This screen shows information about supported features, attained through the Inquiry command.

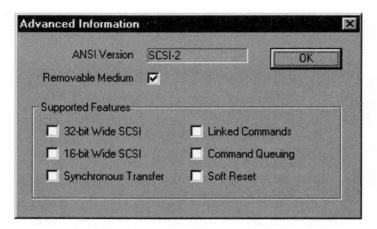

Figure 13-4. Iomega Zip Drive Advanced Information

Let's look at the same screens for a SCSI CD-ROM drive. The basic information screen tells us it's a Sony CD-ROM, set to SCSI ID 2.

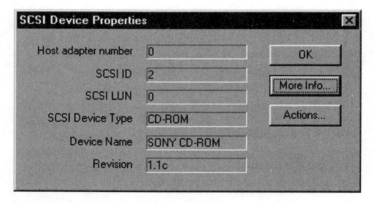

Figure 13-5. CD-ROM Drive Basic Information

Again, a click on "`More Info...`" brings up the advanced information, which tells us that this device supports linked commands and synchronous data transfer.

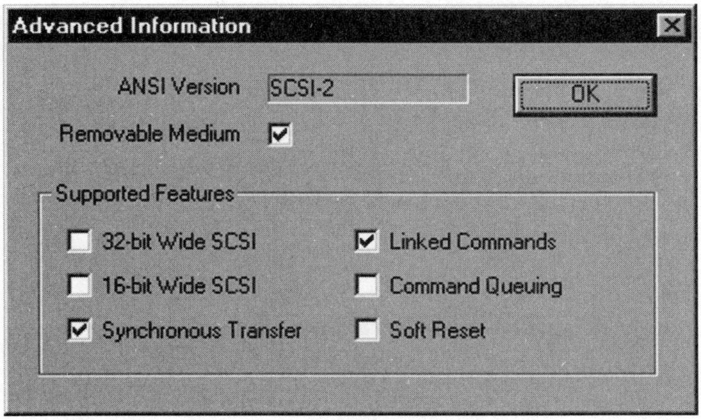

Advanced Information

ANSI Version: SCSI-2

Removable Medium ☑

Supported Features
- ☐ 32-bit Wide SCSI
- ☐ 16-bit Wide SCSI
- ☑ Synchronous Transfer
- ☑ Linked Commands
- ☐ Command Queuing
- ☐ Soft Reset

OK

Figure 13-6. CD-ROM Drive Advanced Information

Clicking the "Actions..." button on the device screen brings up a list of device-specific actions we can perform. For all device types, you'll see the same basic actions: Test Unit Ready, Device Inquiry, and Read Sense. Other actions differ depending on whether the peripheral device type supports them or not. For instance, the Zip drive actions screen shows a list that pertains to direct-access devices with removable media.

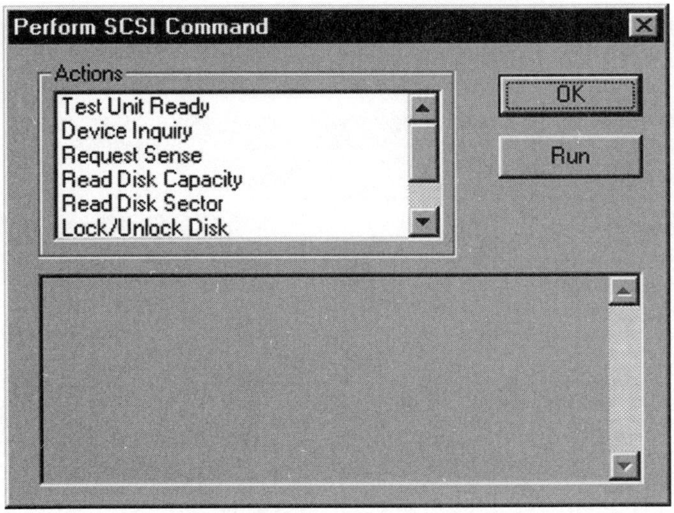

Perform SCSI Command

Actions
- Test Unit Ready
- Device Inquiry
- Request Sense
- Read Disk Capacity
- Read Disk Sector
- Lock/Unlock Disk

OK

Run

Figure 13-7. Zip Drive Actions

Commands for direct access include functions to read the disk capacity, read a sector, and lock, unlock, or unload removable media. Selecting

"`Read Disk Sector`" and clicking "`Run`" brings up a dialog box requesting a sector to read. The results of the command appear in the output box.

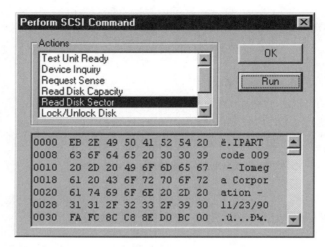

Figure 13-8. Zip Drive Read Sector Results

If the command fails, the output box contains error information and any available sense data.

The actions screen for the CD-ROM is similar to that of the direct-access device.

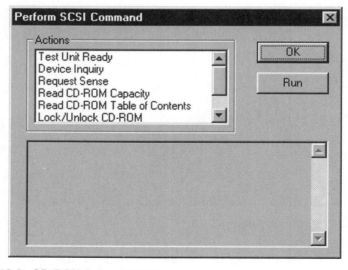

Figure 13-9. CD-ROM Drive Actions

The user may choose to read the CD-ROM capacity, and lock, unlock, or unload the CD-ROM. Instead of a command to read a disk sector, there is a command to read the CD-ROM table of contents. This function displays track information in the output box.

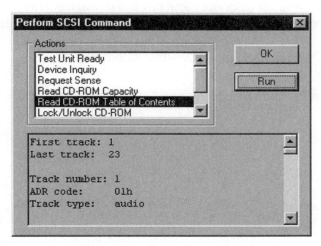

Figure 13-10. CD-ROM Read Table of Contents Results

This version of the SCSI Snooper offers only extended functions for direct-access devices and CD-ROM drives. Actions for other SCSI peripherals such as scanners and tape drives are limited to commands common to all devices. However, it's easy to add support for other device types—we'll show you how as we examine how the application works.

The ASPI Class Library

The foundation of the SCSI Snooper application is the ASPI class library. This library creates a device interface class by applying principles we discussed in Chapter 7. It serves as a wrapper around basic ASPI functions that constructs SCSI Request Blocks, passes them to the ASPI manager, checks for completion, and maps errors.

Note that when we use the term "class," we refer to a C++ class—not a device class or other type of class associated with Windows programming.

The ScsiInterface Class

The ScsiInterface class is the foundation of our class library. It provides a mechanism for software to communicate with devices through the ASPI manager. The ScsiInterface class contains an array of host adapter information and a linked list of devices attached to the adapters. The list approach lets us access a specific device without requiring us to know which adapter hosts it.

Here is the definition for the ScsiInterface class.

Listing 13-1. ScsiInterface Class Definition

```
class ScsiInterface {

    public:

    int AspiIsOpen;
    unsigned NumAdapters;
    unsigned NumDevices;

    AdapterInfo *AdapterList;

    ItemList ScsiDevList;

    ScsiInterface();
    ScsiInterface(int BuildDeviceList, int type=-1,
        int scan_luns=0);
    ~ScsiInterface();

    ScbError OpenAspiLayer();
    unsigned GetNumAdapters();

    unsigned GetNumDevices();
    ScsiDevice *GetDevice(unsigned i);

    int BuildDeviceList(int type=-1, int scan_luns=0);
    void ClearDeviceList();

    ScbError RescanBus(int type=-1, int scan_luns=0);

    ScbError AttachDevice(unsigned adapter, unsigned unit,
        unsigned lun, int type=-1);
    void RemoveDevice(unsigned adapter, unsigned unit,
        unsigned lun);
```

(Continued)

Listing 13-1. (*Continued*)

```
ScsiDevice *FindDevice(char *name);
ScsiDevice *FindDevice(unsigned adapter, unsigned unit,
    unsigned lun);

};
```

An important element of the ScsiInterface class is the `ScsiDevice-List` member. This is a linked list of objects describing the attached SCSI devices. Class member functions help you manage this list or locate specific list items by name or SCSI address.

We have defined a separate class for the objects in this list.

The ScsiDevice Class

The ScsiDevice class describes the attributes and characteristics of a SCSI peripheral, as well as functions to interact with it. It's a bit more complicated than the ScsiInterface class. Here is its definition.

Listing 13-2. ScsiDevice Class Definition

```
class ScsiDevice
    {
    public:

    int Adapter;
    int Unit;
    int Lun;
    int Type;
    char *RealName;
    char *Name;
    char *Revision;
    unsigned int AnsiVersion;
    unsigned int bRemovable;
    unsigned int bWide32;
    unsigned int bWide16;
    unsigned int bSync;
    unsigned int bLinked;
    unsigned int bQueue;
    unsigned int bSoftReset;
    long RetryOnScsiBusy;              // milliseconds to wait
    long RetryOnScsiError;             // milliseconds to wait
```

(Continued)

Listing 13-2. (*Continued*)

```
long RetryOnUnitAttention;        // milliseconds to wait
long RetryOnTargetBusy;           // milliseconds to wait
long RetryOnTargetNotReady;       // milliseconds to wait
long RetryOnTargetBecomingReady;  // milliseconds to wait

ScsiDevice();
~ScsiDevice();

char *GetName()      { return Name; };
char *GetRealName()  { return RealName; };
char *GetRevision()  { return Revision; };
int GetAdapter()  { return Adapter; };
int GetUnit()     { return Unit; };
int GetLun()      { return Lun; };
int GetType()     { return Type; };
unsigned int GetAnsiVersion() { return AnsiVersion; };
unsigned int IsRemovable()    { return bRemovable; };
unsigned int IsWide32()       { return bWide32; };
unsigned int IsWide16()       { return bWide16; };
unsigned int IsSync()         { return bSync; };
unsigned int IsLinked()       { return bLinked; };
unsigned int IsQueue()        { return bQueue; };
unsigned int IsSoftReset()    { return bSoftReset; };
int SetName(char *name);

ScbError Init(unsigned adapter, unsigned unit, unsigned lun );

ScbError ExecuteScb( ScsiCmdBlock &scb, long timeout );
};
```

The ScsiDevice class contains data members that store information about device names, SCSI addresses, host adapters, and supported features. Some of the class functions are defined inline to simply return these values.

The workhorse function of the ScsiDevice class is `ExecuteScb`. This function handles the execution of SCSI commands through the ScsiCmd-Block class.

The ScsiCmdBlock Class

The ScsiCmdBlock class is responsible for building ASPI SCSI Request Blocks and passing them to the ASPI manager for execution.

Listing 13-3. ScsiCmdBlock Class Definition

```
class ScsiCmdBlock
   {

   public:

   ScsiRequestBlock srb;
   ScbError LastError;

   ScsiCmdBlock();
   ~ScsiCmdBlock();

   void Init( unsigned cmd, unsigned adapter=0,
     unsigned target=0, unsigned lun=0 );

   // The following routines assume an SC_EXEC_SCSI_CMD type command
   void SetCdb(void *cdb, unsigned nbytes);
   void GetSense(void *sense, unsigned maxbytes);
   void SetDataBuffer(void *bufp, unsigned buflen);
   ScbError Execute(long timeout = -1L);

   };
```

The `Execute` function passes a SCSI Request Block to the underlying ASPI manager. Other class functions set data buffers for I/O operations and retrieve sense data.

Initializing the ScsiInterface Class

Let's look at these classes more closely to see how they work. We'll start with the second form of the ScsiInterface constructor function.

```
ScsiInterface(int BuildDeviceList, int type=-1, int scan_luns=0);
```

The arguments to this constructor let us tell it to scan the SCSI bus and build a device list. We can also specify a specific device type to look for, and whether to scan Logical Unit Numbers at each address. The default is to report all device types, and only scan LUN 0. This constructor is similar to the default form, except that it calls the `BuildDeviceList` member function. `BuildDeviceList` scans the host adapters for devices, building a linked list of attached devices.

Listing 13-4. ScsiInterface::BuildDeviceList Member Function

```
int ScsiInterface::BuildDeviceList(int type,int scan_luns)
{
    unsigned adapter,unit,lun;
    ScbError err;

    if (!AspiIsOpen)
        {
        err = OpenAspiLayer();
        if (err)
            return 0;
        }

    // paranoia
    assert(NumAdapters <= MAX_HOST_ADAPTERS);

    for (adapter=0; adapter<NumAdapters; adapter++)
        {
        ScsiCmdBlock scb;
        scb.Init(SC_HA_INQUIRY,adapter,0,0);
        err = scb.Execute(3000);
        if (!err)
            {
            unsigned host_unit = scb.srb.hai.HA_SCSI_ID;
            unsigned max_units = scb.srb.hai.HA_Unique[3];
            if (max_units == 0)     // old ASPI managers?
                max_units = 8;

            // Save host adapter information
            if (AdapterList)
                {
                char *s;
                int i;

                AdapterList[adapter].AdapterNum = adapter;
                AdapterList[adapter].ScsiId = host_unit;
                AdapterList[adapter].MaxUnits = max_units;
                AdapterList[adapter].Residual =
                    scb.srb.hai.HA_Unique[2];
                AdapterList[adapter].Align =
                    ((WORD) scb.srb.hai.HA_Unique[0] |
                    (WORD) scb.srb.hai.HA_Unique[1] << 16);

                // Save adapter manager ID
                s = AdapterList[adapter].ManagerId;
```

(Continued)

Listing 13-4. (*Continued*)

```
        for (i=0; i<sizeof(scb.srb.hai.HA_ManagerId); i++)
           *s++ = scb.srb.hai.HA_ManagerId[i];
        *s = '\0';

        // Trim trailing spaces
        while (--s > AdapterList[adapter].ManagerId)
           {
           if (isascii(*s) && isspace(*s))
              *s = '\0';
           else
              break;
           }

        // Save adapter identifier
        s = AdapterList[adapter].Identifier;

        for (i=0; i<sizeof(scb.srb.hai.HA_Identifier); i++)
           *s++ = scb.srb.hai.HA_Identifier[i];
        *s = '\0';

        // Trim trailing spaces
        while (--s > AdapterList[adapter].Identifier)
           {
           if (isascii(*s) && isspace(*s))
              *s = '\0';
           else
              break;
           }
        }

   for (unit=0; unit<max_units; unit++)
      {
      if (unit != host_unit)
         {
         if (scan_luns)
            {
            for (lun=0; lun<8; lun++)
               {
               err = AttachDevice(adapter,unit,lun,type);
               if (err)
                  break;
               }
            }
```

(Continued)

Listing 13-4. (*Continued*)

```
            else
                {
                lun = 0;
                AttachDevice(adapter,unit,lun,type);
                }
            }
        }
    }
    }

    return NumDevices;
}
```

There isn't much mystery to this function. It first checks to see if the ASPI layer is open, calling an initialization function if needed. A side effect of the initialization routine is that it records the number of host adapters present.

The next part of the function loops through the adapters, collecting and storing information about the adapters and attached devices. For each host adapter, it checks all the possible SCSI addresses for active peripherals by calling the `AttachDevice` routine. The `AttachDevice` function performs the actual discovery. Listing 13-5 shows what it looks like.

Listing 13-5. ScsiInterface::AttachDevice Member Function

```
ScbError ScsiInterface::AttachDevice(unsigned adapter,
    unsigned unit, unsigned lun, int type)
{
    ScbError err;
    ScsiCmdBlock scb;
    ScsiDevice *dev;

    if (!AspiIsOpen)
        {
        err = OpenAspiLayer();
        if (err)
            return err;
        }
```

(Continued)

Listing 13-5. (*Continued*)

```
    // Make sure we don't already have it attached
    if ( (dev=FindDevice(adapter,unit,lun)) != NULL )
        {
        if ( (type == -1) || (type == dev->GetType()) )
           return Err_None;
        else
           return Err_NoDevice; // Wrong type
        }

    // See if device really exists by getting its device type
    // This should cut down on init time
    scb.Init(SC_GET_DEV_TYPE,adapter,unit,lun);
    err = scb.Execute(1000L);
    if (err)
       return err;

    if ( (type != -1) && (type != scb.srb.gdt.SRB_DeviceType) )
        {
        // Wrong type
        return Err_NoDevice;
        }

    dev = new ScsiDevice;
    if (!dev)
       return Err_OutOfMemory;

    err = dev->Init(adapter,unit,lun);
    if (err)
        {
        delete dev;
        return err;
        }

    dev->SetName(dev->GetRealName());
    if (!ScsiDevList.AddItem(dev))
        {
        delete dev;
        return Err_OutOfMemory;
        }

    NumDevices++;
    return Err_None;
    }
```

AttachDevice first executes the ASPI SC_GET_DEV_TYPE function to determine the device type attached at a specific SCSI ID and LUN. If the ASPI call returns a valid device type, AttachDevice then calls the ScsiDevice Init member function. The Init function executes a SCSI Inquiry call, then stores device identification strings and capabilities for future reference. Here is what it looks like.

Listing 13-6. ScsiDevice::Init Member Function

```
ScbError ScsiDevice::Init(unsigned adapter, unsigned unit, unsigned lun )
{
    ScbError err;
    ScsiCmdBlock scb;
    SCSI_Cdb_Inquiry_t cdb;
    SCSI_InquiryData_t inq;

    Adapter = adapter;
    Unit = unit;
    Lun = lun;

    scb.Init(SC_EXEC_SCSI_CMD,Adapter,Unit,Lun);

    memset(&cdb,0,sizeof(cdb));
    cdb.CommandCode = SCSI_Cmd_Inquiry;
    cdb.Lun = Lun;
    cdb.Evpd = 0;
    cdb.PageCode = 0;
    cdb.AllocationLength = sizeof(inq);
    scb.SetCdb(&cdb,6);

    memset(&inq,0,sizeof(inq));
    scb.SetDataBuffer(&inq,sizeof(inq));

    {
    long tmp = RetryOnScsiError;
    err = ExecuteScb(scb,3000L);
    RetryOnScsiError = tmp;
    }

    if (!err)
        {
        Type = inq.DeviceType;
        if (RealName)
            free(RealName);
        RealName = (char *) malloc(sizeof(inq.VendorId)+
          sizeof(inq.ProductId)+2);
```

(Continued)

Listing 13-6. (*Continued*)

```
if (RealName)
    {
    char *s = RealName;
    int i;
    for (i=0; i<sizeof(inq.VendorId); i++)
        *s++ = inq.VendorId[i];
    // Trim trailing spaces
    while (--s > RealName)
        {
        if (!(isascii(*s) && isspace(*s)))
            break;
        }
    s++;
    *s++ = ' ';
    for (i=0; i<sizeof(inq.ProductId); i++)
        *s++ = inq.ProductId[i];
    *s = '\0';
    // Trim trailing spaces
    while (--s > RealName)
        {
        if (isascii(*s) && isspace(*s))
            *s = '\0';
        else
            break;
        }
    if (Name == NULL)
        SetName(RealName);
    }

// Save revision string
if (Revision)
    free(Revision);
Revision = (char *)
    malloc(sizeof(inq.ProductRevisionLevel+1));
if (Revision)
    {
    char *s = Revision;
    int i;
    for (i=0; i<sizeof(inq.ProductRevisionLevel); i++)
        *s++ = inq.ProductRevisionLevel[i];
    *s = '\0';

    // Trim trailing spaces
    while (--s > Revision)
```

(Continued)

Listing 13-6. (*Continued*)

```
              {
              if (isascii(*s) && isspace(*s))
                  *s = '\0';
              else
                  break;
              }
         }

    // save other properties
       AnsiVersion = inq.AnsiVersion;
       bRemovable = inq.RemovableMedia;
       bWide32 = inq.WideBus32Support;
       bWide16 = inq.WideBus16Support;
       bSync = inq.SynchronousTransferSupport;
       bLinked = inq.LinkedCommandSupport;
       bQueue = inq.CommandQueueSupport;
       bSoftReset = inq.SoftResetSupport;
       }
    else
       {
       Type = 0x1F;
       }

    return err;
}
```

Look closely at this piece of code. It demonstrates how to build a SCSI Command Descriptor Block, assign the CDB to an instance of a ScsiCmd-Block, set the address of the data buffer, and pass the ScsiCmdBlock on for execution. All SCSI calls in the ScsiDevice class follow this model.

Executing a ScsiCmdBlock

We've finally worked our way down to the actual ASPI function call. It takes place in the ScsiCmdBlock class. The `Execute` member function sets a few flags in the SCSI Request Block and passes it to the `DoAspi-Command` function. `DoAspiCommand` is a static function, and is not a member of the ScsiCmdBlock class.

Listing 13-7. DoAspiCommand Function

```
static int DoAspiCommand(ScsiRequestBlock *p, long timeout)
{
    HANDLE hEvent;
    long wait;


    // get event handle
    hEvent = p->io.SRB_PostProc;

    // map timeout value
    wait = (timeout == -1L) ? INFINITE : timeout;

    ResetEvent(hEvent);

    aspi_SendCommand(p);

    if ( p->io.SRB_Status == SS_PENDING )
        {
        if (WaitForSingleObject(hEvent, wait) == WAIT_OBJECT_0)
        // event completed
        {
            ResetEvent(hEvent);
            return 1;
        }

        time_t elapsed_time;
        time_t starttime = time(NULL);

        while (p->io.SRB_Status == SS_PENDING)
            {
            elapsed_time = time(NULL) - starttime;
            if (timeout != -1)
                {
                if ( elapsed_time > (timeout/1000 + 1) )
                    {
                    if (p->io.SRB_Cmd != SC_ABORT_SRB)
                        {
                        // Abort it now
                        SRB_Abort a;
                        memset(&a,0,sizeof(a));
                        a.SRB_Cmd = SC_ABORT_SRB;
                        a.SRB_HaId = p->io.SRB_HaId;
                        a.SRB_ToAbort = p;
                        aspi_SendCommand(&a);
                        starttime = time(NULL);
                        while (a.SRB_Status == SS_PENDING)
```

(Continued)

Listing 13-7. (*Continued*)

```
                    {
                    if ( time(NULL) > (starttime + 4) )
                        {
                        // Something has gone horribly wrong.
                        // We can't even abort the command.
                        // Ignore the abort, and pretend the
                        // original command timed out.
                        break;
                        }
                    Sleep(10L);
                    }
                }
            // Aborted, return code
            return 0;
            }
        }
    if (elapsed_time > 2)        // is this a long command?
        Sleep(1000L);            // if so, give the OS more time
    else
        Sleep(10L);              // else just give it a little
    }
}

return 1;
}
```

The code should look familiar, as it is similar to the examples in Chapter 7. We use event notification to detect when a command has completed, and add some timeouts and other checks for paranoia.

Some of the constants and structures we use may be unfamiliar. They are defined outside the classes we've examined, and appear separately in the SCSIDEFS.H and ASPI.H header files.

Using the ASPI Class Library

Now that you've seen the low-level workings of the ASPI class library, we'll show you how to use it in an application.

Deriving SCSI Device Types

A useful abstraction for working with SCSI peripherals is to define a generic device type, and derive specialized devices from that. The generic device supports common SCSI functions like Test Unit Ready, Read Sense, Inquiry, and others that apply to all peripheral types. From this base class, we can derive specialized classes for direct-access devices, CD-ROM drives, and other devices.

This is the approach we take for the SCSI Snooper. We start with a base class called ScsiBaseDevice. This class handles common functions and error mapping. Its definition can be seen in Listing 13-8.

Listing 13-8. ScsiBaseDevice Class Definition

```
// Base class for derived SCSI device classes
class ScsiBaseDevice
    {
    public:

    ScsiDevice *Device;

    int IsOpen;
    int LastError;
    int SystemError;
    int LastScsiError;

    unsigned Adapter;
    unsigned Unit;
    unsigned Lun;

    ScsiCmdBlock Scb;         // all commands use this ScsiCmdBlock
    MutexSemaphore ScbMutex;

    union
        {
        SCSI_SenseData_t Sense;
        unsigned char SenseBuffer[SENSE_LEN];
        };

    ScsiDeviceAttributes_t  Attributes;
    SCSI_InquiryData_t      InquiryData;

    ScsiBaseDevice();
    ~ScsiBaseDevice();

    ScsiDevice *GetScsiDevice();

    ScsiError_t Open(ScsiDevice *dev,
        ScsiDeviceAttributes_t *attr=0);
    ScsiError_t Close(void);
```

(Continued)

Listing 13-8. (*Continued*)

```
ScsiError_t DoCommand( void *cdb, unsigned cdblen,
    void *dbuf, unsigned long dbuflen, int dir,
    long timeout );

int ValidResidualCount();
long GetResidualCount();
unsigned MapAscAsq();
ScsiError_t MapScsiError();

ScsiError_t WaitTilReady(long timeout = -1);

ScsiError_t TestUnitReady();
ScsiError_t RequestSense(void *bufp, unsigned maxbytes);
ScsiError_t Inquiry( void *bufp, unsigned maxbytes,
    int evpd=0, int page_code=0 );
ScsiError_t ModeSelect( void *bufp, unsigned nbytes,
    int pf=0, int sp=0 );
ScsiError_t ModeSense( void *bufp, unsigned maxbytes,
    int page_code=0, int pc=0, int dbd=0 );

void QueryErrorString(ScsiError_t errcode, char *bufp,
    unsigned maxbytes);
char *QueryMajorErrorString(ScsiError_t errcode);
};
```

The Device member variable is a pointer to a ScsiDevice object from our class library. This object must already exist, and is passed to the Scsi-BaseDevice object through the Open function.

The higher level functions all call DoCommand, which takes pointers to a CDB and a data buffer as arguments. A simple example is the Inquiry function, which executes a SCSI Inquiry command.

Listing 13-9. ScsiBaseDevice::Inquiry Member Function

```
ScsiError_t ScsiBaseDevice::Inquiry( void *bufp,
    unsigned maxbytes, int evpd, int page_code )
{
    SCSI_Cdb_Inquiry_t cdb;
    char buf[260];
```

(Continued)

Listing 13-9. (*Continued*)

```
    memset(bufp,0,maxbytes);
    if (maxbytes > 255)
        maxbytes = 255;
    memset(&cdb,0,sizeof(cdb));
    cdb.CommandCode = SCSI_Cmd_Inquiry;
    cdb.Lun = Lun;
    cdb.Evpd = evpd;
    cdb.PageCode = page_code;
    cdb.AllocationLength = 0xFF;

    LastError = DoCommand(&cdb,6,buf,maxbytes,Scsi_Dir_In,
        Attributes.ShortTimeout);
    memcpy(bufp,buf,maxbytes);

    return LastError;
}
```

The approach here is simple: build a SCSI CDB and pass it to the DoCommand function along with data buffer information. This makes adding functions for other SCSI commands easy.

The ScsiDiskDevice class inherits the functionality of ScsiBaseDevice, and adds support for other commands.

Listing 13-10. ScsiDiskDevice Class Definition

```
// SCSI direct access device class
class ScsiDiskDevice : public ScsiBaseDevice
    {
    public:

    ScsiDiskDevice();
    ~ScsiDiskDevice();

    ScsiError_t ReadCapacity(DWORD *blklast, DWORD *blksize);
    ScsiError_t ReadSector(DWORD sectnum, void *bufp,
        DWORD maxbytes, DWORD *bytesread = NULL);
    ScsiError_t LockUnlock(int fLock);
    ScsiError_t Eject();

    };
```

We've only added a few device type-specific functions here. The C++ inheritance mechanism makes functions in the ScsiBaseDevice class available to ScsiDiskDevice objects.

It's comforting to note that at higher levels of abstraction the code becomes simpler.

The SCSI Snooper Application Framework

The SCSI Snooper uses the Microsoft Foundation Classes library to provide an application framework and the elements of the user interface. Structurally, the Snooper program is a series of dialog boxes with controls that invoke selected commands.

Much of the application code was generated by Microsoft's Development Studio, and is too bulky to reproduce here. However, it is included on the companion CD-ROM. Feel free to study it, dissect it, and adapt it for your own use.

You may use the included makefile to build the application or create a Visual C++ project file. The ASPI class library files are in a separate subdirectory. Make sure this subdirectory appears in the search path for include files, or the compiler will be unable to locate the class library header files.

SCSI Snooper Application Structure

The application class, CSnooperApp, contains a pointer to a ScsiInterface object. The main dialog class, CSnooperDlg, uses this pointer to locate host adapters and create icon buttons for them. The `CSnooperDlg` initialization routine walks the device list, mapping it to an array. This array is used to create and track device icon buttons by index number.

The adapter information dialog class is CAdapterDlg. The CSnooper-Dlg object passes it a pointer to the application's ScsiInterface object, which it uses to display information about the selected host adapter.

The device information dialog class is CDeviceDlg. It receives a pointer to a ScsiDevice object from the CSnooperDlg object that calls it. Through this pointer, it retrieves the device name and identification strings for display.

The CMoreinfoDlg class is responsible for the extended information dialog. It receives a pointer to a ScsiDevice object from the parent CDevice-Dlg object. SCSI features appear as a series of boxes, which are checked if the device supports them.

The CActionDlg class is more complex than the others. Using the ScsiDevice object pointer it receives from its CDeviceDlg parent, it determines the SCSI peripheral device type and displays the appropriate actions in a list box. On executing the actions, it displays error messages or output in a text field.

Use the SCSI Snooper to examine devices. You may be surprised to see that some devices do not respond as you expect them to. For instance, `Read Sense` command issued after cycling power on a device should report `Unit Attention` condition. However, some devices silently ignore it.

Use the application as a learning tool by extending it. Don't be afraid to experiment!

Glossary of Acronyms

The world of SCSI is filled with strange terms and confusing acronyms. This glossary lists some of the more common acronyms and what they stand for.

General Terms

ANSI   American National Standards Institute—organization responsible for maintaining and promoting industrial standards

ASC   Additional Sense Code—sense value that identifies the source of a specific error condition

ASCQ   Additional Sense Code Qualifier—sense value that provides details about a specific error condition

CDB   Command Descriptor Block—structure used to pass commands and parameters to a SCSI device

CRC   Cyclic Redundancy Check—computed number used to detect errors in data transfers

CCS   Common Command Set—standard command set for direct-access devices

DLL	Dynamic Link Library—file containing shared code or data used in Windows applications
LUN	Logical Unit Number—identifies a subunit on a target device
LVD	Low Voltage Differential—a wiring alternative designed to accommodate higher transfer speeds
SCAM	SCSI Configured AutoMagically—defines a protocol for Plug and Play SCSI configuration

SCSI-2 Definitions

SCSI-2 Protocols

PH1	SSA Physical Level 1—defines Serial Storage Architecture physical layer
S2P	SSA SCSI-2 Protocol—defines SCSI-2 transport over Serial Storage Architecture
TLI	SSA Transport Level 1—defines transport protocol over Serial Storage Architecture physical layers

SCSI-3 Definitions

SCSI-3 Architecture

SAM	SCSI-3 Architecture Model
SAM-2	SCSI-3 Architecture Model, second generation

SCSI-3 Command Sets

MMC	Multi-Media Commands—defines commands for multi-media devices such as CD-ROMs
SBC	SCSI-3 Block Commands—defines commands for block-oriented direct-access devices
SCC	SCSI-3 Controller Commands—defines commands for RAID devices

SES	SCSI-3 Enclosure Services—defines commands for enclosures
SMC	SCSI-3 Medium Changer Commands—defines commands for medium changers such as jukeboxes
SPC	SCSI-3 Primary Commands—defines basic commands for all SCSI-3 devices
SSC	SCSI-3 Stream Commands—defines commands for stream-oriented sequential-access devices

SCSI-3 Protocols

FCP	Fibre Channel Protocol—defines SCSI transport over the Fibre Channel Interface
PH2	SSA Physical Level 2—defines Serial Storage Architecture physical layer
S3P	SSA SCSI-3 Protocol—defines SCSI-3 transport over Serial Storage Architecture
SBP	SCSI-3 Serial Bus Protocol—defines SCSI-3 transport over the IEEE 1394 interface
SBP-2	Serial Bus Protocol, second generation—defines generic transport over IEEE 1394 interface
SIP	SCSI-3 Interlocked Protocol
SPI	SCSI-3 Physical Interface
SPI-2	SCSI-3 Physical Interconnect-2—combines SPI, Fast-20, and SIP
SSA	Serial Storage Architecture
STS	SCSI Transport via SBP-2—defines SCSI-3 transport over SBP-2
TL2	SSA Transport Level 2—defines transport protocol over Serial Storage Architecture physical layers

SCSI Software Interfaces

ASPI	Advanced SCSI Programming Interface

CAM   SCSI-2 Common Access Method

CAM-3   SCSI-3 Common Access Method

SRB   SCSI Request Block—command structure used in ASPI programming

SCSI Resources

A wide range of information about SCSI is available—the trick is to find it. This appendix lists sources of information in both print and electronic form. Use it as a starting point for tracking down information. Keep in mind though, that with the rapid growth of SCSI more information is available daily.

Books

Books about SCSI are scarce commodities. Most books on the topic focus on SCSI hardware, rather than on programming SCSI devices. Some of the books in this list are no longer in print, but are still available through locator services or online bookstores.

ANSI SCSI-2 Standard

Global Engineering Documents
15 Inverness Way East
Englewood, CO 80112
(800) 854-7179

The SCSI Bus and IDE Interface: Protocols, Applications and Programming

Friedhelm Schmidt

> Addison Wesley Longman
> ISBN 0-201-42284-0

The Indispensable PC Hardware Book: Your Hardware Questions Answered, Second Edition

Hans-Peter Messmer

> Addison Wesley Longman
> ISBN 0-201-87697-3

The Book of SCSI

Peter M. Ridge

> No Starch Press
> ISBN 1-886411-02-6

The SCSI Encyclopedia

> ENDL Publishing
> 14426 Black Walnut Ct.
> Saratoga, CA 95090
> (408) 867-6642

The SCSI Bench Reference

> ENDL Publishing
> 14426 Black Walnut Ct.
> Saratoga, CA 95090
> (408) 867-6642

What Is SCSI? Understanding the Small Computer Systems Interface

> Prentice-Hall
> ISBN 0-13-796855-8

In-Depth Exploration of SCSI

> Solution Technology, SCSI Publications
> P.O. Box 104
> Boulder Creek, CA 95006
> (408) 338-4285

Magazines and Journals

"The Advanced SCSI Programming Interface"

Brian Sawert
  Dr. Dobb's Journal, March 1994, pages 154–158

"The SCSI Bus, Part 1"

L. Brett Glass
  Byte Magazine, February 1990, pages 267–274

"The SCSI Bus, Part 2"

L. Brett Glass
  Byte Magazine, March 1990, pages 291–298

"More Than Just Fast"

Rick Grehan
  Byte Magazine, December 1990, pages 361–369

Online Information

The best sources for current information on proposed SCSI standards are on the internet. Web sites offer interactive browsing of documents, FTP sites contain current draft specifications. Here are some lists of useful sites for SCSI programmers.

Web Sites

ANSI X3T10 Committee Home Page—http://www.symbios.com/x3t10/

This is the home page for the X3T10 working committee. Look for current information about SCSI-3 standards here.

ANSI X3T10 Committee Drafts—http://www.symbios.com/x3t10/drafts.htm

This link from the X3T10 home page holds the latest draft documents.

SCSI-2 Specification (Draft X3T9.2 Rev 10L)—http://scitexdv.com/SCSI2/

This site holds a hypertext version of the SCSI-2 draft specification.

SCSI FAQ—http://www.cis.ohio-state.edu/hypertext/faq/usenet/scsi-faq/top.html

> This site—maintained by Gary Field—contains archives of SCSI Frequently Asked Questions from the *comp.periphs.scsi* newsgroup.

Adaptec Home Page—http://www.adaptec.com

> This is the home page for Adaptec, a manufacturer of SCSI controllers and devices. With Adaptec's acquisition of Trantor and Future Domain, support for these devices are also here.

Adaptec Developer Information—http://www.adaptec.com/support/dev.html

> This site holds information for SCSI developers, including ASPI information and documents.

Symbios Logic Home Page—http://www.symbios.com

> This is the home page for Symbios Logic, a manufacturer of SCSI devices and controllers. Symbios grew from the NCR Microelectronics Division, a pioneer in the SCSI industry. Symbios hosts the X3T10 committee home page.

Symbios Logic Articles—http://www.symbios.com/articles/articles.htm

> This page is a starting point for information relating to SCSI.

Ancot Corporation Home Page—http://www.ancot.com/

> Ancot, a manufacturer of SCSI devices and test equipment, hosts technology discussions and pointers to other SCSI resources. They offer a free booklet, *The Basics of SCSI,* that you can order online.

Western Digital Corporation Home Page—http://www.wdc.com/

> Western Digital manufactures SCSI drives and host adapters. Their web site contains useful benchmark programs, ASPI utilities, and testing tools.

Linux Parallel Port Home Page—http://www.torque.net/linux-pp.html

> For information about parallel port devices under Linux, this is the place to go. It contains links to information about parallel port SCSI adapters and the Iomega parallel port Zip drive.

Linux Documentation Project Home Page—http://sunsite.unc.edu/mdw/linux.html

> This is the home of the Linux Documentation Project, and is a good resource for questions about Linux device drivers and SCSI support.

Usenet Newsgroups

Newsgroups are great forums for discussing topics related to SCSI. Users post questions and answers, and lively discussions usually follow.

> *comp.periphs.scsi*—the definitive newsgroup for SCSI information
>
> *comp.sys.ibm.pc.hardware.chips*—a newsgroup with a slant toward SCSI controllers
>
> *comp.sys.ibm.pc.hardware.storage*—good information about SCSI drives and tape devices
>
> *comp.os.ms-windows.programmer.nt.kernel-mode*—questions and answers about SCSI support under Windows NT
>
> *comp.os.linux.hardware*—questions and answers about SCSI devices under Linux

Ftp Sites

I/O Standards Committee Ftp Server—ftp.symbios.com/pub/standards/io/

> This site, hosted by Symbios, holds draft standards, utilities, specifications, and working group proceedings. You'll find documents relating to SCSI-2, SCSI-3, Plug and Play SCSI, and an assortment of other SCSI topics.

Tulane University SCSI Archive—ftp.cs.tulane.edu/pub/scsi/

> This ftp site mirrors the contents of the SCSI BBS. Draft standards, working papers, and other documents appear here.

Linux Ftp Sites
ftp://sunsite.unc.edu/pub/linux/
ftp://tsx-11.mit.edu/pub/linux/
ftp://ftp.redhat.com/pub/

> These are popular sites for Linux distributions and documentation.

Bulletin Board Systems

SCSI BBS—(719) 574-0424

> This is the definitive source for SCSI-related information, maintained by members of the X3T10 working committee.

Manufacturer Contacts

This list gives contact information for manufacturers noted in the text.

Global Engineering Documents

15 Inverness Way East
Englewood, CO 80112
(800) 854-7179

Global Engineering publishes and distributes the ANSI SCSI-2 specification. The document runs over 400 pages of minute detail, but is indispensible for serious development work.

Adaptec, Inc.

691 South Milpitas Boulevard
Milpitas, California 95035
(408) 945-8600

Adaptec manufactures SCSI controllers, host adapters, and other devices. Contact their Developer Relations department to purchase the ASPI Software Developer's kit.

Symbios Logic

Western Sales Division
1731 Technology Drive, Suite 610
(408) 441-1080

Symbios manufactures SCSI controller chips, host adapters, and other devices. They distribute the SCRIPTS compiler for low-level programming of their products.

Iomega Corporation

West Iomega Way
Roy, Utah 84067
(800) 778-1000

Iomega manufactures the popular Zip drive. Available in both SCSI and parallel port versions, Zip drives come in handy for developing and testing SCSI code. The parallel port model comes with an ASPI compatible driver.

Appendix C

Installing the Windows NT ASPI32 Service

The default Windows NT setup does not contain support for ASPI32. Windows NT supports SCSI devices differently than Windows 95, so the ASPI layer is not required. Unless you use an application that installs the ASPI service for you, you'll have to do it yourself.

If you have purchased the Adaptec EZ-SCSI software, it will install the necessary libraries and drivers for you. The EZ-SCSI software is also include in the ASPI Developer's Kit.

If you don't have the EZ-SCSI software, it's not difficult to configure the service manually. The required files are available on the Adaptec web site at www.adaptec.com.

Download the Windows 32 ASPI drivers and DLLs from the Adaptec web site. You may have to hunt around for them. There are four files required for the Windows NT ASPI service.

ASPI32 Support Files

WNASPI32.DLL   32-bit ASPI manager

ASPI32.SYS   ASPI kernel mode driver

WINASPI.DLL   16-bit ASPI manager

WOWPOST.EXE   Support for callbacks in 16-bit applications

Copy WNASPI32.DLL to the \WINNT\SYSTEM32 directory. Copy the ASPI32.SYS file to the \WINNT\SYSTEM32\DRIVERS directory. The other files go in the \WINNT\SYSTEM directory to support 16-bit applications.

Edit the registry to install the ASPI32.SYS driver. Run the registry editor, and create a key under HKEY_LOCAL_MACHINE\SYSTEM\CurrentControlSet\Services called ASPI32. Add the following three values under the new key. Note that they are all REGDWORD values.

ASPI32 Registry Entries

ErrorControl	(REGDWORD) 1
Start	(REGDWORD) 2
Type	(REGDWORD) 1

Exit the registry editor and reboot your system.

When your machine has restarted, go to the Control Panel and click on Devices. You'll see ASPI32 listed among them. It's configured to start automatically when your system starts.

That's it! Your NT system is now ready to support ASPI32 applications.

Appendix D

Companion CD-ROM Contents

The CD-ROM that accompanies this book contains sample code, tools, and documentation that you will find helpful as you explore SCSI further. Keep in mind that SCSI is a rapidly evolving technology. Some of the contents of the CD-ROM may be out of date by the time you read this. Nevertheless, it's convenient to have them at your fingertips.

Sample Code

The SCRIPTS sample code and the source code for the SCSI Snooper application appear on the disk under the *SampCode* directory. You'll find the source code along with the compiled applications.

You'll also find the source code for the TSPI target mode API library under the *SampCode* directory.

SCRIPTS Sample Code

The SCRIPTS sample code contains the routines presented in the SCRIPTS chapter. It contains a makefile for building the sample SCSI inventory program. The makefile is compatible with Borlands' make utility, distributed with their C++ compiler. The makefile assumes you are using Borland C++ and Turbo Assembler. You'll need to modify it if you are porting the code to another compiler.

SCSI Snooper Application

The code for the SCSI Snooper application includes a makefile generated by Microsoft's Visual C++ development environment. You can use it as is, or generate a project file from it. The compiled application and required libraries appear in the *Program* subdirectory.

TSPI Target-Mode SCSI Programming Interface

The code for the TSPI target-mode programming interface appears in the *TSPI* subdirectory. You'll also find sample code from Chapter 9 here.

SCSI Specifications

The SCSI-1, SCSI-2, and SCSI-3 draft specifications appear under the *SCSISpec* directory. The older specifications are plain text files and Adobe Acrobat PDF files. The components of the SCSI-3 draft specification are distributed as PDF and PostScript files. You'll need Adobe's Acrobat Reader to view the PDF files. We have included that in the *Acrobat* directory.

Keep in mind that many parts of the SCSI-3 specification are still under revision. For the latest updates, check the T10 Committee web site at http://www.symbios.com/x3t10.

We also have included a hypertext version of the SCSI-2 specification. This is Gary Bartlett's HTML adaptation of the SCSI-2 drafts, as posted on the web site at http://scitexdv.com/SCSI2. Point your browser to the \SCSISpec\HTML\index.html file on the CD-ROM to view the material offline. If you have installed the Adobe Acrobat Reader plugin, you can also use your browser to view the SCSI-3 specification PDF files.

SCSI Frequently Asked Questions

No SCSI book would be complete without a copy of Gary Field's SCSI FAQ. You'll find it in the *SCSIFaq* directory. This document is posted monthly in the *comp.periphs.scsi* usenet newsgroup.

Symbios SCRIPTS Support

The *Symbios* subdirectory contains tools and sample code for working with the SCRIPTS language. You'll find the NASM compiler in the *Tools* subdirectory, along with the NVPCI debugger.

The *8xxdev* directory contains sample code that demonstrates using SCRIPTS for SCSI initiator code. Other source files in this directory contain utility routines you'll want to use for your own software.

The *8xxtarg* directory contains sample code that demonstrates using SCRIPTS for target mode applications. The sample application creates a virtual SCSI disk drive that can be useful for testing other applications.

Linux SCSI Documentation

Under the *Linux* directory on the CD-ROM, you'll find the Linux HOWTO documents for SCSI support and SCSI programming. The SCSI programming HOWTO document contains an example application that uses the Linux SCSI pass-through feature.

We have also included an archive of the kernel source code for version 2.0.30. You'll need Gnu zip to unpack the tar file, or a Windows utility like WinZip. The *linux/drivers/scsi* directory in the archive holds driver source code for a variety of SCSI host adapters and the code for the SCSI pass-through driver, sg.c. Other SCSI support files are found in the *linux/include/scsi* directory of the archive.

Index